FRONTIERS of KNOWLEDGE

FRONTIERS of KNOWLEDGE

In the Study of Man

---

edited by LYNN WHITE, jr.

President, Mills College

GREENWOOD PRESS, PUBLISHERS
NEW YORK

The Contributors

KENNETH E. BOULDING (Economics) is professor of economics at the University of Michigan. Born in Liverpool, England, he studied at Oxford and taught at the University of Edinburgh, Colgate University, Fisk University, McGill University, and Iowa State College before going to Michigan. In 1949 he won the Clark Medal of the American Economic Association and since 1951 has been a member of the Executive Committee of that Association. He is a member of the Department of the Church and Economic Life of the National Council of Churches of Christ in the United States.

MANFRED F. BUKOFZER (Musicology), professor of music at the University of California, Berkeley, died on December 7, 1955, at the age of 45. He was the most eminent of the younger musicologists in America. Before going to Berkeley he taught at the European Universities of Basle, Cambridge, and Oxford, at the Warburg Institute in London, and at Western Reserve University in the United States.

I. BERNARD COHEN (History of Science) is associate professor of the history of science at Harvard University where, from 1942 to 1946, he taught physics. He is editor of *Isis*, the journal of the History of Science Society, and is a member of the Council of that Society.

THEODOSIUS DOBZHANSKY (Genetics) is professor of zoology at Columbia University. He taught at the Polytechnical Institute of Kiev and the University of Leningrad, and then at the California Institute of Technology from 1929 to 1940, before going to Columbia. On three separate occasions he has been visiting professor at the University of São Paulo, Brazil. He has been president of the American Society for Genetics, the American Society of Naturalists, and the Society for the Study of Evolution. He is a member of the National Academy of Sciences and the American Philosophical Society.

GEORGE HEDLEY (Religion) is chaplain and professor of sociology at Mills College. Born of British missionary parents in China, he was educated in the United States, participated in two archaeological expeditions to Palestine, was ordained a Methodist clergyman, and taught Biblical and Hebrew studies as well as sociology at the College of Puget Sound, the Pacific School of Religion and the Hartford Theological Seminary before going to Mills College in 1940.

EVERETT CHERRINGTON HUGHES (Sociology) is professor of sociology at the University of Chicago, having previously taught at McGill University. He has been president of the Society for Applied Anthropology, and is editor of the *American Journal of Sociology*.

HOWARD MUMFORD JONES (Literature) has been professor of English at Harvard University since 1936, having taught earlier at the Universities of Texas, North Carolina, and Michigan. He is a member of the American Philosophical Society, was president of the American Academy of Arts and Sciences from 1944 to 1951, and in 1956 became chairman of the American Council of Learned Societies.

GEORGE H. T. KIMBLE (Geography) is director of the Twentieth Century Fund's Survey of Tropical Africa. He was professor of geography at McGill University, and from 1950 to 1953 was director of the American Geographical Society. Since 1949 he has been secretary-treasurer of the International Geographical Union.

CLYDE KLUCKHOHN (Cultural Anthropology) is professor of anthropology at Harvard University, and is a member both of the American Philosophical Society and the National Academy of Science.

SUSANNE K. LANGER (Philosophy) is professor of philosophy at Connecticut College, having previously taught at Radcliffe College and Columbia University. Her *Philosophy in a New Key*, first published in 1942, is very nearly the only volume by a living philosopher which continues to be reprinted in a paper-backed edition.

JOHN LOTZ (Linguistics) is professor of linguistics, chairman of the Department of Uralic and Altaic Languages at Columbia, and director of Columbia's Language and Communication Research Center. Born in Milwaukee, he received his doctorate at the University of Budapest and was director of the Hungarian Institute of the University of Stockholm from 1936 to 1947 when he went to Columbia.

GARDNER MURPHY (Psychology) is director of research of the Menninger Foundation at Topeka, having formerly taught at Columbia University and the College of the City of New York. In 1943-44 he was president of the American Psychological Association.

ALFRED NEUMEYER (Art History) has been professor of art history and director of the art gallery at Mills College since 1935. Since coming to the United States from Germany he has served as visiting professor at Stanford University, the Santa Barbara College of the University of California, Harvard University and the Free University of Berlin.

PETER H. ODEGARD (Politics) is professor of political science at the University of California at Berkeley. He had previously taught at Columbia University, Williams College, Ohio State University, Amherst College, and had been president of Reed College as well as assistant to the United States Secretary of the Treasury. In 1951 he was president of the American Political Science Association.

ANATOL RAPOPORT (Mathematics) is associate professor of mathematical biology in the Mental Health Research Institute of the University of Michigan. He had taught mathematics at the University of Chicago and in 1953-55 was president of the International Society for General Semantics.

LYNN WHITE, JR. (History) has been president of Mills College since 1943. Previously he had taught medieval and Renaissance history at Princeton and Stanford Universities.

GORDON R. WILLEY (Archaeology) is Bowditch Professor of Archaeology at Harvard University, having previously served on the faculty of Columbia University and as anthropologist in the Bureau of American Ethnology of the Smithsonian Institute.

Contents

What This Book
Is About

The original purpose of this book was to tell in nontechnical language about the new methods of research, the new puzzlements, and the new qualities of insight which students of human nature have been developing in recent years, and to share some sense of the exhilaration and excitement of the scholar's quest for self-understanding.

Because their practical results in medicine, engineering, industry, and warfare are so spectacular, the feats of scientists in advancing our knowledge of the natural world have deservedly caught the imagination of the public. But in the long run the more significant part of the intellectual adventure of our age may be the revitalizing of "the proper study of mankind," the effort to comprehend man himself—or ourselves. Today's humanists are using means of investigation and forms of thought which make their fields as different from the humanism of the past as pre-virus is from post-virus biology, pre-atomic from post-atomic physics, or pre-galactic from post-galactic astronomy.

The chapters of this book reflect the normal academic trade unions into which the humanists of our time are divided. But while they are written by specialists they are not written in a mood of specialization, for each represents no more than one angle of approach to the human phenomenon. Nor are these chapters conceived as summaries of the present state of studies in a given field. As in the natural sciences, so in the humanities, much rewarding work is being done and remains to be done by traditional methods on traditional subjects: novelty is not the greatest of virtues. Here we set ourselves the task of describing the growing edges of the humanistic enterprise.

But the most significant thing about this volume is the way it outgrew its first intention. As the chapters converged on my desk it became clear that they added up to far more than the sum of the parts. *Frontiers of Knowledge* is not a manifesto—none of the authors is responsible for more than his own chapter. Yet it announces not the ideal but the fact of a new kind of humanism: a humanism stripped of provincialism and preciosity, one no longer bound by an exclusive concern for the Western tradition of culture or by the interests of an aristocratic society.

In the last chapter I have tried to extract the common denominators of the seventeen other independently written chapters. One of the most rewarding ways to read this volume might be first to peruse Chapter 18 and then to judge to what extent its conclusions are justified by what goes before. Where have I been blind? Where have I followed the patterns of my own presuppositions? The riches of the substance of the book should provoke every reader to write his own Chapter 18 and thus to share its editor's adventure. In any case, this volume should stimulate and help to orient the thinking of all those who are searching for principles of intellectual and spiritual order in our generation, and who want to know who they are.

LYNN WHITE, JR.
Editor

Mills College
Oakland, California

FRONTIERS of KNOWLEDGE

GENETICS

Inside Human Nature

by Theodosius Dobzhansky

ALL MEN may be created equal, but assuredly no two of them are made alike. Equality among men does not mean identity, just as variety does not necessarily imply inequality. Men are thought of as equal before God and before the Law. Such equality is an ethical concept derived from the Judaeo-Christian and certain other religious traditions. Diversity in physical appearance and in behavior is, on the other hand, a matter of direct observation. It is enough to have a pair of healthy eyes to see that some men are taller or heavier than others, and a superficial acquaintance suffices to show that men are not alike in character and disposition.

Whence comes the diversity among men? There is no universally agreed upon answer but modern geneticists and biologists are hard at work looking for one. Opinions have ranged, and still range, widely. Hereditarians like to ascribe most or all human differences to variations in "nature" or heredity; environmentalists ascribe them to "nurture" or environment. Galton, the father of eugenics, wrote that "The instincts and faculties of different men and races differ in a variety of ways almost as profoundly as those of animals in different cages of the zoological gardens." His modern follower Darlington believes that "Some men are born to command, others to obey, and others again are intermediate." By contrast, the anthropologist Mead found it possible to say: "We therefore 'hold human nature constant' and assume, for the present, that human nature may be regarded as similar for Bushmen, Hottentots, Americans [of 1941], etc." The truth probably lies, as usual, somewhere between these extremes; human diversity is due in part to diversity of natures and in part to that of nurtures.

The idea that biological heredity may be a determinant of the intellectual and emotional life of human beings is intensely repugnant to many people. Since the present state of the evidence shows that this idea is to some extent a valid one, we may just as well take cognizance of this repugnance. It is due to two causes: frequent misuse of biology as a specious justification of war, slavery, and exploitation of the weak by the strong; and widespread and persistent misunderstanding of how biological heredity operates.

Flushed with the success of the Darwinian theories of evolution, some biologists, particularly around the turn of the century, thought that they understood social phenomena better than the sociologists. Is not the competition and struggle between races and classes the same thing as the struggle for existence which brings about organic evolution? If biological progress stems from "the stern discipline of nature which eliminates the unfit," does it not follow that "War is an element of the order of the world established by God"? It is only natural that ideas of this sort appealed to those who were busy eliminating their economic and political competitors for nonbiological reasons. Modern evolutionists, or most of them, are more sophisticated in their views and less presumptuous in their claims. Yet the prostitution of biology is not entirely a matter of the past. The race theories of the Nazis are the most notorious example, but similar views are still widespread in some parts of the world, not excluding America.

The nature of heredity is, however, becoming better known today. Heredity is no longer looked at as a sinister force against which man is necessarily powerless. Hereditary traits can often be influenced and modified by the environment. The possibilities of such control of development increase as our knowledge of biology increases. There is no hard-and-fast distinction between hereditary and environmental traits, since all traits are really both. The supposition that human psychic traits are influenced by heredity is, as we shall see, compatible with personal freedom and democratic ideals.

Most of what modern geneticists are discovering depends on the work of a humble Augustinian friar. Slightly more than a century ago a young man by the name of Gregor Mendel failed an examination for the position of schoolteacher. Disappointed, he retired to a monastery at Brno, Czechoslovakia, and found consolation in experimenting with plants in a little monastery garden. He crossed different varieties of plants, as others have done before him. But while others simply observed the hybrid offspring, Mendel counted the numbers of individuals showing different characteristics. It is hard to tell whether he had the slightest suspicion that he was discovering some of the most fundamental laws of life. Nobody paid any attention to his findings when he published them in 1865. To his contemporaries Mendel was an even greater failure as a scientist than he was as an aspirant for a teacher's job. Yet he did come closer than anybody else to solving the riddle of heredity, which the sceptical Montaigne, in the sixteenth century, had already recognized as the most mysterious of biological processes.

Montaigne believed that he inherited from his father a stone in the gall bladder. But his father first felt signs of this disease years after Montaigne was born. How could a father's heredity transmit to his son something which the father himself did not have when the son was conceived? "Explain this to me," wrote Montaigne, "and I will believe as many miracles as you like." Mendel's plants furnished the explanation. Montaigne did not inherit a stone; what he did inherit from his father were tiny particles, mere molecules, which modern biologists call genes. These genes caused the propensity to develop a stone in the gall bladder at a certain age, when living in a certain environment. There is no mystery when one realizes that the father and the son both had certain genes during their entire lives.

The misunderstanding of heredity is due in part to the confusion of the biological heredity with legal inheritance in most of the

European languages. The two things are very different. When one inherits a house or a jewel, certain material objects change their owners without necessarily changing themselves in the process. Inheritance of, say, the skin color or of a good disposition cannot possibly mean the same thing. An individual arises from the union of just two sex cells, and the sex cells have no skin of any color, and assuredly no ascertainable disposition. In a sense, the two sex cells are all that we inherit biologically from our parents. More precisely, we inherit the genes which the sex cells contain. Now the genes are neither pieces of skin, nor granules of skin pigment, nor stones in the bladder, nor essences of intelligence or behavior. And yet the genes do condition all these things and many others in the organism. All the genes that an organism has, jointly and severally, make the fertilized egg develop first into a fetus, then an infant, an adolescent, an adult, a senescent, and finally a cadaver. What the genes do, then, is to cause the development to follow a certain path. Depending upon which path the development follows, the skin may be light or dark, there may or may not develop stones in the gall bladder, and the individual may exhibit a greater or lesser degree of intelligence.

The gene theory is atomistic, since the hereditary endowment of the organism is shown to consist of a large number (of the order of twenty thousand in the case of man) of separate units, genes. The proof of the existence of these units, given by Mendel, was certainly one of the great attainments of modern science. But the atomism of heredity should not be exaggerated. Even before the rediscovery and the recognition of the importance of Mendel's work in 1900, Weismann speculated that heredity is a mosaic of separate entities, which he called determinants. Weismann's determinants were, however, conceived to be the units not only of heredity but of the development as well. Weismann supposed that each determinant was a rudiment of a certain body part: each part of the eye, each muscle, and perhaps even each cell of every organ was supposed to be represented in the sex cell by a separate determinant. A sex cell contained, then, all the determinants for all parts of the body; the development consisted of sorting out these vestiges, until every cell came to possess only the determinant which uniquely determined its nature.

Weismann's theory postulated that the body is, in effect, already present in a sex cell, though in the form of tiny determinants of each organ and cell. This way of looking at things has a venerable tradition in biology; it had flourished since the seventeenth century when the pioneer microscopists (Leeuwenhoeck and others) imagined that they could see a miniature human form, a "homunculus," within the male sex cells. The alternative view is that the sex cells contain nothing like a diminutive copy of the mature organism, and the latter arises by stages during the process of development of the living matter. This alternative view corresponds better to modern biological knowledge. Mendelian genes are clearly not rudiments of separate organs. There exist, for example, genes which determine the size or the coloration, or the chemical composition of the entire body. But the apparent simplicity of the earlier way of looking at things was too beguiling; the genes became the determiners of "unit characters" —body size, pigmentation, intelligence, presence or absence of this or that disease, etc.

But what, it may be asked, is a "unit character"? Every bone composing the skeleton may be considered a character of the human body. But so may be every tubercle, ridge, pit, aperture, etc., which a large manual of anatomy distinguishes in every bone. A physiologist may, instead, designate as "characters" each kind of enzyme, or each chemical substance of which the body is composed, regardless of the body part in which this chemical may be found. Clearly, a "character" is a convenient but arbitrary abstraction which a biologist makes for the purpose of describing the aspects of the organism that he wishes to study. But the genes surely do not determine the abstractions that we may choose to make.

It is customary to speak of genes "for" blue or brown eyes, for hemophilia, or for intelligence. These are legitimate shorthand expressions. The trouble is that the shorthand is often taken too literally. It is evident that the gene "for" blue eyes cannot by itself make an eye of blue or of any other color. This gene does so only as an integral part of an organized complex of genes, which makes the whole organism develop in a given way in a given environment.

The development of the organism does not consist of piling up one "unit character" upon another until a complete body is formed. The development is cumulative and continuous from conception to death. Each developmental event determines the course of later events. The development as a whole is determined jointly by the genes present in the fertilized egg and by the environment in which the development occurs. The insistence of modern biologists on saying that genes determine the paths which the development may follow, rather than that they hold "unit characters," is not a matter of mere semantic finesse: if there existed a gene for intelligence, then those who failed to inherit it just could not be intelligent, while those who did could not help being intelligent. If, on the other hand, genes determine patterns of developmental reactions, then the outcome of the development is, in principle, modifiable by manipulation of the environment. In the former case heredity is inexorable fate; in the latter it is only conditioning. The extent to which the outcome of development can be controlled depends on our understanding of the developmental processes involved.

Genes are often said to be remarkably stable, resistant to environmental change, and even independent of the environment. These are again shorthand expressions, which lead to appalling confusion when taken too literally.

A human fertilized egg cell weighs approximately 0.000,000,05 of an ounce. Supposing that the weight of the adult body is some 160 pounds, the increase in mass between fertilization and maturity is approximately 50 billionfold. The source of the material for this increase is obvious—it is the food consumed and assimilated. During the growth as well as during maturity, the organism transforms a part of the environment, food, into its own constituents. The path of this transformation is directed by the heredity of the organism. Roughly the same foodstuffs can be fed to a man, a dog, and a pig;

they will be transformed into characteristic constituents of the human, canine, and porcine body respectively.

The matter may be looked at also from a different angle. A fertilized egg divides into two cells, then into four, eight, and eventually billions of cells. The cell division takes place usually by way of a remarkably precise maneuver called mitosis, during which the chromosomes of the cell nucleus are each split into two halves exactly alike, and the halves pass to the daughter cells. The evidence is conclusive that most of the genes are carried in the chromosomes. The genes are then duplicated between every two successive cell divisions. Just how the gene duplication occurs is not known yet; one thing is clear enough, however, that the genes somehow construct their own copies from materials which are not genes, in the last analysis from food. Self-duplication or self-copying may be the chief or even the only function which the genes perform in the cell. Self-copying is, indeed, the most fundamental function of living matter. The development of the organism is a consequence of gene reproduction; in a sense, the body is a by-product of gene copying.

It is evident that the genes constantly interact with the environment. Quite likely the genes are among the most chemically active cell constituents. In what sense, then, are they stable and independent of the environment? The gene stability is of a peculiarly active kind—the genes work to transform the susceptible part of the environment, food, into their own copies. The process of copying does go wrong occasionally. Most of the imperfect copies happen to lack the ability to reproduce themselves; hence, they are no longer genes. Only a small minority of the altered genes do reproduce themselves; they are the mutant genes, and some of them furnish the raw materials of the evolutionary process. The genes may be said to be resistant to environmental influences only because it is much easier to destroy a gene than to have it changed and remain a gene.

At this point let us be on our guard against a confusion of a different sort. Genes are in all likelihood giant molecules of a class of substances known as nucleoproteins. The process of gene reproduction takes place on the molecular level, and as shown above, this process is cyclic. The development of the organism is, to be sure, brought about by the activities of a constellation of genes. But these activities are so integrated that, on the organismic level, the development is a coherent whole. The individual goes through a succession of developmental stages, first fetal and then postnatal, and eventually reaches the reproductive age and kindles new life.

Individual development, in contrast to gene structure, is fairly easily modified by environmental influences. Food, diseases suffered, upbringing, education, relations with other persons, all affect the development. Furthermore, the effects of the environment on a person are cumulative. Barring mutation, the genes which you have at present are true copies of those which you had as an infant. But the condition of your body, your appearance, personality, and disposition are changing continuously. This is the reason why in modern biology a distinction is made between the genotype and the phenotype. The genotype is the sum total of genes which the organism has inherited from its parents. The phenotype is the appearance of the organism at a given moment or stage of its development. Your genotype now is about the same as it was during your infancy. But your phenotype is quite different now, and it changes all the time. At any given moment your phenotype has been the result of the interaction of your particular genotype with your environment. But the environment which has determined your present phenotype is obviously not alone that which prevails at the moment when this line is being read; it is rather the whole sequence or succession of all the environments which you have faced in your lifetime.

It is clear that all the developmental processes without exception, as well as the outcome of the development at any given moment including all the body structures and physiological, psychological, and cultural characters which a person may have, arise from interactions of the genes which this person carries with the sum total of the environments met with in the process of living.

This disposes at once of the traditional dichotomy of hereditary and environmental traits which still continues to be perpetuated by many biology and psychology text books. In reality, all traits are both hereditary and environmental. Consider a disease such as the common head cold, or a cultural trait such as the language spoken. Head cold is due to an infection with a virus, and therefore is of environmental origin. A person must be exposed to an environment containing the virus of the cold to acquire the infection. But let us not forget that to be liable to infection with this virus one must have human genes. Cats, or mice, or flies, do not as far as known become infected with this virus. Furthermore, it is not impossible that some people are more and others less susceptible to infection with the cold virus. Language is unquestionably a learned trait, though the quaint medieval legend had it that children who are not taught any language begin to speak Hebrew, because Hebrew is the language of God. However, only possessors of human genes can learn any language, and even in some humans, such as congenital idiots or deaf-mutes, the learning process is uncommonly difficult.

The above considerations may seem self-evident, but their significance is nevertheless by no means generally appreciated; a "hereditary disease" is still synonymous in the popular mind with incurable disease. In reality, the curability depends more on the degree of the understanding of the bodily functions which are disturbed than on how much the genes are involved in the origin of the disease. No remedy is known for many diseases which are as clearly environmental as the head cold. On the other hand, myopia, which sometimes has a genetic basis, is corrected by glasses; certain kinds of diabetes can be corrected by injections of insulin. Of course, glasses do not "cure" myopia and insulin injections do not enable the diabetic body henceforth to manufacture its own insulin. But neither does being cured of a head cold prevent another infection after a lapse of a certain time. Glasses, insulin, aspirin, immunizations, vaccinations, etc., are environmental agencies; a myopic person needs glasses and a diabetic needs insulin in their respective environments to enjoy a reasonable degree of well-being.

To make the distinction between hereditary and environmental traits meaningful, modern biologists try to relate this distinction to the degree of the genetic and environmental diversity found in the materials studied. The language spoken is not hereditary, because any normal person can, at least as a child, learn any language. Learning comes from the environment, and one learns different languages in different places; the capacity to learn is basically genetic, but almost all children and many adults possess this capacity. The head cold is not a hereditary disease, because all, or at any rate most, humans contract it when exposed to infective environments. Whether people do or do not suffer from colds depends more on their environments than on their heredities. Diabetes can reasonably be called hereditary because some people do and others do not develop this disorder when living in apparently similar environments. But physiologists can induce so-called experimental diabetes in laboratory animals by means of certain drugs or certain surgical operations. Here, then, are experimental environments which force the development of diabetes in possessors of nondiabetic genes. Of course, an animal with an experimental diabetes has no more acquired genes for diabetes than a sufferer from the gene-induced diabetes has lost it because of insulin injections. The manifestation of the genes has changed, but the genes stay the same. The blood group to which a person belongs is determined by his genes; almost any large group of people (except some American Indian tribes) will contain persons with O, with A, B, and with AB bloods. The inheritance of the blood group occurs according to the rules discovered by Mendel, and no methods are known whereby one could modify, even temporarily, one's blood group.

The relativity of the distinction between hereditary and environmental traits can be shown also in another way. We know that the skin color in man is hereditary because some people have very light and others very dark pigmentation while living in similar environments. The skin color is also, however, an environmental trait, because the same person may be lighter or darker depending upon the amount of exposure to sunlight. Is, then, the heredity or the environment more important in the determination of the skin color? The answer turns out to depend on the group of people which is studied. In a small town in Northern or in Northeastern Europe, the environment might seem the more important of the two, since the extremes of pigmentation would probably be encountered among those leading outdoor lives on one hand and those confined indoors on the other. In New York, or in Alabama, or in Rio de Janeiro, the heredity would appear to be the primary factor, since great differences in the pigmentation often occur without corresponding environmental diversity.

The relative importance of heredity as a cause of differences among men evidently increases as the environment becomes more uniform, and vice versa. This shows the futility of trying to decide once and for all whether nature or nurture is the more important factor in susceptibility to some disease, in intelligence, personality characteristics, in criminal conduct, etc. Indeed the reasonable way to state the problem is about thus: "What part of the observed variance in the trait X is due to the variety of the genes existing in a given population, and what part to the variety of environments to which this population is exposed?"

The answer which is valid for one population may not be valid at all for another, since the genetic and environmental diversities are by no means uniform in different populations. The observed variance in the intelligence quotient will contain a relatively larger environmental component where cultural and economic opportunities are unequal than where they are relatively uniform. It can be argued that only where a reasonable equality of opportunity for all people is available can meaningful estimates of the genetic diversity for some particularly labile traits be obtained.

Darwin has shown that man is a product of organic evolution and kin to all life. The work of biologists since Darwin has demonstrated that the mechanisms of biological heredity are fundamentally the same in man and in other sexually reproducing organisms, and similar to those in any other living beings, down to simplest microbes.

Yet, in man biological evolution has transcended itself. A modern evolutionist tends to emphasize more and more that man is a singular and unique product of organic evolution. Man's separation from other animate creatures is just as interesting and significant as his relations to them. Man alone, among animals, is capable of abstract thought. The use of sounds as warning signals and as expression of emotions is common among higher animals. A dog can make so many different sounds that it "almost talks." But in man alone the sounds have acquired symbolic meaning and have become language. The ability to think in abstract ideas and symbols has enabled man to create and to maintain a body of learned traditions and skills, which is culture.

The transmission of culture from generation to generation is basically different from that of biological heredity. Heredity is transmitted by genes in the sex cells; it is transmitted only in the direct line of biological descent. Culture is transmitted by instruction, learning, precept, and imitation; in principle at least it can be transmitted from any human person to any other person. Transmission of culture is, then, vastly more efficient than that of the biological heredity; by the same token, heredity is more stable than culture. At a risk of oversimplification it may be said that man has two heredities, the biological and the cultural, while other living creatures have only one. Man is biologically unique.

Failure to appreciate the biological uniqueness of man has made ridiculous many a biologist who ventured solutions of human problems based on the assumption that man "is nothing more than an ape with a few extra tricks." But to assume that biology in man took a long holiday is equally fallacious. Human nature is neither uniform nor constant, and heredity and culture are not in watertight compartments. The capacity to acquire, hold, and transmit culture occurs only in possessors of human genotypes which are free of gross pathology. It is absent in animals, even in the great apes, and is severely limited in victims of certain human hereditary diseases. It is also variable from person to person.

The fundamental consideration is, however, that the contents of a culture are not determined by the genes, although the capacity of developing a culture in the human species is so determined. In other words, human genes are a necessary but not a sufficient condition for the cultural development taking one direction rather than another. Human history, particularly the history of cultures, is nonbiological in the sense that it could have taken a variety of courses with the genetic endowment of its protagonists being held constant. Gobineau and all the biological racists who followed him assumed that every form of culture is uniquely determined by the biological heredity of its creators. This is bad biology, bad ethnology, and bad history. There are no specific genes for such things as preferred art styles, grammatical forms, kinship systems, totems, taboos, and other cultural forms. Genes simply do not transmit such things. Man became the most successful biological species not because he acquired genes for cooking food, for parental care, for hygiene, or for trade. His success has been due rather to the possession of genes which make him capable of developing various art styles, different forms of cooking, different techniques of parental care, different taboos, etc.

Biological racism has confused biological heredity and transmission of culture. Making clear the distinction between them is an important recent achievement of the science of cultural anthropology. Culture is learned, not inherited. Alas, it is one of man's most cherished foibles, to which scientists are especially prone, to suppose that their particular experience explains the universal. Hence, the gratuitous assumption that human nature is everywhere uniform with respect to cultural development. A child learns to be the kind of person which he eventually becomes; there is in any culture a process of socialization, whereby an individual is trained to respond to his environment in ways which are approved or at least tolerated by his neighbors. But it does not follow that a newborn infant is a *tabula rasa*, or that he is equally susceptible to all possible socializing influences.

Perhaps the most basic assumption of evolutionary biology is that organic diversity is an adaptive response of living matter to the diversity of environments on our planet. However, no single form of life is universally adapted. No organism combines the capabilities of a bird in the air, of a mammal on the ground, of a fish in the sea, and of a plant which binds the energy of sunlight. The multiformity of life observed in forests, in fields, on sea beaches and in sea depths is a device to eke out a living from all possible environments. In the eternal struggle with death, no opportunity for life is too small to be overlooked.

The diversity within a biological species is, in the main, also adaptive. The same species may occur in different countries, or in different sections of the same country, and therefore may be exposed to different climates, grow on different soils, eat different foods, and cope with different enemies. Hence, many species are differentiated into geographic races, each race being a product of a gradual adaptation, by means of natural selection, to its particular environment. Finally, individuals within a race also vary. Some of them grow large and strong when abundant food is available; others may be smaller but may survive on less food; still others may be immune to some infections, etc. In species which reproduce sexually the variety of patterns of genes is so great that no two individuals except identical twins have exactly the same genes.

Both geographic-racial and individual-intraracial diversity arose in the human species at the dawn of its history. This genetic diversity still persists in modern mankind. But while it may have sufficed in the remote past to adapt our species to the heterogeneity of its environments, the progressing complexity of human life far outstripped the adaptive potentialities of the genetic diversity. Indeed, while technology has rather reduced the importance of climatic and other physical variables in man's environment, the diversity and the importance of cultural variables has increased by leaps and bounds. Man has learned to keep the temperature of his immediate surroundings steady during winter cold or summer heat; he even can, if he so chooses, have about the same diet in all latitudes and at all seasons. But the variety of occupations in which men have to engage, and of social functions which they have to perform, is immense, growing continuously, and changing rapidly.

The genetic variability proved inadequate for adaptation to the diversity of the specifically human environments. Changing the biological heredity is too clumsy and slow a method to keep up the adaptedness to the rapidly transforming social conditions. A novel adaptive instrumentality, the genetically conditioned ability to absorb by learning a body of tradition called culture, has become superimposed on the genetic variability. Indeed, it is primarily through training and learning that men become adapted to perform different functions and to engage in different occupations. Although all human cultures exact more or less conformity to certain accepted standards from their members, learning and education do not level down the personality differences among men. On the contrary, these differences are accentuated and made use of. Equality of opportunity would not mean erosion of individual differences; it would mean their unobstructed development and utilization by the society.

That genetic variability is one of the causative factors which brings about the observed diversity of personality characteristics is quite obvious. Only the widespread and persistent misunderstanding of the nature of heredity is responsible for the confused thinking about this matter. It stands to reason that the whole personality, behavior, choice of occupations, pleasures, and diversions are often influenced by physical defects, malformations, and diseases, many of which are caused by known gene anomalies. But the influence of heredity on personality is just as evident in "normal" and healthy people. Not every boy can be trained to become an outstanding athlete. Some boys do not have a physique needed to make the training successful, while others take to such training like ducks to water. Not everybody can become an outstanding composer or performer of music, because most of us lack the requisite sensory and motor equipment. Some boys and girls possess bodily and facial features which conform to the popular ideas of comeliness, while others do not. That the body build, physical and facial features, and the degree of refinement of the sense organs are in part (but only in part) genetically conditioned cannot be doubted. That these things, in turn, influence the emotional and the intellectual life is apparent. The "inheritance" of athletic, musical, or intellectual aptitudes does not, however, mean that an individual is destined to become an athlete, or a musician, or an egghead regardless of circumstances. Genes do not work that way. The individual's personality is settled neither in the fertilized egg nor in the newborn infant: it develops gradually and by stages in the process of living in a certain sequence of social and cultural environments. It is never finally fixed, and continues to change until death.

Evaluation of human nature is one of the basic issues concerning which men never have succeeded in reaching unanimity or agreement. There have always been optimists, who held that normal men are naturally good and reasonable, and who trusted that, given some opportunity and some education, most men will act decently most of the time. However, there has never been a shortage of pessimists, who felt passionate contempt for their fellows and regarded them as weak, foolish, treacherous, and deceitful. Traditional Christianity, especially the Calvinist faiths, inclined on the whole toward the pessimist end of the spectrum. Human nature is permanently corrupt because of Original Sin; however, the Grace of God can make a man good and keep him good, and any man can hope to receive this Grace. Optimism was the fashion especially during the Age of Enlightenment, the eighteenth century. Man is born good, and he would continue to be good if left in the "natural" state of innocence and "noble" savagery. Alas, he is made bad by living in badly organized societies. The way to make him good again is to build a good society for man to live in. The dissensions, discontents, and conflicts which rend asunder our modern world may not be caused by people disagreeing on the evaluation of human nature, but they at least reflect these disagreements.

What, if anything, has modern biology to contribute toward a better understanding of this issue? The views that human nature is intrinsically good or bad both imply that men are destined to be good or bad regardless of circumstances. These views are equally wrong. Both as men and as biologists we can still hold the ground common to Christianity as well as to the Enlightenment, that men, by their natures, may become good or bad in different circumstances. We may, however, add a significant detail: there is no single human nature but many different human natures. All human societies about which we know anything are or were utilizing the diversity of human natures for the performance of different functions: We may infer that the cultural and intellectual development of mankind was conditioned by human diversity; diversity has acted as a leaven and a driving force.

In contrast to other animal societies, e.g., to social insects such as ants and termites, human societies have not evolved towards genetic specialization of individuals for the performance of a narrow range of functions. The biological uniqueness of man lies precisely in the fact that his biological natures permit wide ranges of developmental patterns in different circumstances. Any normal person can be trained to perform any one of several functions. And yet different persons may require different environments for their optimal developments. Among the types of social organization which have been observed in operation rather than in theoretical blueprints, democracy comes closest to providing a practical recognition and utilization of human diversity. In this may lie its greatest virtue and its best chance for survival.

We have attempted to disentangle the often hopelessly confused problems of human diversity and human equality. Diversity is a biological, equality an ethical phenomenon. Equality is not predicated on biological uniformity, since the utility of equality lies precisely in that it facilitates cooperation between different men and most efficient utilization of their diversity for common good. Biologically considered, human diversity is an adaptation of our species which permits different social functions to be performed most efficiently. As in other organisms, human diversity is partly genetically and partly environmentally conditioned. However, human environments are determined chiefly by the cultural tradition transmitted by instruction and learning, not by physical and biotic factors as in other organisms. There is no sharp cleavage between human heredity and human environment: genes do not transmit any "unit characters," either physical or psychological or cultural; the genes determine, jointly with the environment, the path which the development of a person will follow.

2

PSYCHOLOGY

New Ways to Self-discovery

by Gardner Murphy

In addition to the ways of self-discovery known to the prophet, the philosopher, and the poet, an amazing variety of new ways to self-knowledge has recently come into being. Man, the rational animal, has learned since the time of Darwin to grasp something of the irrational impulsiveness that comes from his descent from an animal ancestry; and since Freud he has learned to understand that much of what he feels and thinks is the expression of these impulsive forces through more complex channels. In the very era in which these discoveries have come from biological and medical science, a host of further types of inquiry, all broadly psychological—some psychological in a more technical sense—have piled up before us at a rate which makes the sheer unwrapping of the packages difficult indeed, quite aside from their careful inspection. It is an age of Christmas presents about the nature of man, some beautiful, some, at least on first inspection, in bad taste; but all challenging.

These discoveries come from the physical sciences, from the biological sciences, and from the cultural sciences. To begin with the physical sciences, it has long been understood by biologists that "chemistry is the central science." But only within the last few decades has it been grasped in what an intimate sense man's feelings and attitudes, literally his loves and hates, may express the balance

of chemical reactions going on within him; how the slight acceleration or retardation of metabolic processes may relate to enthusiasm
and apathy; how the administration of a hormone may, as William
James said of a cup of coffee, transform one's philosophy of life.
Passing, however, beyond the piecemeal stage of knowledge which
existed in the era of William James, we have today a reasonably
systematic picture of the way in which the chemistry of the blood
stream and, in particular, the activity of the glands of internal secre-
tion, may sensitize the nervous system to one way of perceiving
rather than another, to one train of fantasy rather than one presenting a contrasting mood. A psychologist who has at the same time the
basic training in biochemistry has within his hands one of the powerful instruments of the next few decades. He will, for example,
understand the meaning of the newer drugs in psychiatry, those
extraordinary preparations which are today cutting down much of the
suffering in many types of mental disorder and indeed, in some cases,
blotting out the symptoms in an almost magical fashion. He will
have before him the avenue which leads from biochemistry through
physiology to a more intimate knowledge of the functioning of the
cells of the central nervous system, and that intricate chain of nerve
cells and their fibers which lie the length of the spinal cord and are
known as the autonomic nervous system, the regulator of much of
our vital activity.

Here the domain of "psychosomatic medicine" points at last to a
clear manner of envisaging as two-way streets the functional relations
between biochemical process on the one hand, psychological process
on the other. No longer can we speak today of biochemistry as regulating the mind. We must, in the same sense, speak of the mind as
regulating the biochemical system. Or rather, as the more sophisticated students of the problem recognize, we are dealing always
with a psychophysical unit in which sometimes the mental aspects,
sometimes the biochemical aspects have to be recognized first; but
the other aspect is always likewise present. To "know thyself" means
no longer the mastery, by an immaterial principle, of a blind and

inert material stuff; or the belief, as with nineteenth-century materialists, that "the brain secretes thought as the liver secretes bile." Today we seek progressive recognition of the mutuality of two ways of describing humanness.

The problems which are important for science no longer lie neatly in long narrow boxes, belonging to one or another discipline. Biochemistry, physiology, medicine, and psychology are intertwined in a delicate strand with which we fish for truth. He who would work on psychological problems may sometimes be simply a psychological specialist with awareness of what lies in all directions from his subject matter. Sometimes he may be a biochemist, often a medical man. We are concerned more with the reality of function than with the sharp demarcation of academic disciplines.

There are, however, problems which are pursued mainly by psychologists, such as the question of the way in which we learn. Even here, however, material from the biological sciences is utilized. There has been an extraordinary convergence of information about the way in which human nature takes shape. Following upon the "nature-nurture controversy" which for decades told us that certain traits are inherited, others acquired, we have come into an era of recognizing that everything human, or indeed everything biological, is both inherited and acquired, the fulfillment of a potential contained within the genetic potentialities, but released, guided, and developed by specific environing conditions. We have now the specific question of "how human nature is acquired." Following the logic of the newer approach, we cannot conceive a fixed human nature planted within all members of the species, or indeed planted in any individual person. We can see human nature taking shape.

One process which has been observed closely within the last few years is the process of maturation within the nervous system and the discovery that, despite the supposedly foreordained or clock-work fashion of development which earlier embryology had suggested, the form of development depends partly upon function. Much basic work can be done with animals; indeed if the problem cannot other-wise be studied at the necessary level of complexity, monkeys or anthropoid apes may be used.

But even puppies can teach us much that we want to know, and give us a frame of reference from which to approach other species. In the McGill University psychological laboratory the question arose whether it is innate or instinctive in the puppy to retreat or yelp in response to injury. Deeply ingrained in all our assumptions is the belief that whatever is universal and automatic must be inborn, in-evitable, foreordained from the beginning. In the McGill laboratory, however, some puppies were isolated from all other members of their species, while control animals grew up in the normal way with their litter mates. The isolated animals grew up healthily, ate well, and when observed later by those who had not known their history of isolation, were judged to be typical and healthy members of their group. When, however, these puppies encountered a candle flame, they pushed their noses into it. In the same way, when accidentally the animals' toes were stepped on they showed no tendency to with-draw. This suggested that what we regard as fixed or instinctive be-havior is actually a result of a particular cycle of experiences; and indeed the control puppies which had been cuffed and pushed about by their litter mates and had had the "normal" canine growing-up experiences behaved in a way which we would regard as normal in response to these traumatic situations.

This fragment of evidence fits in with a great deal of other material about the learned nature of much that we usually call instinctive. Let us turn to the investigations by the Continental naturalists known as "ethologists." They have this to report about how instinctive be-havior is built up: the grey gosling, like other well-behaved fledglings, follows its mother. Let the experimenter, however, take care that mother is away at the time when the grey gosling is ready for loco-motion. The experimenter starts to walk away, and the grey gosling follows him. After experiences of this sort, the grey gosling has under-gone a process known as "imprinting"; the experimenter is now the object which calls forth this response of following. Indeed, the agitated mother can now walk or wheedle and the little fellow ignores her, following only the experimenter whose image is somehow imprinted within the nervous system of the fledgling. Such habits are in the main irreversible. They constitute cases of "acquired instincts."

Is there anything like this in man? There certainly seems to be. There is a process, much like that of the imprinting just described and perhaps identical with it, in which the human young form profound attachments to particular individuals, usually the mother, and build into the character structure a dependency relationship from which much else springs. As regards infants whose mothers, through illness, death, or desertion, have dropped out of the child's life, there have been remarkable studies of many who have gradually undergone personality deterioration in the form of an apathy and the disintegration of the normal emotional life; if this goes on too long, apparently complete recovery does not occur. There appears to be irreversible damage.

It might be held that the processes described up to this point relate only to the organization of the *impulsive life*, the chaining of responses to specific environmental stimuli, so that the stimuli forever afterwards call them forth. There has been much evidence however, in recent decades, that the *intellectual life also* is molded and shaped by the earliest months. For example, the self-evident three-dimensional world which we see around us is itself a construct depending upon a series of specific experiences in childhood. Those blind from birth, but operated upon for cataract in the preadolescent period, do not, when they first receive their vision, actually "see" in the usual sense. It takes time to organize the meaningless blurs into a meaningful world. While animal studies of space-perception show the slow development of the normal ways of perceiving, human studies show that an even longer time is required to organize the world of sight, hearing, and touch into the three-dimensional form which we think is so self-evident, so much the "inborn" and necessary way of perceiving.

Amazing new experiments in this field have emerged from the psychological institute at Innsbruck, Austria. These studies, working with young adult subjects, made use of "distorting lenses," which broke up the familiar world so that everything was seen wrong; and then over a period of weeks the careful daily observations permitted a study of the way in which the world came right again, the way in which the utter confusion, the baffling bewilderment of an upside down or crazy-quilt world was, while one still wore the lenses, rebuilt into a normal and acceptable world. While earlier investigators had contented themselves with showing the ways in which the person learns to *behave* normally while wearing inverting lenses, the newer studies have shown that perception itself can be built and rebuilt. With complex lenses, lines which are *bent* gradually *come straight* as one learns to react to the world, and to *re-see* the world while wearing them.

Relevant to all this are the much discussed recent American experiments, which began at Dartmouth and have been continued at Princeton and elsewhere, in which distorting rooms of various sorts are used to present the individual with a fundamental conflict between two ways of seeing. If he looks into a small room through an observation hole, the room appears to be perfectly cubical. Actually, however, the room has a sharply tilted floor and tilted ceiling, and the walls recede at strange angles. Through this peephole the projection of all these surfaces upon the retina is identical with that which would ordinarily be projected by a cubical room, and so we see the familiar cube. If, however, we must act within this space— for example, throwing a ball to hit a spot of light which moves about from place to place—we rapidly learn (typically within thirty or forty minutes) not only to throw the ball more accurately, but what is the more extraordinary, to see the distorted room *as it is*. In other words, we rebuild the cues, we reconstitute the world of experience. From such material comes the beginning of a new empirical theory of cognition, a view of the processes by which the familiar world is built up in the normal course of individual development by taking the fragments acting upon the sense organs and throwing them into order. We act in a world which requires, in the long run, order and stability. We furnish ourselves with such a world. This has implications for philosophy, but it is here the sheer psychology which delights the experimenter: the possibility of controlling, step by step, the world of the known, as well as the world of the felt and the world of the willed.

Some of the experiments that have just been described could be called experiments in the formation of personality, because they deal with ways in which knowledge, feeling, and impulse are built together. In many points they come into contact with psychoanalytic theory, with its rich conception of the forming of the person through the interaction of biological drives with social requirements. This is no place to do any sort of justice to the rich intricacies of the psychoanalytic system to which Sigmund Freud, one of the great geniuses of modern times, gave his life, and represented now by the largest single body of observational material about human nature which exists. The psychoanalytic system is based almost entirely upon clinical observation, is lacking in many types of scientific control, and is shot full of inference and bias of the analyst himself and the socially shared biases of those who have helped to develop the factual underpinnings and the lofty theoretical structures reared upon them. It is far too early to sift the reality from the fantasy here.

However, three things should be noted about psychoanalysis as a way of observing human nature. First, the profound relaxation and the dependency upon the doctor which characterize the course of psychoanalytic treatment make possible the direct observation of much that is ordinarily concealed. The vast new world of the unconscious discovered by this method would make psychoanalysis forever important in the history of human thought, even if no specific factual discoveries could as yet be claimed.

Second, much of the material gleaned in this way checks with material directly observable in infants, for example, with reference to the enormous importance of their instinctive life: the emotional cravings which appear as the forerunners of those emotional cravings, including the sexual, which play such a large part in adult life, and the cross-references which the child gives us to the child in other cultures. The different forms of social organization in other societies help us to see how the raw material of human nature is guided in different ways through the social pressures, taboos, constraints, distortions, which the tightly structured world of adult society inevitably entails.

Third, psychoanalysis as a system has offered a rich field of collaboration between clinical practice on the one hand and experimental studies of perception and instinct on the other hand. Typical of this is one type of investigation which is often called today the "new look psychology," an investigation of the ways in which psychoanalytic dynamics reflect themselves in the very process of perceiving.

In addition to the newer knowledge of perception summarized above, there is a large area of investigation in which we begin to see the role of drives, needs, fears, and aversions, reflecting themselves in the way in which the world is perceived, recalled, understood, and imagined. We begin to see that the world is no longer simply registered upon the sense organs, and that even though we may allow a huge role for past experience in the formation of associations about the world, as in the Dartmouth and Princeton studies already quoted, we have still not told even half the story.

The investigations may be said to have begun with the genius of Hermann Rorschach, who, during and immediately after the First World War, discovered that complex and irregular, though symmetrical, inkblots—some in black, some in color—made upon a semiabsorbent surface, gave rise to a rich variety of interpretations by different persons, throwing light upon the intellectual habits, the unconscious needs, the basic poetic, scientific predisposition of the observer. Rorschach thus brought out differences between the people of various cantons of Switzerland, for example, and differences between normal and disturbed, or between the various types of disturbed personalities. This Rorschach test initiated an era of "projective tests," devices for showing the way in which perception reveals the emotionally toned and impulsively directed outlook of each individual.

During the 1930's it began to be realized that in addition to these clinical instruments, many laboratory methods existed which could be developed to permit fuller understanding of these personality dispositions, as reflected in the different ways of perceiving and understanding the world. In the Harvard laboratory picture tests of various sorts were developed, some, for example, showing that different meanings were assigned to the pictures depending upon the number of hours since a person had eaten a meal. In the City College laboratory in New York, it was shown that this time-since-eating altered the way in which figures behind a ground glass screen were perceived: the hungrier the subject, the more of these objects were perceived as food objects. Other studies from the City College laboratory showed that simple rewards and punishments, as in receiving money and losing money from time to time, tended to standardize the visual situation, so that a person in an ambiguous situation saw it as he had seen while he was being rewarded, not as he had seen while he was being punished. Nonsense sounds recorded on a disc were found at the Worcester State Hospital laboratory to have definite meanings for various groups of mental patients. A series of definite laws began to evolve relating to the way in which a person accepts or rejects certain aspects of the perceptual field. One of the specially favored investigations of recent years has been the inquiry into "perceptual defense"—the process by which threatening or otherwise disturbing visual material shown under conditions requiring great alertness may actually be shut out or mutilated, while other material initially of the same level of difficulty may be seen perfectly well. Perceptual defense is one of the many areas in which the psychoanalytic concepts of unconscious dynamics as they influence perception have been especially stressed.

A stimulating integration of these laboratory studies with psychodynamic modes of inquiry has appeared in connection with studies originally aimed to contribute to the war effort, but continued now for over fifteen years as fundamental devices for the understanding of individual differences in perception. The initial task in these studies is to ascertain how well our laboratory subject can identify the vertical, report what is straight "up" and "down." He must tell us when a shaft is straight upright, although the large frame within which it is placed is tilting one way or another by a few or a great many degrees. The individual in a tilting chair must tell when he himself is upright, although the cues around him are often misleading. In one striking series, for example, his tilting chair is placed within a tilting room. The whole room, with pictures on the wall, with a well defined molding and baseboard, and accepted as a room, can be made to tilt back and forth; and now the individual sitting within the room and tilted in his chair must tell when his own body is vertical. As a result of all these studies, we find it possible to state the individual ways of responding to these situations by defining a dimension of personality: "field dependence." This is the degree to which a person under these conditions is dependent upon the visual field, and in this dependence fails to take accurate note of the cues from within the body which tell him actually when he is upright. Some individuals are incredibly field dependent. They must be as much as fifty or sixty degrees tilted to the right or left before they know it, so dependent are they upon the belying cues, as from the tilted room which they accept as upright. Other individuals, however, accept the testimony of their own bodies, the pressure upon the hip as one tilts, the sag of the muscles, and so on, so that two or three degrees of tilt suffice to betray the reality to them, and permit them to reject the misleading evidence of the visual field around them.

Field dependence is next brought into relation to a series of personality dimensions. Six different types of personality assessment, beginning with the Rorschach inkblot method already described, are used. Persons thoroughly trained in the use of these clinical devices are forced to predict "blind," that is, with absolutely no further information about the individual than his response to the projective test, just how field-dependent each individual will be in the laboratory studies of detection of the vertical. In all of these six different methods the predictions are remarkably good. We have, moreover, a study of children, year by year, made in order to see how each individual achieves his own characteristic adult degree of field dependence. In such investigations we see a personality dimension slowly taking shape, as a result of growth and learning; clinical instruments are in each case brought into relation to laboratory findings.

All of the foregoing begins to suggest that growth is more than the release of a potential. It is actually the interaction with a personal-social reality. This leads us into modern social psychology, which has proliferated at an incredible pace in the last few decades. The social psychology of the era of World War I was still essentially a descriptive study of groups, "mob mind," or propaganda. Laboratory investigations of individuals in group situations began during the 20's and soon made tremendous gains. Some of these situations involved competition and leadership; others picked up the thread already noted, viewing the influence of the structure of a social group upon the way in which each member of this group perceives a situation. Contemporaneous with these uses of the laboratory in understanding the basic dynamics of social psychology, came the influence of sociological theory and of practical business demands for better methods of assessing public opinion; and during the 30's public opinion techniques grew like Jack's beanstalk. Finally, during World War II, these methods of assessing public opinion, so important in the Army, were brought into relation to the depth dynamics, psychoanalytic modes of thought, projective tests, and so on, to throw further light upon factors involved in each individual's opinion and attitude. This naturally interested those whose approach had been defined in terms of cultural anthropology; thus public opinion research as a nose-counting adventure evolved into public opinion research as a mode of assessment of group-structured attitude patterns seen against the backdrop of the culturally ingrained uniformities of a social group. The psychoanalytic theory of cathexis became useful: a theory to the effect that each individual invests his emotional life in certain objects from which he never thereafter fully withdraws it. This theory, which had already been useful in terms of habit formation, as in the imprinting process described above, came to be seen as describing a factor shared by all members of cultural groups, so that irreversible value patterns constituted much of the cohesive force of society.

The view of individual personality and of human nature which derives from all of these studies so far described is inevitably much oversimplified. The laboratory method is in general a simplifying method and, as we noted, it makes comparisons of man with simpler forms of life. Even when dealing with his more complex social behavior, it tries to envisage simple drives and simple ways in which they are molded. The simplicity is not to be damned, but there is a place for complexity, too. We can here only list a few of the directions in which the struggle to deal with complexity has been manifest.

First, the role of language in marking off the things in the environment, grouping them together, and permitting conceptual thought (as recognized since Greek philosophy) has come in for intensive study in the last few decades, with the psychological laboratory playing its modest but genuine role in connection with linguistic investigations of many other types.

Second, there has been general recognition that all of the higher phenomena of psychology are organized around the *self* or ego, and that it will not suffice to describe either instinctual energies or perceptual integrations, or simple acts of memory or fantasy without bearing in mind that these are the acts of an experiencing individual who to some degree is aware of his own individuality, as well as of the things with which he is directly dealing. Psychoanalysis, after thirty years of primary concern with the life of instinct and its manifestations, became more and more oriented to "ego psychology," and in a series of brilliant papers during the 1920's Freud defined the issues from which a psychoanalytic ego psychology finally took shape in the 30's and 40's. Psychoanalytic ego psychology is a psychology of complex integrative acts, ultimately derived from instinctual energies, yet carrying out intricate processes of "reality testing" and processes of gauging the soundness or unsoundness of ideas and the wisdom or folly of projected lines of action. It is a long way, indeed, from the commonly held view that psychoanalysis is an impulse-glorifying scheme to the modern psychoanalytic ego psychology of perception, recall, judgment, and conceptual thinking.

Despite the range of activities in which psychology is involved, and the far-from-systematized nature of the little islands of fact discovered in a sea of the unknown, the implication should not be given that psychology moves quickly in response to the individuality of the investigator. Psychology has grown mostly within the university structure. This was indeed one of the reasons for the slow recognition of the importance of the psychoanalytic movement. When once a pattern of thought becomes crystallized, the inertia becomes tremendous, partly because it is so hard to get out of prepared grooves and partly because of the enormous vested interests which consciously or unconsciously keep us thinking as we have learned to think. It takes something really new, really heroic, to see man in terms of his animal ancestry and also to see him in terms of historical and cultural richness; and our psychological training is still inadequate to the job, as is evident if one looks either at most research on the learning process, or at the present state of thinking about religion, ethics, art, and law. The blinders and straitjackets are more serious than we realize. Countless topics have been clamoring for investigation but only given a nod. Thus, when at the end of the eighteenth century a peculiar form of sleep was shown to be related to some of the roots of mental disease and the possibility of its cure, its proponent, Anton Mesmer, became for the respectable simply a quack; and forty years later the English surgeon, Elliotson, had a similar fate. Psychoanalysis took several decades to win its place.

But the most important combatant for a legitimate place among the sciences is parapsychology, or psychical research, a type of inquiry into telepathy and other types of knowledge transcending the use of the known senses, and of various poorly understood relations between living individuals and environment which began to come in for serious experimental work in the 80's of the last century. Dozens of distinguished figures in science and medicine have gone their way, decade after decade, each asserting the reality of some of the phenomena described, and each has been pooh-poohed. An elaborately controlled experimental demonstration of telepathy, for example, at Groningen University in The Netherlands in 1921, involving transmission of numbers from experimenters in one room to a blindfolded subject in another room, was simply ignored. A somewhat better fate was accorded J. B. Rhine at Duke University in the early 30's and thereafter, since, despite a long series of attacks, the mass of evidence which his laboratory (and now many others) have accumulated, including long-distance experiments, appears to be no longer capable of such absolute rejection. Indeed, the recent massive investigations of Soal and Bateman at the University of London, including successes in telepathic experiments between London and Antwerp, fully confirm and extend the case for the realities of types of knowledge not transmitted through the senses.

Parapsychology is in itself a vast field, a field with a research literature comparable in size and importance to that of experimental psychology. Several dozen young psychologists have recently had the energy and courage to devote themselves to the development of experimental methods in this field, and a number of principles of general validity about such paranormal types of functioning appear to have been tentatively established. It is a safe bet now that within the next two or three decades parapsychology will be one of the areas of experimental psychology in which fundamental progress will be made—an area, moreover, of special importance, because we do not at present know of any way in which to integrate our knowledge of the physical and biological sciences with the realities which are emerging in the laboratory. It is that which is most repugnant to the "common sense" of today which has the greatest promise of bursting the shackles and giving a new synthesis. It is that which does not fit into the existing world view which offers the greatest promise of new worlds for old.

3

CULTURAL ANTHROPOLOGY

New Uses for "Barbarians"

by Clyde Kluckhohn

IN A WORLD where educated people now recognize that the ways of other clans and nations cannot remain matters of indifference or contempt or antiquarian curiosity, anthropology suddenly finds itself fashionable. Anthropologists have returned from the natives and are thinking and talking about the wide contemporary world. Some of this talk is hasty and immature, but at any rate some essential questions are being posed. It is these fundamental new questions that will interest us here rather than the attempts to apply anthropological knowledge to ease the transitional period for American Indians, or to improve communication with the Hindus, or to help management understand the tribal organization of the factory or hospital.

To Herodotus and to many writers of the Renaissance and Enlightenment, the "barbarians" provided a cabinet of human curiosities. Tacitus, Voltaire, Chateaubriand, and Melville used the "noble savage" as a weapon of social criticism. Nineteenth-century anthropologists illustrated stages in a supposedly uniform social evolution culminating in the "progress" of the Victorian Age.

Anthropologists of the first four decades of this century prided themselves on their factual and "objective" descriptions of exotic ways of life. They lived among "primitives" and noted scrupulously what they saw. They asked the "savages" what they did and why.

Psychologists and psychiatrists, however, know that there are things true about any personality that even the most cooperative subject or patient cannot reveal because he is himself unaware of them. Similarly, the anthropologist today realizes that some of the most significant things about a life-way are so taken for granted by the participants in that culture that they can't talk about them. This growing edge in the analysis of human uniformities and variants starts largely from four basic problems:

1. What can we say about a total culture that would not emerge from a list of its various parts?
2. How does one become an American or a Russian or a Choctaw?
3. To what extent are unconscious patterns of thought, emotion, and action conditioned by or revealed in different languages?
4. Are all values relative?

When Americans meet, they shake hands. Japanese bow. The intent is the same in both cases. And Japanese-Americans shake hands as "naturally" as other Americans. "Culture" is a set of historically derived regularities in behavior that distinguish one group from another. Cultures are storehouses of group experience. Almost all of anthropology's contributions to the intellectual mainstream derive from this central idea which explains as much about human behavior as does the idea of gravity in the physical world. Much of what we do cannot be understood in terms of biology or of the situation in which we find ourselves at the moment, but only by looking at the blueprints supplied by our cultures.

The details of culture patterns take their origin in the accidents of history. Yet, in the large, when they first develop they also make some kind of sense in providing orderly habits for meeting biological and social needs under given circumstances. But once established, both the accidental and the originally functional elements are usually resistant to change even when conditions which brought them into being have changed radically. An expensive example of the stubborn persistence of historical accident is the absurd spelling of our language which squanders time and money in printing and creates needless trials both for our own children and for foreign students of English. A patent instance of the survival of a once useful but now vestigial social organ is our Electoral College.

Any alteration of a culture is commonly felt as a threat. Unless the mores are stable one cannot predict or interpret correctly the acts of one's fellows. Hence the innovator is accused of "attacking our sacred customs." Cultural habits are also all too tempting as instruments for distinguishing the in-group from the out-group, citizens from "foreigners," the "civilized" from the "savage," the "intelligent from the "benighted heathen," even "the good" from "the bad." Human beings are not organic machines who give fixed responses to stimuli. The cultural animal responds to stimuli only as these are defined and interpreted in accord with conventional, man-made categories. These unseen screens which interpose between organisms and their environment are largely cultural. Hence, any culture is a bar to the free exercise of rationality.

To be sure, human creatures can stand only a little uncertainty. We all need some order in our lives and some semblance of predictability as to what we can expect from others if our own conduct is thus or so. Life would indeed be chaos, weird and unthinkable, if each of us were truly "spontaneous" in his behavior, acting out freely the impulse of every moment. It is fortunate for all that even the most iconoclastic among us most of the time follow established patterns not of our own making. Human life is a cultural life and a moral life precisely because it is a social life. In the case of the human species, cooperation and other necessities of social life are not taken care of automatically by instincts as with the bees and ants.

Yet it remains a serious question both for societies and for persons as to how much an individual should become the automaton of his culture. The healthy man is probably he who accepts, protects, and fulfills his own nature as a unique organization of experience but at the same time manages to identify himself wholeheartedly with the conserving and the innovating forces of his culture alike. For man is the creator as well as the creature of culture. New patterns are woven not only from the tangled web spun by the accidents of history but also from the stuff supplied by the uniqueness of biology and private experience. Cultures do change, albeit sometimes too slowly and too late.

Such change often exhibits remarkable regularity. This is notably true of language, that aspect of culture which is most mountainous and anonymous and unconscious. Everyone knows of Grimm's Laws and other "sound shifts" of Indo-European languages. Recently it has been shown that the common words of languages have a "half-life" not unlike those of organic compounds, the age of which can be dated up to thirty thousand years by the Carbon 14 method. If two speech communities have been separated for a thousand years, 66 per cent of the basic vocabulary in the two languages remains recognizably similar. It is now known, for example, that the Eskimos and the Aleuts were a single people roughly three thousand years ago. This date (and others) fits well with dating established by Carbon 14 and geological and archaeological methods.

Because the study of culture is the study of regularities, the anthropologist is not ordinarily as much preoccupied with figures as is the public opinion poller or the social psychologist. If you want to analyze the grammar of standard American English, any normal educated adult or any widely read and accepted book will do for a source. Only if you are interested in individual peculiarities or regional or dialectical variations do you have to worry about the nature of your "sample." Or, if you observe in a dozen middle class houses that on semiformal occasions men rise when a woman enters the room, you would be foolish to go on counting cases unless you are looking for the occasional deviation and the precise circumstances under which it occurs. Since they are studying culturally standardized behavior, anthropologists use "informants" and incidents much as an historian uses documents, rather than as a public opinion poller uses "respondents" or a psychologist experimental "subjects." The issue for the anthropologist and historian is that of the specimen in the series: how does the new information illuminate a general context or a style?

The anthropologist is skeptical of mechanical quantitative methods that dismember a context which in the actually experienced world is a whole. Since the field worker is often alone he must cover the waterfront. He must observe and hear about everything from the techniques of basket-making to the tuning of drums and the nursing of infants. He has learned from experience that "religion" and "economics" and "politics" do not stay dammed up in the neat little pools of our Western categories. A Hindu may give up his farm tools and sell his female children into slavery before he will consume the flesh of his cattle. If the anthropologist's central interest really lies in power ("who does what to whom, when, and how") he finds that some of his best clues come from noting how a mother treats an unruly youngster as well as from watching formal deliberations in council.

Cultures are wholes. Everything is somehow related to everything else. The problem of investigation is that of finding the point of entrance in the study of a circle. Whether you start with witchcraft or the exchange of goods or the graphic arts, you ought to end up in about the same place if you follow out your data in every direction in which they lead. For cultures have organization as well as content. Even the most complete listing of separate traits will produce only that kind of utility possessed by a telephone directory or by a Sears Roebuck catalogue. Anthropologists look at the web as well as the strands. Each strand gains its significance in part from being at a particular point in a network of relationships. The Hopi and the Navaho Indians both make sandpaintings, but the cultural meaning —the place that sandpaintings have in the total life of these two peoples—is quite different. The Hopi sandpainting is an incident in a complicated annual ceremonial calendar. The Navaho drypainting is an important technique used to cure an individual patient, selected to suit that individual's ailment, and made at a time chosen by him and his relatives.

Not only is almost everything in a culture interdependent and interrelated; much of the interrelationship must be understood as the actualization, with varying materials, of a theme central to the whole culture. Such a theme is that of "aesthetic nicety" in Japanese culture. The tea ceremony and flower arrangement are hackneyed illustrations. But the same note is struck in many details in etiquette: the subtle gradations of bowing; the wearing of kimonos corresponding to the month and the precise age grade of the woman; the refinement of court and academic procedures. Food among the upper classes is prepared more for the gratification of the eye than for the satisfaction of the stomach. In Kyoto trout are cooked in such a way that they curve in a shape harmonious with that of the dish, and they are garnished with a bamboo container filled with colored pebbles to simulate the brook. The language is saturated with minute prescriptions that have aesthetic overtones. Some sounds appear too harsh to Japanese ears for women to utter. There are the intricately complicated honorifics. A monograph could be written upon the niceties of choice as to which personal pronoun to choose in addressing one's wife, friend, acquaintance. Two little articles, wa and ga, used to identify various types of subject and object of the verb, have so many nuances as to perplex the Japanese themselves.

To say that a culture is a complex of interrelated parts, often ordered with respect to a number of rather pervasive themes, is not to say that any culture is "perfectly integrated." All cultures, like all personalities, have their contradictions and inconsistencies, their quirks, and their blind spots. Nor is there any suggestion that anthropologists have mastered the secret of analyzing a multidimensional order. To be all-embracing is not the same as having embraced all. The best that can be said for anthropologists is that they have recognized the problem and are trying.

In many ways this problem of how to cope with a multidimensional order is the present grand dilemma of chemistry and genetics and other natural sciences as well as of the study of human behavior. In the seventeenth century Western men learned to solve problems of ordered simplicity such as those of the classical mechanics. The well-known mathematician, Warren Weaver, uses the example of the motion of a single ivory ball as it moves about on a billiard table. Here the unknowns are limited and a relatively simple calculus involving dimensions, angles, and force will solve the order of events.

The later development of probability theory and statistics has enabled us to tackle problems of disorganized complexity where a large number of events was involved and where the relevant question is "Can such a distribution be due to random chance?" No insurance company can predict that a particular individual will die in an automobile accident six months hence. Yet while such individual events are helter-skelter, a dependably accurate prediction can be made as to about how many highway fatalities will occur among the millions of automobile passengers.

But this is not enough: statistical techniques are not appropriate to realms of organized complexity where some statements can be made only of two or more things considered in their interrelationship, where the pertinent fact is not the presence or absence of something in such and such quantity but rather the nature of the arrangement of the observable entities. The selfsame atoms, present in exactly the same number, may constitute an organic molecule of either a food or a poison, depending solely upon the fashion in which these atoms are arranged in respect to each other. If we throw a crystal to the ground, it breaks; however, its dissolution is not haphazard The fragmentation proceeds in a complex but organized manner following lines of cleavage predetermined by the particular structure of the crystal, invisible though this structure is to the naked eye. Such a realm is that of culture, where patterning reigns supreme.

From ordinary experience we know that each personality is in certain respects completely unique, in other respects similar to certain others, in a few ways like all human personalities. The same may be said for each culture. Is there any systematic relationship between similarities in culture and similarities in personality? The Greek physician Hippocrates, and many writers after him, have argued this point. During the last generation the joint effort of psychiatrists, psychologists, and anthropologists has tried to transform clinical speculation into exact research. There is no doubt that laughing and fainting and other outward expressions of personality are culturally patterned. There remains doubt as to how deep-going these influences are and as to the extent to which we are justified in speaking of a "typical" personality for each culture.

A clinical psychologist gave Rorschach ink blot tests to Navaho Indians, Zuni Indians, Spanish-Americans, and Mormons living in the same area in New Mexico. On his return from the field he gave his records to an experienced student of this test. All culturally identifying materials were removed, and she was asked to sort by personality type alone. She made five piles, but only one of these conformed in large part to the cultural group. However, the experiment was repeated and the second Rorschach expert's groupings corresponded to the cultural divisions to a degree considerably beyond chance expectation. The difference in these two results cannot be attributed to variations in the skill and intelligence of the two experimenters. It may be traceable to the fact that the experience of the first had focused her attention upon the uniqueness of each personality, while the second was more trained to look for similarities cutting across variations. But the cautious verdict would be that such trials need to be repeated many times before we can be sure how deep-going are the influences of culture upon personality.

An anthropologist and a psychologist examined facts from thirty-seven cultures distributed over the world to test the psychoanalytic theory that cultural habits as to weaning children have an effect on personality development. They found a significantly greater amount of emotional disturbance among children in the societies where weaning took place at two years or less. They also found that anxiety about aggression was markedly higher where there was a cultural belief that illness could be caused by animal spirits. These and other correlations established are matters of detail, but they have been made so carefully that we may infer that studies of the relation between culture and personality are promising.

The Russian Research Center of Harvard University interviewed, observed, and tested a sizable number of recent escapees from the Soviet Union. Some of these had come to maturity before the Communists took over. Others had grown up under the Communist regime. Members of both groups exhibited to varying degree the traditional Russian "national character" as familar from literature. But there was much evidence that some of the younger people, and especially those who had been actively identified with the Party, were being made over into the image of "the new Soviet man." These latter were much more formal and controlled; less warm, expressive, and expansive. They were more distrustful, less identified with the social group in which their day-to-day lives were spent, far more committed to "doing" as opposed to "being." The Russian escapees were also compared with a matched group of Americans on whom the same information was obtained. Some of the contrasts between the more "traditional" Russians and the Americans stand out. The Russians were less interested in achievement, more in personal relationships. They welcomed others into their lives but were not tensely anxious about what others thought of them. The Russians expressed fear, depression, and despair more frequently and openly than Americans. Americans and Russians were about equal in their love of material things, especially gadgets.

These investigations, too, demonstrate a relationship between culture and personality as well as the wide range of personal variation within any cultural group. From the point of view of the contemporary scene, the most hopeful conclusion is that even the most brutal and totalitarian schemes to make a new man of the human animal meet with stubborn resistance. Nevertheless, human nature can be changed within limits, and the Communists are engaged in a persistent experiment on the grand scale.

Human speech approaches being pure culture. Our vocal apparatus allows us to make a great variety of sounds. But we soon learn to make a particular set of sounds selected by our culture out of a considerable number of biological possibilities. As youngsters we can still learn another language quite easily, but by the time we are adults cultural crystallization has taken place. Since language exemplifies the cultural process in such a pure form, many anthropologists use language as a theoretical model for the study of culture generally. It is also in the field of anthropological linguistics that the most rigorous methods have been developed and where the frontiers of cultural anthropology are being swept back the most dramatically.

Only in language do we have clear-cut units of culture comparable to the atom in physics or the gene in biology. However, talk about these "phonemes" gets immensely technical. Here we can only note that there is certainly order, system, and predictability in this sphere of human behavior. Once the student of an undescribed language discovers one "ejective" (abrupt closure and release of the glottis) as a distinctive sound-class (phoneme) he can be sure that certain other sounds of similar type in the language will conform to the same pattern. For example, I hear in the Navaho Indian language a t sound that is unlike any we ordinarily make in English. It strikes me as if it were flicked off the end of the tongue with some effort, and I can see something happening in the region of the Adam's apple. I can therefore anticipate that other sounds of this type (voiceless—vocal cords not vibrating—and where the sound is produced by a stoppage of the breath at some point) will also be made in this fashion. And indeed there is in Navaho a whole series of such ejectives or "glottalized consonants."

Phonemes constitute not a natural but a conventional or cultural category. For most people all of language belongs to the class of the "taken for granted." Native speakers seldom indeed have to stop to think about how to make a sound or what grammatical form to use. Talking takes on almost the automatic character of an "instinctive" response. But the characteristic way in which certain questions are begged in the customary turns of speech tells us something about the manner in which people dissect their experience. The Navaho show an intense, almost pathological, avoidance of the dead. This is reflected in their language. In telling a story one must add a special suffix whenever the name of someone belonging to the past is mentioned. The Wintu Indians pay little attention to the distinction between singular and plural which is stressed in "good" English. They lavish this care on another contrast, that between the particular and the generic: the man and Man, these acorns and all acorns.

The Western type of subject-predicate proposition is absent in Chinese. Chinese thought is not based upon the "law of identity" but rather upon the relation of opposites. In literary Chinese the English phrases "A relates to B" and "A is related to B" would be expressed by one and the same form. The traditional Western type of subject-predicate proposition (which is the basis of the Law of Identity) is lacking in Chinese. The Chinese think of relations rather than of substance. The Chinese language focuses on the how-priority, Western languages on the what-priority. Chinese ideographs point, as it were, to specific objects by signs or symbols. The structure of the sentence indicates a relation between the signs or symbols. The language goes no further. The number of ideographs is legion, and they are not grouped into classes except on the basis of how one character was gradually modified into others. Western languages are much more concerned with categories which get at the substance "underlying" the concrete entities brought together. Some scholars see a connection here with Chinese civilization's relative neglect of nature and science, its centering on human affairs.

Anything can be expressed in any language, but the structure of each different language favors certain kinds of statement and hinders others. Japanese is a language in which the relative status of the speakers is precisely defined but the rest of the content of a conversation is left rather ambiguous. In the tongue of the Trobriand Islanders of Melanesia, causation cannot be expressed—only propinquity in time or space. Any grammar acts, to some extent, as an unconscious philosophy.

Perhaps the most important contribution of anthropological linguistics has come from the difficulties the anthropologist goes through in trying to express the meanings contained in forms of speech completely foreign to the pattern of all European languages. On the basis of a critical examination of languages of widely different ground plan, some anthropologists have questioned the universality and the necessity of such central Western concepts as time, velocity, and matter. The "time" of the Hopi Indians varies with each observer, does not permit of simultaneity, and cannot be given a number greater than one. The Hopi have constructed a consistent picture of the universe with a "psychological time" (like Bergson's "duration") altogether different from the mathematical time of our physicists. Edmund Wilson, on working through the Hebrew text of the Old Testament, is baffled by the translation problems arising from the early Jewish conception of time. He comments:

The Hebrew line of eternity ends by slipping away from all . . . points and retaining only the property of extending indefinitely in either direction. . . . Our myths are the temporal myths of Caesar and Pericles, of Charlemagne, Washington, Hitler, but the myths of the Jews are timeless—the patriarchs and prophets who never die, the Messiah who never comes.

We see now that our categories are not "given" by the external world. Experience actually comes in a kaleidoscopic flux of impressions which is organized by our minds in accord with the constructs developed in and favored by our culture. The "real world" is unconsciously built up, in part, on the language habits of the group. But much more work will have to be done before we know whether linguistic patterns limit perception and dictate thought or whether they merely direct perception and thinking into habitual channels. It seems likely that language both determines and is determined by the rest of culture. And there is small case for the view that reality itself is relative; rather, different languages tend "to punctuate and categorize reality in special ways." Yet we will do well to remember that language, in the cross-cultural as well as in other senses, is fetter to thought as well as its key. As Edward Sapir remarked, "To pass from one language to another is psychologically parallel to passing from one geometrical frame of reference to another."

One of the massive movements of recent intellectual history has been that toward relativism. Anthropology, along with psychoanalysis, Marxism, and logical positivism, has contributed to the crisis of values in the Western world. Anthropological research and writing have persuaded a good many educated men and women that all values are culture-bound, relative to given times and places: some

Arctic tribes strangle their grandmothers, whereas Englishmen usually don't.

Now there are senses in which the principle of cultural relativity is sound. Comparison of cultures leads quickly to recognition that they are differently weighted in their values. This is important. True understanding of a culture necessarily involves seeing its values against the perspective of the historical experience and the present situation of the people. We cannot fully comprehend or appraise a moral judgment without taking the whole way of life into account.

On the other and, the inescapable fact of cultural relativism does not justify the conclusion of some that cultures are in all respects utterly disparate and hence incomparable entities. There is a generalized framework that underlies the more apparent and striking facts of cultural relativity. All men face the same inevitable problems, whatever their cultures: they must get food and shelter, and learn to cope with birth, illness, love, and death. (This is a platitude, but nothing becomes a platitude unless it is interesting and important.) All cultures constitute many somewhat distinct answers to the same dilemmas posed by human biology and by the generalities of the human situation. Every society's patterns for living must provide approved and sanctioned ways for dealing with such universal circumstances as the existence of two sexes; the helplessness of infants; the need for satisfaction of the elementary biological requirements such as food, warmth, and sex; the presence of individuals of different ages and of differing physical and other capacities. The basic similarities in human biology the world over are vastly more impressive than the differences.

Equally, there are certain necessities in social life for this kind of animal regardless of where that life is carried on or in what culture. Cooperation for obtaining food and for other ends requires a certain minimum of reciprocal behavior, of a standard system of communication, and indeed of shared values. The facts of human biology and of human gregariousness supply, therefore, certain invariant points of reference from which cross-cultural comparison must start. The response or performance potentialities of the species are the building blocks from which cultures are constructed.

Any science must be adequate to explain both the similarities and the differences in the facts with which it deals. For two generations anthropology focused its attention preponderantly on the differences. They are there; they are real and significant. There must be no attempt to explain cultural relativism away or to deprecate its importance because it is inconvenient, hard to take, hard to live with. Some values are almost purely cultural and draw their meaning from the matrix of a single culture. Even the universal values have their special phrasings and emphases in harmony with each distinct culture.

At the same time one must never forget that cultural differences are still so many variations on themes arising from raw human nature and from the human situation. In broad outline the simple but precious things that people all over the world and throughout historical time have wanted are about the same. Quarrels, both physical and intellectual, have developed mainly over modes and means of attaining these ends. Millions have perished and many more millions have suffered in struggles over means, and doubtless this will go on and probably worsen so far as the numbers affected are concerned. It is tragic that the similarities in basic wants should be so obscured. The common understandings between men and women of different cultures are broad, general, easily obscured by language and many other observable symbols. Yet the cultural trappings make up, in some ways, a comparatively superficial veneer. True universals or near universals (in content as opposed to form) are, to be sure, apparently few in number. But they seem to be as deep-going as they are rare. Anthropology's facts attest that the phrase "a common humanity" is by no means meaningless.

Anthropology today, though an importer from both the humanities and the sciences, is perhaps too imperialistic, a trifle intoxicated by the fantasy of the anthropologist as philosopher and king. Every profession—like every individual and every culture—has its own pathology. And, if passion bulks too strongly in anthropological utterances that reach the wider public, monographic paleness is still preserved in the great bulk of its writing. In any case we must never allow ourselves to be intimidated by the caution of the specialists who are usually lacking in contrastive perspective.

We can rejoice in the excitement which prevails in contemporary anthropology. The new wine is threatening to burst the old bottles. Major intellectual developments are usually initiated by changes in what scholars regard as "real" and legitimate objects of study. Such a change may be represented by anthropology's concern with relations as well as things, by the respectability suddenly acquired by "values" as a proper object of anthropological enquiry. There is a decent chance that the varyingly labeled studies of man may halt the flight to the irrational, the terrified retreat to the older orthodoxies of which we see so many alarming symptoms on the present horizon. As E. R. Dodds suggests in his great book, *The Greeks and the Irrational*, an outstanding contrast between ourselves and the Greeks at the dawn of the Hellenistic Age is that, while the Greeks "were deeply and imaginatively aware of the power, the wonder, and the peril of the Irrational," they could describe this kind of behavior only in mythological or symbolic language. They had no systematic intellectual instruments for analysis and understanding. Anthropology and psychology, along with the other human studies, have created at least the beginnings of an understanding of nonrational (e.g., customary) and irrational behavior. This is no vitalism, no abdication to the irrational. Rather, it is an extension of the area that reason can deal with and, conceivably, control in some measure.

4

ARCHAEOLOGY

The Snows of Yesteryear

by Gordon R. Willey

ARCHAEOLOGY'S preoccupation is with the oddments of the dead because these hold within themselves the secret of what once was life. The stone axe and the broken urn have their esoteric role in science, but underlying this is the deeper significance that they are the objects which long ago felt the hands and breath of other men. The archaeologist seeks to reestablish that kindredness which binds humankind together even across the millennia of time. It is his task to fashion an image of the past and to infuse it with a semblance of living. He is the new Pygmalion.

The past is both inescapable and irrevocably lost. We are irresistibly swept away from it, and yet the form of the present bears the imprint of what went before. Our thoughts, our emotions, the physical shape of the world in which we live—all these are conditioned by our predecessors, and if we are to achieve self-knowledge, we cannot disavow or disregard them. Heartening and tragic, this past is mankind's great storehouse of experience, and we are wise to turn to it.

But can any part of it truly be recaptured? Gibbon with all his narrative power stirs the imagination; but is it really Rome, Caesar's Rome, which he describes, or only a vision distorted by eighteenth-century eyes and minds? Perhaps the most successful recapture of times gone by is the sensitive, evocative creation of Proust, and yet

48

even within the single and intimate confines of the consciousness of a great novelist one wonders what is real and what is the magic of illusion. Has the archaeologist the temerity, then, to try where these masters have failed? Can he, with nothing more than scraps of stones and bones, recapture the past?

The answer is both yes and no. He has, and must ever have, the courage to try. At the same time he should have the wisdom to know just how far short from his goal his efforts bring him. He can at best construct a replica pieced together from the residue of antiquity which, embarrassingly, shows the handiwork of his own generation and his own self. Nevertheless, this poor creation of the archaeologist is all that we have of the surge and fury of much of life that lies behind us and is forever still.

How does the modern archaeologist meet this challenge and what are his victories against heavy odds? What does he do and how is he doing it better?

To begin, he is an historian in the broader sense of that term. Like the historian, his studies are directed toward retelling the human past, and his story should be a dynamic and integrated one, not a series of static facts. He is a scientist, too, or strives to be one, in that archaeology is a part of anthropology, and he is interested in cause and effect as well as generalizations about human social behavior and the development of civilization. Finally—and this is in no way incompatible with his scientific interests—he is a humanist. He deals with facts objectively, adds them up, subjects them to statistics, but he also loves them. Because he deals with broken pieces of something that was once vital and whole he searches constantly for patterns into which these pieces fit, and glories in their reassembly. At the same time he loves, and dares not forget, the fragment that does not fit the pattern, for it, too, in its isolation, carries with it the essence of humanity.

It has been traditional for the archaeologist to confine himself mostly to the mute evidences in mankind's record and to leave the written word for his historical colleague, although this working arrangement is by no means binding. The inscriptions of ancient Egypt or the Near East are generally considered to be within the domain of archaeology in that the total context of these writings is, for the most part, a reconstruction based upon the material remains of these civilizations. Conversely, the historian has often been as concerned with the architectural remains of the European Middle Ages as he has with their documentary sources.

There is, however, a difference of emphasis between archaeology and history which has profound implications and which also reveals the important complementary relationship shared by the two disciplines. In treating chiefly with the nonliterate record—the palace foundations, the tombs, the potsherd debris—the archaeologist is a seeker after patterns. He must, perforce, look for the grand similarities and differences in these *disjecta* of vanished peoples and civilizations. He must "play the percentages," try to capture the main trends over the centuries, and when he speaks he speaks at best of probabilities. There are both strengths and weaknesses in his approach. His fundamental advantage is that the vast preponderance of man's history on this planet lies in the archaeological past, not in contemporary written records. The hundreds of thousands of years of the Paleolithic, the millennia of the Neolithic, and much of the Bronze Age extend deep below the last five thousand years of even partial textual recording. With this kind of perspective the archaeologist is able to see and compare the rise and fall of cultures and civilizations over immense spans of time.

On the debit side, the archaeologist must usually struggle against the bleakness of a picture bereft of recognizable human faces, of the color and zest of personalities. The military power of a long-dead state may be traced through its expanding systems of fortifications or the spread of its dynastic art, but it is difficult to portray these events as something more than abstractions of human affairs. If fifteenth-century Europe had left no written records, archaeologists might have made a fair job of describing the warlike tendencies of the feudal period. From arms and other devices found in France they could have identified the invaders of that country as Englishmen.

Possibly some of the actual campaigns could have been plotted, and with skill the slow defeat and withdrawal of the invading forces might have been reconstructed. But not even the most brilliant archaeological imagination could have conceived of Joan of Arc in this total setting. This inability to delineate the individual—and the individual human being is ever the main focus of interest for other human beings—is archaeology's greatest failing. Here written history must take over.

As we have said, archaeology is anthropology as well as history. The archaeologist must apprise himself of the ethnology of the area which is in any way concerned with the problems he is investigating. In this way he is able to project present and observed behavior back into the inert forms of past life. As an example, archaeologists working in the prehistoric Pueblo Indian cultures of the Southwestern United States are able to explain the meaning and function of strange underground chambers that appear in ruined villages of otherwise above-ground structures. These subsurface rooms are *kivas*, similar to those still used today for Pueblo Indian ceremonials and intimately tied up with the Puebloan clan systems and religious life. This knowledge, which derives from ethnological observations and not written records, enables the archaeologist not only to identify the prehistoric below-ground rooms as *kivas* but to make further inferences about the social and religious organization of the deserted villages. In much the same way the European archaeologist is able to interpret and understand his Neolithic findings in the area of the Baltic States and other parts of Northern Europe. Here, he finds that the present-day peasant follows customs and uses agricultural, hunting, and fishing implements that differ little from those of three or four thousand years ago.

Archaeology also interprets its data within a more general anthropological frame of reference. If man's biological makeup and needs are much the same the world over, it is logical to expect some general similarities in the various ways he has attempted to satisfy these needs through the medium of his culture. It is a major and unsettled problem of anthropology as to what kind and what degree of similarities or regularities exist. Certainly there are some. Man builds dwellings, organizes families, and worships gods. Out of these activities certain analogies may be drawn and inferences made that will aid the archaeologist in his interpretations when more specific and historically related ethnological parallels are lacking.

Today, archaeology is being carried out in almost every region of the world and under almost every conceivable physical condition. The jungle decay of Mexico and Guatemala has been cut away to reveal carved stone temples and lifelike frescoes of the ancient Maya. These buildings and their portraits of priestly dignitaries presiding at ritual sacrifices date from the middle of the first millennium after Christ, and bear testimony to the richness and splendor of one of the world's unique civilizations which flourished and died several hundred years before Cortez sighted the Mexican shores. At another climatic extreme the frozen ground of the Altai mountains, near the Siberian-Mongolian border, has yielded the dazzling and multicolored felt tapestries and rugs, along with the handsome leather horse-trappings, from the tomb of a long-dead nomadic prince. The remnants of this Scythian, or Scythian-related, civilization as they were found at this Siberian site of Pazyryk are probably as old as 400 B.C.; and they provide a fascinating glimpse into the life of the Asiatic pastoral peoples who once spread from Hungary through Siberia and whose descendants played such important roles in later European history.

Archaeology is not all spectacular new discoveries, although these are an exciting part. Sometimes findings of the highest significance are made in settings of the familiar. A good example of this was the accidental spotting of a faintly carved design on one of the stone columns at the well-known prehistoric site of Stonehenge in England. Of all ancient monuments, Stonehenge has been one of the most often reported and frequently visited of any in Europe. Yet recently a British archaeologist, in walking among its ruins, noticed, in a certain slanting of the sunlight, the carved outline of a Mycenean battle-ax. This peculiar battle-ax design, originating in the pre-Hellenic cultures of the Grecian peninsula, was indisputable proof of contact, some 3800 years ago, between the Mycenean world of the Mediterranean and remote Britain.

The range of the subject matter of archaeology is enormous. From the crude chopping tools of the Lower Paleolithic of Southeast Asia to the walled cities of the Middle Eastern Bronze Age—all is in the province of the recovery of prehistory. Similarly, the approach to the subject varies greatly. In many places the archaeologist's task is still the primary one of establishing relative sequences and geographical distributions of artifact or architectural types. It is through this rather humdrum work that the foundations of the science are constructed. There remains a great deal to be done along these lines, and some of the current results are of special interest. In the Americas the possibilities of interrelating widespread regional chronologies are just beginning to emerge as the result of such routine, systematic work. Recent archaeological test digging in both Colombia and Ecuador has disclosed sequences of pottery types which relate rather closely in both type and sequential order to similar series in Mexico and Peru. Such similarities—although based upon broken pottery refuse—have outstanding importance in linking the early pottery-making, agricultural civilizations of Peru and Middle America, the two principal centers of pre-Columbian cultural achievement in the New World.

In those areas or localities where much of the basic chronological and distributional spadework has been done the archaeologist feels freer to devote himself to the reconstruction of "cultural contexts." This refers to the total setting of any archaeological discovery. It may pertain to the position of actual objects in the ground or their association with buildings or graves. Context may also have a wider orientation. Much of our archaeological knowledge of Maya civilization is that which has been obtained from excavations and explorations of the handsome palaces and temples. It is in these that the hieroglyphics and art of the priestly ruling class are best exemplified. But this is only a part of a society. To what did these temples and palaces refer in a larger social and demographic setting? Where did the masses of the people live whose energies helped support this handsome superstructure? To answer such questions the archaeologist must turn to studies of total community settlement. For the Maya problem, specifically, it means searching several square miles of jungle surrounding any single ceremonial and political capital.

In pursuing his objectives the modern archaeologist leans heavily upon methods and techniques that have been developed in other sciences. From physics and chemistry he has recently obtained the means of dating many of his finds. Fluorine content of bone is an indicator of relative age. The radioactivity of carbon in charred, or otherwise preserved, organic materials can be measured for age in absolute years. Geology has long provided that mainstay to archaeological digging, stratigraphy, which is simply the principle that deposited strata—whether of natural or human origin—are oldest at the bottom of a series and most recent at the top. Paleontology, soil sciences, and paleobotany contribute increasingly to the dating of man and his works; they also offer evidences of environmental context. Spear points found with the bones of a mammoth in the Western United States not only prove a considerable antiquity for these points and their makers but let the archaeologist know that these ancient men in question lived in a colder, wetter climate than that of the present—a climate and an environment in which the great mammals could flourish. Pollen analyses of buried soils are another way of determining the nature of past climates and flora. These environmental and climatic reconstructions are often of greatest importance in providing an insight into the tool and weapon types which prehistoric men used at any one time or place. Long, large spear points make sense as the means by which to kill the mammoth or mastodon, but not the jackrabbit. Abundant hafted axes might readily be expected in a region that was once wooded, but not on the open plain.

One interesting sidelight is the assist which archaeology has received from aviation. Shortly after the First World War it was noticed that archaeological features often stood out in aerial photographs when they could not be readily detected on the ground. Roman and other ancient encampments and fortifications in Britain were first discovered by aerial surveys in some instances, and in many places, such as Mesopotamia and coastal Peru, detailed site maps of complex palace and dwelling compounds were made from aerial photographs.

One of the most dramatic frontiers of archaeology today is that of man's origins. Although this question cannot be reduced to anything so simple as the formula of the "missing link," prehistorians are gradually piecing together the story of human evolution from the primate forms. Up until the last decade the remains of fossil men, such as the famed Java or *Pithecanthropus erectus* or the Peking or *Sinanthropus pekinensis*, were all definitely on the hominid side. In posture, facial structure, dentition, and cranial capacity these early beings were men, albeit somewhat ape-like in certain characteristics. But the discoveries of the man-ape, or *Australopithecine*, skeletons in the caves of South Africa present clear evidence of what the anthropoid stock must have looked like during the late Tertiary geological epoch. The *Australopithecine* remains do not date back this early, but are associated with strata which are middle to late Quaternary or Pleistocene. As such, they are actually contemporaneous with more advanced forms of men. Nevertheless, their physical makeup is such as to indicate their intermediate position in an evolutionary series. Presumably, they represent a somewhat retarded offshoot from the main stream of development from the higher apes to man. These man-ape skeletons range in adult body size from a stature somewhat smaller than that of modern pigmies to an average man. Their skulls have brain-jaw proportions closer to the gorilla or the chimpanzee than to man, but their tooth structure is entirely human. It is clear that they were bipedal and upright. It is possible, although not proven to the satisfaction of most scientists, that the *Australopithecine* manufactured crude pebble tools and practiced cannibalism. It is certain that they lived together in what might be thought of as relatively large bands or societies.

On the hominid side of the line dividing man from the apes is Peking Man or *Sinanthropus pekinensis*. Remains of these individuals have been found in caves near Peking, China. Biologically more primitive than *Homo sapiens*, Peking man is, nevertheless, considerably farther along the road of human evolution than *Australopithecine*. Geologically, he is of about the same age. Culturally, however, he is representative of what archaeologists have termed the Lower Paleolithic or the earliest phases of the "Old Stone Age."

The evidences which confront the archaeologist working with Paleolithic remains, and the manner in which he interprets these, are well exemplified by the Peking finds. The actual cave sites, at a place called Choukoutien, are dwelling locations of *Sinanthropus*. From the fact that many of the long bones of *Sinanthropus* were found cracked or broken, and that skulls often show lesions or depressed fractures, it is believed that these early men were cannibals. In any case they were not addicted to a raw diet, as remains of fires and hearths have been found, indicating the importance of the fire-making discovery for cooking, warmth, and protection against animals. Refuse at Choukoutien reveals abundant animal bone, largely deer but with gazelle and horse also represented. To supplement their meat diet the inhabitants also ate a small cherry-like fruit, the hackberry. Chopping and pounding implements were manufactured from flint cores and from large flakes. Presumably, these were used in the food quest. It is of interest to note that *Sinanthropus* did not bury his dead.

Several hundred thousand years later, in that cultural substage known as the European Upper Paleolithic, the archaeologist has more data with which to work, and his vignette is sketched in greater detail. Human life by this time appears to have been a bit more expansive than at Choukoutien. Dwellings were not only in caves but in the open. Little, however, is known of houses or structures. That these open sites were permanent, year-around settlements is attested to by the fact that the animal bones from these sites show that the animals were killed and eaten at all seasons of the year. Burials, with funeral implements accompanying the dead, imply a concept of an afterlife. The special burial treatment accorded some individuals suggests that these were chiefs, priests, or leaders and that society was, therefore, organized along some formal lines. Moreover, for the first time we find conscious striving for beauty. Magdalenian art of the Upper Paleolithic of France and Spain is justly famous for its cave wall paintings and sculptures in monochromes and polychromes and for its small artifactual carvings in stone, bone, and ivory. The significance of this art, whose themes are largely concerned with game animals, was probably magico-religious and directed toward securing or propitiating game and the dead spirits of the animals. It seems unlikely that a primitive hunting community, living in an exacting environment, could have supported an art that was purely decorative and artists who had no other function than to provide for aesthetic pleasure. Nevertheless, it is clear that the artists were skilled and gifted individuals even though a part of their energies were probably given over to priestly or shamanistic duties.

In much later times, when men in the Eastern Mediterranean regions began to farm and a knowledge of the important food plants as well as domesticated animals spread northward over Europe, the potentialities for archaeological interpretation are increased, but the factors available for consideration are more numerous and complex. In fact, it is virtually impossible for the archaeologist to deal successfully with any isolated element of prehistoric cultures. It is by a kind of cross-referencing and triangulation of his facts that their meaning emerges. The long story of the dissemination of an agricultural way of life throughout Europe cannot be understood by tracing the presence or absence of domesticated grain, harvesting tools, or the implements of food preparation alone. This complicated history is also intimately bound up with climate and climatic change, soils, forest cover, settlement patterns, and demography.

An example of archaelogical sleuthing which combines a variety of factors is that of the small kiln-like buildings found in the Orkneys, the Shetlands, and parts of Northern Scandinavia. These little structures date from the Late Iron Age. In spite of the fact that there was some historic evidence for buildings of this type being used for grain storage, their prehistoric relationship with agriculture was unclear. For one thing, it was known that agriculture had been introduced into these regions several millennia earlier, but the kiln-like edifices were not built at that time. The relationship is not revealed, and interpretation remains impossible, until the climatic element is examined. In this case it is known that the climate of Northern Europe deteriorated rapidly during the Late Iron Age. Marginal lands of the Far North became less well adapted for growing. One result was the necessity of constructing special shelters or kilns for drying the grain at that particular period of prehistory.

Studies on prehistoric European livestock demonstrate, even better, this same kind of analytical cross-checking and subsequent synthesis. The British archaeologist, J. G. D. Clark, has noted that a careful counting and identification of the animal bones from a number of prehistoric sites in England, Denmark, and Switzerland indicate that swine were the most common farm animal during the Neolithic stage but that by Iron Age times sheep and goats had replaced them in importance. He correlates this directly with the decrease of forests and the increase of cleared land, particularly around farming settlements. Pigs, being well adapted to the forest environment, were able to thrive in the earlier periods, whereas sheep and goats are animals of the open country. Somewhat the same pattern, but with a greater span of time involved, is observed for the horse. The wild horse seems to have been reduced to comparative insignificance with the spread of forests over Europe in the postglacial period. He did not begin to revive until agriculture and land clearance got under way several millennia later. His revival was, of course, as a domesticate.

Knowledge of these important climatic and vegetational changes comes to the archaeologist from detailed investigations of mud and peat deposits in England and the Scandinavian countries. Pollen readings from these stratigraphies indicate that in glacial and early postglacial times the landscape was open or sustained only birch trees and grasses. This open environment was modified by the addi-

tion of pine and hazel trees, and these were followed by the deciduous oaks and elms that confronted the first European farmers. It is
of utmost significance—and provides the support for the deductions
cited above—that the decline of pollen from the deciduous trees and
the reappearances of that from grasses corresponds exactly with the
emergence of the first agricultural communities.

These interrelationships between man and his natural environment impinge upon those of man and his social environment. The
archaeologist lays no claim to explaining ultimate causality in human
affairs, least of all by the oversimple claims of environmental deter-
minism. Nevertheless, the natural settings in which man and his
societies developed played an important role. In Neolithic times the
Danubian Valley was the principal route by which peoples and new
ideas from the Eastern Mediterranean diffused throughout Europe.
We know that the farmers of that time worked the oak-covered loess
soils from Moravia eastward to Galicia, over Poland as far as the
lower Vistula, and northward and westward into Germany. There
were several different groups, "nationalities," or "tribes," each characterized by their own distinctive pottery wares, and their rapid
movement from place to place was consistent with their farming
methods of small forest clearings, easy crops, and subsequent shifting
to uncut parts of the woodland. There is every evidence that this was
a time of relative peace among tribes. Land was plentiful and to be
had only for the clearing of it. But toward the close of the Neolithic,
with the increase in the number of settlements of this kind and with
less chance for the regeneration of the forests and the soil, there are
signs of strife and warfare. Warrior peoples, equipped with battle-
axes, invade the Danube and prey upon the older farmers. Clark
has summed up his interpretations of these ecological and social
changes in stating:

Prehistorians have indeed vied in emphasizing the contrast between the
early peasants and the later warriors, without, however, offering any
very satisfactory explanation. Yet surely one is dealing here with the
effects upon human history of an immense ecological change wrought

unthinkingly by the neolithic farmers and their livestock. The crisis when it came extended far beyond the sphere of animals and plants and involved not merely the economic basis, but the whole outlook of large segments of the population of prehistoric Europe. In many parts at least the fat times of forest farming were over for good and all. The stored up fertility of the virgin soil had been taken and the potash from the burned woodlands had been absorbed.

A convergence of the natural sciences with archaeology in order to increase our understanding of past behavior is also exemplified in the study of prehistoric trade and exchange. Stone materials for artifacts or the clays and sands for making pottery can be identified as to their natural sources by petrographic analyses, and by this means the archaeologist may get some idea of ancient trade routes and contacts between prehistoric peoples.

For instance, during the Neolithic a particular type of banded flint, derived only from Galicia and Southern Poland, was widely traded in the form of axes and other tools. Implements made of this kind of stone are found all the way from the Carpathians to the Baltic. In this same geographic zone, and in the same graves along with the weapons and tools of the banded flint, are ornaments made of Baltic amber. Here is an obvious example of prehistoric trade, and it is likely that these two substances, or the objects made from them, were exchanged for each other. A knowledge of the presence of such a trade route is of vital importance to the archaeologist attempting to interpret the prehistory of Central and Eastern Europe. The route demonstrates that contacts among widely separated peoples once existed and leaves open the possibility that ideas as well as objects and materials may have spread along the same path.

The relationship of trade and trade items to the diffusion of technological ideas is a case in point and is illustrated by the bronze industry in prehistoric Denmark. At the close of the Neolithic the region that is now Denmark developed a bronze-working tradition of high attainments. As there are none of the raw materials necessary for bronze-making in Denmark or the immediately surrounding territory, it is obvious that both the materials and the ideas reached the area from elsewhere. Trade objects alone were insufficient to produce a local bronze-smithing craft. Various items of bronze had been reaching Denmark from the south as early as the Danish middle Neolithic, but the technical knowledge of how to work the metal had not passed with them. When the Danish Bronze Age finally got under way two major lines of bronze trade into Jutland were in existence. One of these originated in Central Germany and seems to have been in the hands of organized middlemen or traders. This is inferred from the fact that huge hoards of German bronze goods of the period have been discovered along the trade routes, attesting to the wealth and organization of the trade. Although this Central German trade undoubtedly stimulated an interest in bronze ornaments and tools among the local inhabitants, it does not seem to have been crucial for the development of the Danish bronze industry. The second line of trade was from Britain. Its volume was much less, and there is no evidence that it was as well organized as its German counterpart; however, the British trade appears to have been in the hands of merchant-smiths. These traveling smiths were the key men in the passage of the knowledge of bronze-working into Denmark. This is clearly seen in the particular techniques and designs of many of the Danish manufactures. Although the bulk of the metals which fed the Danish industry continued to come up from the south, such important items as the pile type of flanged axe were of British inspiration.

These various developments in Europe, from the Paleolithic through the Mesolithic, Neolithic, and Metal Ages, do not, however, reveal the story of the origins of plant and animal domestication and the profound effect these inventions had on human society and culture. Agriculture and animal husbandry began in the Near East, and it is in Iraq, Egypt, and the Indus Valley that the archaeologist can best trace the gradual transformation of hunters and gatherers into food-producers and, eventually, city-dwellers. Of all of these regions, Iraq (the Mesopotamian Valleys and the bordering hills) has not only the most complete sequence of events spanning this important phase of human history but appears to be the locale in which agriculture is most ancient. The archaeologist Henri Frankfort has shown convincingly that pre-Dynastic Egyptian civilization received its initial stimulus from Mesopotamia, while Harappa and Mohenjo-Daro of the Indus Valley are clearly derived from the same source. Iraq, then, appears to have been a kind of "forcing-bed" for civilization and for the farming upon which it was based.

In the Kurdish hills of Iraq there are chipped stone implements comparable to some of those found in European and Asiatic Paleolithic contexts and which probably date the presence of man in this area as early as 100,000 years ago. This ancient hunting and gathering mode of life must have changed slowly, for at the site of Karim Shahir, in the same Kurdish hills, archaeologists have found small flint blades, crude mortars and milling stones, and other utensils indicative of very primitive living down to as late as 6000 B.C. The most significant difference between the older Paleolithic sites and Karim Shahir is the presence of pig, sheep, and goat bones at the latter. It is not certain if these animals were domesticated at this time, but their presence, together with the remains of man, suggests their importance as food.

The next links in the chronological chain of human occupation in Iraq territory are the two ancient agricultural sites of M'leffat and Jarmo. These represent the oldest settled agricultural villages ever to be explored by an archaeologist. M'leffat, in Northern Iraq in the Greater Zab River basin, probably dates from 5000 B.C. or even earlier. Its inhabitants did not make pottery but they farmed as evidenced by grain impressions found in the mud ruins. According to radio-carbon dates, Jarmo was first settled about 4700 B.C. Robert Braidwood, the American excavator, describes the site as a hillock of village debris some three acres in extent and as much as twenty-five feet deep. Like Karim Shahir and M'leffat, it is situated in hill country. The Jarmo houses had been made of mud set up on stone foundations. Braidwood and his associates cut down through twelve architectural levels, each one constructed over the one below. In the lower levels there was no pottery, but clay ovens and fire-basins, baked through use, were found in place in the houses. Small flints, used in sickle blades, and axes and hoes of ground stone reflect the agricultural pursuits of the builders of the houses. Moreover, impressions of wheat, barley, and peas were found in the mud walls of the structures where they had been accidentally mixed with straw as binding for the mud. Most of the animal bones from the Jarmo refuse are those of domesticated species, with the majority of the sheep and goats of yearling age, suggesting a selection resulting from domestication rather than hunting. The religious or magical side of life is seen in numerous little clay animal and "mother-goddess" figurines, possibly votive offerings or fetishes connected with fertility. These figurines are of unfired clay, but true pottery finally appears in the late levels of the site. From all of this it is clear that Jarmo marks an important step on the way to civilization, not only for the region of Iraq but, because of its priority, for much of Eurasia. From about 4700 B.C. forward, the settled village, supported by crops and farm animals, became the focus of life in the Near East.

After Jarmo, the Hassuna and Halaf cultures, at approximately 4400 and 4100 B.C. respectively, show a continuation of the village farming tradition in Iraq. By 3900 B.C. the Ubaid culture of Southern Mesopotamia, discovered near the later famed Ur-of-the-Chaldees, marks the beginning of large towns. These towns, constructed of uniformly molded mud bricks, appear to have grown up around temple and trading centers. Reckoning back from historical knowledge of later Middle Eastern cities, it is likely that the Ubaid temples were combined with a market system. The first copper and bronze tools also date from this time, and there is a significant shift from the rainy hill country down to the drier alluvial flats of the great rivers. In this river plain country irrigation would have been necessary to sustain the population of the large towns, and the fact that the movement from hills to plains did not take place until populations and technologies were of sufficient size and complexity to cope with the problems of irrigation is undoubtedly correlated with this.

After 3500 B.C. the trends toward urban concentration achieve city proportions in what Delougaz has called the "Proto-Literate" phase of Mesopotamian prehistory. Although the term "civilization" is in many respects a highly subjective one, its basis and its original meaning are connected with idea of the city and all that it signifies. In this sense, the Mesopotamian "Proto-Literate" phase is on the threshold of civilization. Towns become cities. Temple structures are of monumental proportions and elaborately decorated. From what we know of the later literate periods it is likely that city states were formed at this time. The construction of large scale canals implies technical "know-how," social and political controls, and, probably, land laws and riparian rights. As the name suggests, clay tablets with pictographic signs make their appearance during the "Proto-Literate" phase. These were probably records or accounts related to the temples and the markets, and they are the obvious fore-runners of the later Sumerian and Babylonian cuneiform writing.

In sketching this story of the rise of civilization it must be re-membered that the archaeological record is unavoidably biased upon the side of the material and the technological. These are the things and the evidences that remain after all else has perished in the earth. True, they have an importance. The individual genius is limited by his particular milieu. The artisan of the Lower Paleolithic, no matter how gifted, did not stand upon the accumulated technical knowl-edge that was available to Benvenuto Cellini or Christopher Wren. Population increase and concentration and the general availability of leisure time is made possible only by a fully efficient food pro-duction and by adequate tools. Nevertheless, we cannot measure the other significant aspects of civilization by economy and technology alone. They offer certain possibilities, but they do not determine the form and the kind of political organization, laws, morals, religion, and aesthetics. Sir Mortimer Wheeler, an archaeologist long devoted to the craft, writes:

In a classic sentence it has been observed that a great nation may leave behind it a very poor rubbish-heap. And are we, as practising archae-ologists, to award the palm to the unknown Sumerian who was buried at Ur with sixty-three helmeted soldiers, grooms, and gold-garlanded damsels, two chariots and six bullocks, or to the Nazarene in a loin-cloth who was nailed up on Golgotha between two thieves? I merely ask the question, but cannot help feeling that, were archaeology alone the arbiter, the answer would not be in doubt. Give us helmets and gold garlands every time; bread and circuses give us, provided that the bread is carbonized and the circuses well-furnished with good solid bronze and marble. But let us at least, in our gratitude for these things, remember the missing values that cannot be appraised in inches or soil-samples or smudges in the earth.

In turning from the story of civilization in the Old World to that of the New, the archaeologist is confronted with the problem that has intrigued explorers, historians, and philosophers since that day when the first conquistadores of Spain saw revealed before them the amazing cities of Mexico and Peru. Were these native civilizations of the Americas independent creations of the men of this hemisphere, or were they in some way linked to Asia and the Near East? It is not at all impossible—in fact, it is even likely—that there were some pre-Columbian contacts across the Pacific between the high cultures of the American middle latitudes and those of Asia. The common possession of certain domesticated plants, such as cotton and the yam, as well as man-made items or technical ideas of a rather specific nature, are difficult to explain otherwise.

The fundamental question is whether or not these contacts were significant in the growth of New World civilization. Most American archaeologists feel that they were not of great importance. The American aborigines are distinct racial types whose relationships to the Mongoloid peoples of Asia are only of a general sort. The American Indian languages of Mexico and Peru do not have affinities with Old World linguistic stocks. Finally, most of the content—the manufactures and customs—of the pre-Columbian civilizations is unique and distinct in its style and form from that of Asia, India, or the Near East. In spite of this, there are a number of striking similarities in the modes of growth or change in the Old World civilizations and those of America. These are parallels of the sort that Spengler, Toynbee, and others have reviewed—parallels in the rise and fall of great civilizations the world over.

For example, the American archaeologists have discovered evidence for the beginnings of a native agriculture in Mexico and Peru, based upon maize, in the second and first millennia B.C. The early settled agricultural villages of the Peruvian coast do not differ greatly from the Old World community of early agriculturists uncovered at Jarmo. These early Peruvian sites were, in turn, succeeded by larger settlements in which temples and public buildings were incorporated, and these, still later, gave way to large towns or cities of mold-made mud bricks in which commerce and political control were centered. All this occurred centuries before the Inca Empire which finds its own parallel in some of the historically documented conquest states and kingdoms of Mesopotamia.

Obviously, we cannot yet answer the question as to why these similarities in culture development exist between the Old and the New World. The effects of contacts between peoples and civilizations follow no set rules, or if they do the archaeologist and anthropologist have not yet discovered what they are. It may be that a boatload of Asiatic voyagers could have wrought profound changes and could have exerted powerful long-term influences on the peoples of the New World. On the other hand, the possibility of essentially independent developments cannot be discarded.

This consideration—that historically unrelated peoples and societies follow similar courses of change in their development of civilization—leads us back, again, to the nature of archaeology or to any related discipline that takes as its subject the full gamut of human history. If we are to profit, now and in the future, from a knowledge of history and prehistory we must extract generalizations or "laws" from the multitude of particulars. At the same time the archaeologists must be sufficiently humanistic in outlook to search for and appreciate the multiple and complex causes that lead to culture growth or decay. There may be "laws" or regularities in those courses of human events which lead to civilization, but it is unlikely that these will prove to be simple materialistic-deterministic formulations. Man has, indeed, lived within limits set for him by his very biological self, the landscape, climate, and by other men. The record shows that he has always struggled against these limiting influences. At first, ages ago, he was dwarfed by the unknown and fearful world of the Ice Epoch, by his pitifully few possessions, and his few numbers. Gradually he freed himself from these fetters to enjoy creativeness of material and nonmaterial riches. In so doing it may be that he fashioned new chains, binding himself to an urban existence that again threatens and minimizes him. But if archaeology instructs at all it teaches us that man is tough, flexible, and determined.

5

HISTORY

The Changing Past

by Lynn White, jr.

HISTORY too has its history, and today far more
is happening in the quiet studies of historians than most people
suspect. For one thing, history is being made faster than we can
absorb it. In our time, for the first time, it has suddenly become
worldwide and the mere quantity of the stuff is overwhelming. East
and South Asia, Russia, and pre-Columbian America can no longer
be treated as fine-type footnotes to Western Civilization. As yet no
mind, not even Arnold Toynbee's, has really digested the new material. But even the most specialized historian senses the job to be done.

The busy spades of archaeologists are further complicating matters
by digging up not only objects but whole cultures unknown even a
few years ago. In 1900 the Hittities were hardly more than a name
in the Bible. Today Yale is publishing a bulky Hittite dictionary.
The jungles of Cambodia have been torn aside to reveal the astonishing remains of Ankor Vat and the vanished Khmer civilization.
Moslem fanatics still prevent excavation of the South Arabian ruins
of Saba whose queen may have visited Solomon nearly three thousand years ago, but in the Indus valley a cluster of cities perhaps as
old as Babylonia or Egypt has come to light. On Crete and in the
Aegean the Minoans are emerging from the mists. In 1953 a British
architect who had worked on Nazi spy codes during World War II
cracked the most common form of Minoan writing. Studies of the

early Germans and Celts are fast changing our notions of what the Romans found when they marched north of the Alps. And in the Americas, Aztec and pre-Aztec, Inca and pre-Inca cultures, always curious and sometimes magnificent, are turning up in most embarrassing profusion. We really don't what what to do with all the history we now have.

But historians these days are not just excited about the quantitative expansion of history in time and space. The most fascinating part of their business is the recent discovery of new ways of quizzing the dead, fresh methods of interpreting and understanding the traces left by old thoughts, deeds, and passions. History is changing its quality too.

The growth of the natural sciences in our time has put novel power-tools into the historian's kit. In 1949 a counter was perfected which would measure the amount of radioactive carbon in animal or plant material up to 25,000 years old. In 1953 at the Universities of Manitoba and Chicago two types of scintillation counters were developed which promise eventually to date such objects over a span of some 45,000 years as compared with the present 30,000 years. While puzzling problems remain in the use of these machines, especially as regards material from moist regions, we can now take a few splinters from a beam, charcoal from an ancient campfire, a bone or a shred of cloth from a tomb, and attempt to give them pin-point dates. Within a decade we may have for the first time a worldwide chronology which will connect events in the regions of written records to those in the far larger areas which have lacked either writing or dates.

Mere literacy has never been identical with intelligence or vitality. For an understanding of the movements of history, the unlettered but not necessarily stupid or uncultured barbarian is often as important as the city-dweller. Indeed, the latter has often awakened to discover himself subject to that same barbarian and required to modify his arts and social order to suit his new master's taste. Moreover, it has already helped our time perspective to learn that while the Athenians were building the Parthenon, the temples and tombs of Monte Alban near Oaxaca were under construction; that when Augustus was boasting that he had found Rome a city of brick and turned it into a city of marble, the vast Pyramid of the Sun at Teotihuacan near Mexico City was already ancient and subject to enlargement over old cores.

Ever since the invention of agriculture, people have been so mixed up with plants that the current development of botany has opened up entirely new kinds of historical evidence. The study of fossil pollen, for instance, is throwing new light on the history of Northern Europe. All the way from Ireland to Finland there are peat bogs, and annually a new layer of peat moss is laid down in them. As the breezes blow, some of the local pollen is deposited on the summer's growth of moss, and this pollen, despite its delicacy, is so well preserved that the species of each grain can be identified under a microscope. Climatic changes may be detected in shifts in the kinds of trees and plants surrounding a bog as reflected in changing pollens in the levels of peat. These levels can be dated rather exactly, so that we now have a climatic history of the regions around the Baltic and North Sea extending over several thousand years.

One of the most startling results is the discovery of a sudden worsening of climate about 1300 A.D. which made farming so difficult that during the next three generations thousands of villages in Northern Europe were abandoned. No change in physical climate can account entirely for the almost terrifying changes in the intellectual and emotional climate of the fourteenth century. It has been long recognized as an age of turmoil, agony, soul-searching, and new departures. But the careful counting of grains of fossil pollen has given us new insight into the sufferings and discontents of the Northern peasantry, and into the economic hazards and consequent neuroses of their feudal overlords.

The botanists also have renewed old controversies by finding good evidence of two-way contact between Asia and South America since very early times. The skipper of the *Kon-Tiki* has popularized the fact that the sweet potato, a New World plant, was found by the first white explorers all over Polynesia bearing its American Indian name. The yam, originally from the East Indies, was known in the Caribbean before Columbus's time, while a gourd which is native to India is found in Peruvian graves earlier than 1000 B.C. A cotton with thirteen long chromosomes was domesticated early, presumably in India. It was taken to America, where it crossed with a cotton having thirteen short chromosomes. The hybrid seems to have been carried westward again to the Pacific Islands before Europeans reached those waters.

Certain specific things common to Asia and to the New World have long been noted (parcheesi, blowguns, the abacus, hieroglyphics, four-wheeled pulling-toys, zero, decorative motifs, and the like) although most historians have brushed the matter aside as pure coincidence. But as one botanist has remarked, "plants are not constructs of the mind." Their wanderings back and forth across the Pacific having been proved, the question of the spread of the other items is reopened. The cultural history of mankind may have far more unity than hitherto we have thought possible.

The present growth of historical studies, however, is due only in small part to techniques and novel kinds of evidence provided by the natural sciences. A new idea can be a more important instrument of research than a Geiger counter or electronic microscope. And the new ideas are burgeoning.

Historians have recently waked up to the extent to which they have been document-bound. The written records upon which they depended in the past with the rarest exceptions were the product of the upper classes, and reflect their interests and the things they cared to talk about. Record-keeping began with a tiny dominant group of priests and rulers. Gradually through the centuries more of the nobility, and eventually some of the greater merchants, entered the charmed circle of the "historical." But even as late as the eighteenth century, what do we really know—and in terms of the written records what can we know—about the nine-tenths of the people, even in literate societies, who were themselves illiterate and voiceless? Not until the age of the American and French Revolutions did the great masses become articulate and emerge clearly into the historical records.

There is a vast subhistory which is like prehistory. It must be explored if we are to have a history of humanity rather than just of the aristocracy. The task is by no means hopeless: there are ways of gleaning the fields which conventional historians thought they had harvested. We have archaeological data, pictures, even the casual metaphors of the upper classes. How many readers of Dante realize that the first evidence of the windmill in Italy is found in the last canto of the *Inferno* where Satan threshes his arms "like a mill which the wind turns"? A poet does not use such a figure unless it is immediately recognizable: windmills must have been common in Italy by Dante's day. Yet no one who could write had bothered to mention one. We may be sure that the people who sweated for a living were not so indifferent to this major power-machine.

It would be wrong to picture the submerged nine-tenths as dumb brutes. If there is anything in genetics, we can't permit ourselves to think so for we are all descended from them. There was much originality and creative force in those who did not get into the records. To a great extent (although not entirely) changes in the so-called fine arts and literature are refinements of the folk art and oral literature of the common people. Just as many traits of the modern American novel sprang from the supposedly contemptible "penny horribles" of our nineteenth century, so it appears that such things as harmonic music and rhymed poetry are humble in their origins.

Indeed, since aristocracies breed themselves out, in every age the ambitious and able have managed to upgrade themselves socially, bringing their basic attitudes with them. Perhaps peasants are more responsible than philosophers for the ideas which we all take for granted.

Anyone who has become acquainted with educated and sensitive Asians traveling among us to explore our minds has been told, not once but often: "The thing which fundamentally separates you Americans and Europeans from all the rest of mankind is that you live on nature, not with nature." To which we refrain from replying, "Why, yes! This accounts for our superiority!" and, with evasive amiability, pour another martini for our guests.

Where did we get this distinctly Western notion of our relation to nature? From the earliest times land was distributed among peasants in allotments sufficient to support a family. Although the peasant paid rent for his land, usually in produce or services, the assumption was subsistence farming. Then, in Northern Europe and there alone, a great change took place in agricultural methods. During the early Middle Ages a new kind of heavy plow came into use with a moldboard to turn over the sod. Friction with the soil was so much greater than in the case of the older two-ox scratch-plow that normally eight oxen were needed. But no peasant had eight oxen of his own. So the peasants began to pool their ox-teams to work a single plow, each taking strips of plowed land in proportion to his contribution. Thus the standard of land distribution ceased to be the needs of a family and became the ability of a new machine to till the land. No more fundamental change in the idea of man's relation to the soil can be imagined: once man had been part of nature; now he became her exploiter.

We see the emergence of this same attitude in the illustrated calendars available from Roman times onward. The oldest of these show the twelve months as allegorical ladies holding flowers, fruits, and other symbols of the season. The mood is passive, contemplative. Then gradually during the Middle Ages the pictures change to scenes of human activity: planting, harvesting, wood-chopping, people knocking down acorns for the pigs to eat, pig-slaughtering. Man and nature are two things, and man is on top. We who are the children of the peasants of Europe take this for granted, but it deeply disturbs many Asians.

Probing into subhistory, the historian finds relationships which have had tremendous effects on the "higher" culture but of which there is no written record. Before the invention of the spinning wheel about 1300 A.D., spinning the yarn was the most expensive process in producing ordinary, nonluxury textiles. The spinning wheel, which was gradually perfected, greatly reduced the price of cloth, the market for it expanded, and ordinary people began for the first time to use linen shirts, underwear, kerchiefs, sheets, towels, and the like. As a result the price of linen rags, then the chief raw material for European paper, sank, and with it the cost of paper itself. Until paper became much cheaper than parchment it was not likely that anyone would undertake the arduous task of developing printing with cast movable type. Even if printing had cut the labor cost of the scribe, books would have remained a luxury commodity, unsuited to mass production, so long as the raw material for them was as expensive as parchment. We who read are no more indebted to Gutenberg than to the unknown and lowly inventor of the spinning wheel who provided the context for Gutenberg. And the person who made the first spinning wheel had an excellent mind: he invented the belt-transmission of power, too.

This sort of thing bothers many historians, professionally trained as they are to provide a documentary footnote to "prove" every statement. But much of life escaped the documents. If we are to discover the history of our race and not merely that of the literate upper crust, the historian must create his patterns of probable truth less in terms of specific records and more in terms of relationships intuitively evident to him as he deals with the records.

This is a dangerous game, for it increases the chance that unscrupulous forces may manipulate history for present purposes. We have seen it so used in every totalitarian state. But dangerous or not, the game cannot be avoided. While he can never afford to lose touch with all the recorded facts he can get, the historian is forced by the development of his field to become more and more like the critic of literature. Clio is resuming her place in the sisterhood of the arts.

The part which intuitive perception must play in the study of history is heightened by the insights of psychology into the interconnection of all parts of human experience and into the importance of the unconscious. We are beginning to be able to trace the prenatal history of ideas and attitudes in the unconscious of people who perished centuries ago.

For instance, why did the atomic theory of the nature of matter appear so suddenly among the ancient philosophers of the Ionian cities? Their notion that all things are composed of different arrangements of identical atoms of some "element," whether water, fire, ether, or something else, is an intellectual invention of the first order, but its sources are not obvious.

The key is to be found in the saying of Heraclitus that "All things may be reduced to fire, and fire to all things, just as all goods may be turned into gold and gold into all goods." He thought that he was just using a metaphor, but the basis of the metaphor did not exist until shortly before his time. The distinctive thing about Ionia, the chief stimulus to the commercial prosperity which provided leisure for the atomistic philosophers, was the invention in Asia Minor of coinage. The age of barter was ended: now every commodity could be bought and sold for officially stamped pieces of metal of guaranteed uniform weight. Probably no Ionian was aware of any connection between this unique new economic device and the brainstorms of the local intellectuals. But that a causal relationship did exist can scarcely be doubted, even though it cannot be "proved" but only perceived.

There are times when our rummagings into the unconscious of the past are so detailed, and the conclusions so firm, that we have the illusion of "proof" in the old-fashioned documentary sense. But the method of research is in fact completely new and revolutionary: we are stretching the past out on the analyst's couch.

It is becoming clearer, for example, that in the later twelfth and thirteenth centuries a seismic shift began to take place in the nature of Christian piety. What people said in words is less revealing than what they said unconsciously in religious art. Only a conservative Spanish bishop, Luke of Tuy, sensed what was happening: he denounced pictures of "one-eyed Virgins," by which he meant representations of St. Mary in profile. His fears were well grounded.

Christian art up to that time had been largely frontal, as that of the Eastern Church still is. Such images establish a direct and almost hypnotic relationship with the worshiper whom they fix with their eyes: they form an art capable of conveying power and spiritual grace. But as soon as the eyes of the image shift from the worshiper, religious art becomes drama rather than sacrament, and the worshiper tends to become merely a spectator. Any spiritual value which the new art has, comes from the spectator's personal psychological reaction to the scene observed.

Nowhere is the new religious focus better shown than in the changing ways of representing the Last Supper. The early pictures of it are inspired by the moment when Christ (always shown frontally) takes the bread and says, "This is my body broken for you." It is the institution of the Mass: Christ is the first priest, and the disciples are gathered about him as congregation. The emphasis of the picture is completely sacramental.

Then a new way of showing the Last Supper came into fashion: the moment is no longer the breaking of the bread but now it is the sop given to Judas. To the late medieval mind this was an episode of terrible significance: what should have been the bread of salvation was in fact confirmation of Judas's damnation. The intention of God is defeated by the sinfulness of man. The scene combines in equal measure sacrament and drama.

In the later thirteenth century a third style appears: the moment shown is that at which Christ says, "One of you shall betray me." Judas recoils. The other disciples are thrown into consternation, crying, "Lord, is it I? Is it I?" Through the generations each disciple became psychologically differentiated, and the tradition of this form of the Last Supper culminated in Leonardo's masterpiece. For our purposes the thing to be noted is that in this representation, sacrament has vanished entirely and drama is everything. The human situation has displaced the transit of divine grace as the center of attention.

A related change is seen in pictures of the Annunciation. In the earlier period St. Mary is going about her housekeeping and is startled by the sudden intrusion of the Archangel Gabriel with his message. But in the thirteenth century the Virgin is increasingly shown at praye᷈ or reading holy writ. In other words, in early Christianity when God speaks Man hears. In the later period the mind must be prepared for the divine message. The focus of religion shifts away from the saving power which comes from outside Man and centers on the problem of human adjustment. For the last seven centuries this tendency, despite periodic reactions, has continued. In our own time Christian Science, psychosomatic medicine, and psychoanalysis have made not merely salvation (renamed "adjustment") but physical health itself dependent upon the subjective psychological state of the individual. From his standpoint, Bishop Luke of Tuy was entirely correct.

Are interpretations of this sort valid? Are they "objectively there," inherent in the historical material? Or are they "subjective," imposed by the mind of the historian? To most of us who live in the middle of the twentieth century they will seem objective because they reflect the typical mental processes of our age. But to historians of even fifty years ago, not to mention the educated public, such forms of thought would have been unintelligible.

The enigmas of human nature may of course be studied in the living men and women around us, and in ourselves. But the billions of our fellows who are dead, and the vanished pageant of their generations, have left traces equally instructive, and instructive in new ways each decade. The past does not exist. What we call the past is our present thinking about what went on before us. Today the past is changing with incredible rapidity because our ways of thinking are in flux and expansion.

The research of historians, however, is far more than a passive reflection of the change of values which is at the heart of the turmoil of our time. What they are discovering and how they are discovering it is a major part of our present intellectual adventure, and affects all other parts of it. Like every humanistic scholar, the historian is trying to show people the meaning of what they are up to. By making men aware, conscious of the implications of their actions, history is to some extent modifying and molding the historical processes which it studies: the historian is actor as well as spectator. The airplane has unified the globe physically, but only the mutual respect which comes from an increasing sense of the global history of mankind will turn geographical shrinkage from bane to blessing. The democratic revolution of the past two centuries has in some ways been frustrated by the carryover into our new society of educational and cultural assumptions suitable only to the age of aristocracy. The historian's discovery of subhistory is helping us slowly to create a world which will prize all originality and not merely the kinds which were valued by the upper classes of the past. And in an era when rapid change breeds fear, and fear too often congeals us into a rigidity which we mistake for stability, the historian's exploration of the unconscious of past generations, and of the ways in which their real beliefs and tendencies were so often at variance with their professions, may lend us a healing humility when we look at ourselves. The way the past is changing may foreshadow a better future.

6

SOCIOLOGY

The Improper Study of Man

by Everett Cherrington Hughes

THE PROPER study of mankind is man. But what men shall we study to learn most about mankind, or simply about people? Those long dead, those now living, those unborn? The learned or the unlettered? The lowly, or those of high degree? Those nearby and of color and deportment like the student's own, or men of strange mien and demeanour? The men of the kraal, or those of the city? Faithful or infidel, the virtuous or the vicious? Are all equally human, or are some a little more so than others, so that what one learns about them is of wider application? Where should one start? At the earliest possible beginning, working toward the present by way of the peoples who were in some sense more directly our ancestors? Shall we produce the future from the lines of the past? Or should we, exploiting our experience of living men, apply to both past and future the lessons of the present?

And by what means shall we learn of those whom we choose to study? Suppose we elect to study living people. Shall we put our trust in studying great numbers, or at least such numbers as, properly selected, will represent all sorts and conditions of men in true proportion? Or shall we pick a few whose doings we observe as under a microscope and whose minds we probe for thoughts, desires, and memories, even for such as they themselves know not of? By what ideas, schemes, and formulae shall we reduce what we find to order?

And, not least, how much of what we learn shall we tell those whom we have studied, the larger public, or our colleagues? What principles shall guide us in the discovery of men's secrets; what, in the telling of them?

Shall we wait for those crucial things to happen which offer most increase to our knowledge of this or that aspect of human life, and travel fast and far to catch events on the wing? Or shall we set up experiments, bringing people together under circumstances so controlled as to get precisely the answers we want next? Shall we study people in small groups and communities, and hope to find ways of expanding our findings without distortion to the big world? Shall we look at people where nothing happens save the turn of seasons and generations, and where men are of one breed and of one mind, taking that as man's normal state? Or shall we study men in the seething flux of cities, migrations, crusades, and wars, wherever breeds mingle and minds clash?

To what of people's doings shall we more closely attend: their politics, their religion, their work, their play, their poems, their philosophies, their sciences, their crafts? What, finally, should be the form of our questions: "What were people like and what did they do?" "What are they doing?" "What will they do?" or "What would they do if—?"

The academic departments which study people are distinguished from each other by their choices from among these and similar possibilities. Some species of academic man insist on a single answer, explicitly stated. Most of us combine explicit answers with less conscious predilection for some kinds of human material rather than others. Some like to think of themselves as scientists; others as artists, critics, or moral judges. Some love the adventure of digging up manuscripts long buried in dust. Some like to crack a script, or to put together the fragments of ancient pots or temples. Others like to express behavior in mathematical formulae. Still others like to study living men, to discover new things about their own kind still warm, or to detect commonplace motives under the apparently strange ways of exotic people. But preference for one kind of study does not prevent scholars from having a try at other kinds and methods of study now and again. Again and again some academic people, or even rank outsiders, discontent with the set ways of academic study, go off on some new path of discovery, or simply take as their major preoccupation what others have considered a side issue.

So it was, in the century of evolution, that a number of naturalists, philosophers, historians, and students of the law assembled, classified, and sought to put into "evolutionary" order the varied customs reported as practiced throughout the world, and especially by those peoples most removed from nineteenth-century Europe in time, distance, civilization, and race. Some of these men called their work sociology. Toward the end of the century English and American philanthropists and reformers visited the slums of the great and growing cities, described the ways of the people who lived there, counted and tabulated the things that appeared the best indicators of their misery. Their surveys were called sociology. Some French legal scholars sought explanations for the alleged penchant of modern people to follow the crowd rather than their ancestors in both virtues and vices. A sharp-tongued Yale professor, Sumner, and, a decade later, an Italian engineer and economist, Pareto, got concerned about those aspects of human social behavior—usages and sentiments—which did not yield good price curves. They wrote treatises on sociology.

In addition to a name, these varied pursuits had in common a concern with the classifying of human doings, with the relations of events rather than with the events themselves. They also cut across that organization of the academic studies of man by which the state, the church, economic life, literature, and the like, as well as the various periods of history and the various regions and countries of the world, were each the special domain of some organized group of scholars, and of one department of a university. As historians of human learning have been quick to say, others had gone off on these tangents before. What was new was that these sociologists, and people influenced by them, gained a footing in the universities, especially so in the newer American ones. The older scholarly guilds cried, "Trespass," and those of classical bent slew the sociologists with the true but irrelevant accusation that their name, although of noble lineage, was a bastard, being half Latin, half Greek. As do the members of any budding profession or academic specialty seeking access to the sacred precincts, the sociologists sought and found ancient and honored ancestors, founded a society and journals, and have since been arguing about what academic ways to get set in. In the debate and in their deeds they are moving toward a certain combination of answers to the questions raised about the proper study of mankind.

By predilection rather than by logic, most sociologists work on the here and now. Although vast apparatuses have been set up to catch and spread knowledge of current doings, not all is recorded; and of what is recorded, not all is spread abroad. There is an economy of observing, recording, and disseminating the news. There is also a politics of it, a balance between revealing and concealing, in which all people and all organized institutions are in some measure involved. It has become part of the mission of sociologists to catch the goings-on of people and institutions at the time; or at least to catch those parts of them which tend to be overlooked by students of politics and economics, and by those who report on and criticize what are considered the serious works of art and of the mind. The lives of the families across the tracks; the reactions of housewives to the morning soap opera; how the men down in the garage unconsciously weave their own inarticulate anxieties and yearnings into their talk of what happened to L'il Abner this morning; the slow moving changes in the level of schooling of those Americans who are called Negro. These things don't make the news, but they make the big story comprehensible when it breaks into the headlines. One might say that part of the calling of sociologists is to push back the frontier of the news so as to get at the news back of, or below the news, not in the sense of getting at the lowdown, but in that of giving the reported events another dimension, that of the perspective of culture and of social processes.

One part of this job is undertaken by the surveyors of opinion. They have invented all sorts of devices for getting at what people think and do about a great variety of matters, large and small. No one of the particular opinions or actions they report would make the news columns, as does the fiftieth home run of a big league player or the visit of a monarch to a country fair. Neither the actors nor the actions, taken singly, are thought worthy of note. Put together, they are the ground swell on which prominent figures and great projects rise and fall, run their courses or founder. Mr. Unnamed Millions is, as many have noted lately, more and more a gentleman of leisure, a grand consumer of goods and of the popular arts and of the innumerable "services" of our civilization. His choices make or break the great institutions and enterprises. Keeping abreast of him is a job which, like woman's work, is never done. Predicting what he will do, even in the short run, has some of the features of predicting the weather. Many sociologists specialize in these very jobs; they are the quantitative historians of their own times. One of the risks of their trade is that their errors of prediction are more quickly discovered than those of people in some other lines of human study.

Working on this frontier is not a matter merely of setting up machinery to watch people and to inquire of them what they do and think. For one immediately strikes that other frontier, that of conscious and unconscious secrecy. Even a willing informant seldom can or will tell all that he thinks, knows, or does about a matter; nor is he able to show or explain the many connections between his different thoughts and actions. He will tell more about some things than about others; more in some situations than in others; more to some people than to others. It is common knowledge that a human group—a family, school, business concern, a clique— keeps together and keeps going only by maintaining a delicate balance between discretion and frankness. Students of group behavior have achieved great skill in inserting themselves as participant observers into the interstices of groups so as to observe things which can be perceived only by an insider, but whose significance can be conceived only by an outsider free enough of emotional involvement to observe and report accurately and armed with concepts with which to relate what he sees to other groups. Learning the role of participant observer, including the subtle practice of its ethic, is a basic part of training people for social discovery. Each observer, himself a member of society, marked by sex, age, race, and the other characteristics by which people place one another in various roles or relations, must find out not merely what the significant kinds of people are in the groups and situations he wants to study; he must also learn to perceive quickly and surely what role he has been cast in by the people he is studying. He must then decide whether he can effectively and on honest terms get them to see him in such light that they will trust him.

The role of participant observer can be difficult and trying. A young sociologist spent a considerable time as observer in a public mental hospital. The patients would not believe he was not a physician; they pestered him to help them get out. The other doctors were somehow, they insisted, in a plot with relatives to keep them wrongly locked up. The attendants, accustomed to being spied upon, thought him another and more ingenious kind of detective sent to catch them breaking regulations or stealing public property. The physicians, although used to the idea of research and although briefed about his project, were a bit inclined to consider him a spy, too. Only by skillful and strict adherence to his role of seeing much and to his bargain of telling nothing that would harmfully identify any person, did he succeed in staying and in finding out the inward structure of the social groups which even the mentally ill and their keepers and therapists form.

The author of a well-known book on corner gangs "hung on the corner" with a group of young men in a New England city for three years, always torn between whether to get as involved as they wished, which would have bound him to secrecy; or whether to stay just on the edge, where there was a bit of a question whether they could trust him. Except for one essay into helping them get a man elected to public office by voting several times, he stayed on the edge.

As it turned out, that was the way the gang wanted it. He wrote the book and is still friends with several members of the group.

It is conceivable that there are social groups so closed and so suspicious that they cannot be studied by participant observers. They may be so tight that they have no place for people of neutral role. Fanatical religious or political sects, criminal gangs, groups planning some secret strategy for either good or ill, bodies charged with knowledge which must be kept close for the common good, people living in great and vulnerable intimacy with each other, these do not welcome even the most trusted outside observers. However, a great deal can be learnt by projecting on these groups what is known of others which approximate them in some degree, and by setting up experiments which simulate them. A group of social scientists has indeed set up an organization to assemble, evaluate, and draw conclusions from the small amounts of information which can be got about people in the Iron Curtain regions. Some of them have written an intriguing book on how to study cultures from a distance. The problems are in part those of the historian, who is limited to the documents left around, since he cannot ask the dead to write documents to his order; but they are also in part the problems of evaluating the testimony of renegades and converts, people who have left some secret group and from various motives tell, or purport to tell, about what they have left. All of these are the problems of the social rhetoric common to all human intercourse.

The fears which lead people to make it difficult for investigators are often enough well-founded; more than that, they lie in the nature of social life. A family has secrets, or it is no family. It is not the public's business, ordinarily, what goes on in the bosom of a family; but it is a matter of basic human and scientific interest to know what kinds of families there are, what makes some hold together and others break up, and what happens to children brought up in one kind of family rather than another. The sociological investigator cracks the secrecy, but buries the secrets, one by one, in a tomb of silence—as do all the professions which deal with the problems of people. This means, of course, that the student of human groups must remain willingly and firmly a marginal man in relation to those he studies; one who will keep, cost what it will, the delicate balance between loyalty to those who have admitted him to the role of confidant and to his colleagues who expect him to contribute freely to the accumulating knowledge about human society and methods of studying it.

While some prefer to study people in situ, others take them aside and learn from them in long interviews, reassuring their subjects, showing sympathy for the problems of each, and refraining the while from even the gesture of censorship. One of the most powerful of modern social inventions is the psychoanalytic interview, in which the patient is led painfully through a maze of hindrances of conscience, shame, and fear to a fuller expression, hence to fuller knowledge, of his own mind. It is based on the assumption that the injunction to know one's self is one that few of us can follow without help. The prolonged sympathetic interview of the social investigator is less dramatic, but is an effective instrument of social discovery. But every device must be valued by its results. Some students have found that there are situations in which contradiction, calling the subject's bluff, facing him with his own contradictions, and even questioning his sincerity bring out depths and ambivalences which might otherwise remain hidden. Some have undertaken experiments to discover how differences of tactical rhetoric on the part of the interviewer affect the rhetoric of the subjects.

Some investigators prefer to go even further than experimenting with methods of interviewing and observing; they set up their own situations and create their own groups. The social research of the University of Frankfort on the Main used such a method in study of political attitudes in 1951. They got up a letter in which an American soldier who had spent some years in Germany tells the people back home in the United States what he thinks are the German attitudes towards the Nazis, Jews, Americans, and democracy. Germans of various backgrounds were called together in small groups to discuss social and political issues; the letter was read to them from a tape made by a speaker with an English accent. In the conversation following the reading, attitudes such as have not been caught by any political questionnaire in postwar Germany came to light.

Similar methods have been used in study of various matters in the U. S. A. A team of social scientists engaged to find out how juries arrive at their unanimous decisions, has had the record of a damage suit read on to tape, using different voices for the various persons in the court: the record is played to groups of twelve who are then left alone to decide the case as if they were a jury. A silent observer with a recorder sits unobtrusively in a corner. The subjects play the role of jurymen with great seriousness. The doings of real juries are properly kept secret; the experimental device provides an approximation with much better observation than one would in any case be likely to get by asking people what had happened in juries on which they had sat. For the observer keeps a record of those who talk the most, those who change their minds, and what alliances are made in the course of the wearing on of the argument. Combined with surveys of the ways in which people of various incomes, education, and other traits say they would judge various cases submitted to juries, these experiments are teaching us a great deal about the operation of one of our cherished institutions.

Some investigators would eventually replace all study of "natural groups" by experimental devices. Only so, they contend, can the many variable factors in social behavior be kept to such number that one can keep track of them and measure their influence. Some would go further than the Frankfort institute or the jury team. For in these projects, the experimenters were interested in the substance of their findings—the political attitudes of the Germans, and the operation of juries in the United States, respectively. The pure experimenters make the substance suit the experiment. They assemble a group of people, and give them a problem to solve to which the experimenter and the subjects are alike utterly indifferent. It is the interaction between people, the influence they have on each other, the way and the mood in which they communicate with one another that is the object of study. For instance, what difference does it make in the interplay among a number of people whether one of them is so placed that the others can talk to each other only through him, or whether they can all talk to each other at once? One may study the forms of social interaction—social choreography— as a student of poetry may study meters and periods without attending to thought, or as the philologist may analyze grammatical forms and phonetic modulations free of concern for meaning and mood. It is but a narrow step from such study of form in human conduct to the study of form and style in art; one is on the fluttering edge between the abstractions of science and those of art. It is perhaps no accident that Simmel, the German philosopher who first proposed the study of pure interaction, attention to form rather than to content, as the basic concept of sociology, should also have written about money and about art in the same spirit. The more abstract one's way of conceiving things, the more likely one is to make generic discoveries which apply to many concrete fields of natural and human phenomena. As the experimenters penetrate further into the mathematical symmetries of human converse, they may well add to knowledge of other systems of things as well.

If men were gods, big gods with solar systems at beck and call, they might set up control planets, plant people on them, and reproduce millions of years of history, intervening now and then to see what would happen. But students of human society are mortal; our subjects live as long as we do, and usually have as much power over us as we over them. One experimenter has seriously played god by pretending that, in his laboratory as in heaven, a minute is as a hundred years. His naïvete only highlights the problem of translating the findings of small, limited experiments to larger organizations and to the time-scale of history; it does not prove that the transfer cannot, with care and in limited degree, be made.

Social experimenting has also raised the problem, both ethical and practical, of manipulating other people. There has been quite a hue and cry about this lately. A psychologist "running rats" is playing a game; the rats play for keeps without even knowing that it is a game. I believe it is suspected that now and again a sly one makes a game of the experiments and laughs up his metaphoric sleeve at the serious psychologist. No one has objected to playing with the rat, but many believe that to manipulate people is an improper way of studying man. But, of course, all politics and much of social life consist of the more or less successful attempts of people to influence one another. Every profession that deals with people is suspected of looking with an experimental and manipulative eye at its clients; indeed, no one would think of going to a lawyer, physician, or even a clergyman who did not look upon his case as one among many from which they had learned their trades. The real problem of manipulating (hence of experimenting upon) humans is not that of manipulation or no manipulation, but that of the proper conditions, limits, means, and ends thereof.

Some sociologists combine the mood of the experimenter with the roving eye of the reporter. They frequent the places where events of the kinds they are interested in are bound to happen, or they get a wide knowledge of some order of human occurrences or problems, and chase down the crucial cases which will give them the combinations of circumstances on which a more general and abstract, yet more refined and useful, knowledge can be built.

Not long ago some social psychologists were studying what happens to a group of people when a great promised event does not occur as predicted by their leaders. When they were in the midst of their project, a small sect gathered about a man who was predicting an early end of the world. Now this has happened many times before, and there are some records of the cases. For instance, when the world didn't come to end on the due date in 1843, the Millerites decided their arithmetic was wrong. A century later their successors, the Seventh Day Adventists (some of them at least) are beginning to say that while Jesus is indeed coming again in the flesh to establish his Kingdom on earth, it is sinfully presumptuous of men to think they can calculate the day and the hour. For did he not say, "Ye know not the day nor the hour"? But the team of psychologists mentioned above quite properly were eager to see a group of living people go through the experience of waiting for the world to end, and they did. Seldom do scholars have such luck.

We are in a time when we have more than common reason to want to know how people will react when disaster strikes. Flying squadrons have been sent in the wake of floods, tornadoes, explosions, and fires to find out tactfully, before memories are clouded and distorted, how people meet such adversity; who rises to the occasion to help others, and who must, on the contrary, be helped. Immediately after a great fire that destroyed half their town, the citizens told a field worker what a hero a certain obscure sister superior of a small convent-hospital had been. The nun, they said, had simply taken over and run the rescue services and the whole town. Sometime later the proper order of things had been restored; people appeared to believe that the mayor and an ecclesiastical dignitary had saved the day. In another disaster, the minister of one rather popular church went completely to pieces while the representative of a minority church and a school teacher saw the town through its tragedy. The minority minister's hair came out in handfuls some days later when reaction set in; it was the price of his courage. In many cases of such "firehouse" social research, two reports are issued. One is a newsy and perhaps immediately useful report, the other more general, and so phrased as to be useful to others who study human behavior.

If one frees his curiosity of the pecularities of some one time and place by developing a good set of abstract ideas for comparing one case or situation with another, he will see many situations in various parts of the world comparable to those that originally aroused his interest. He will fall into the delicious conflict between wanting to learn more and more detail about the one dear case and the desire to go elsewhere to add both breadth and nuance to his knowledge. A number of students of American race relations have gone off to Africa, the most tumultuous and massive Negro-white frontier of these days. The relative numbers and the historical situations of people of Negro, European, and other ancestries on the racial frontiers of Africa are varied, and are everywhere quite different from the North American racial frontier. Race relations are still vivid in the United States, for we still consider a man's race an important thing about him. Furthermore, these relations are at a crucial point in which much of both practical and theoretical interest is to be learned. Adventure lies at our own door. But there is also much to be learned by going afield. Race relations have occurred in many historical epochs, in a great variety of circumstances, accompanied by various degrees of cultural differences; their course has been influenced by intervening events. Sometimes peoples meet who are alike in race, but different in almost all else. The irreducible core of race relations, as distinguished from the relations of peoples different from each other in other regards, might be found by comparing various communities.

To be sure, one's ability and will to learn languages, his health, the adaptability and sense of adventure of his wife, his knack for playing roles such that he can live among various peoples, not to mention the human life-span, limit the number of cultural situations one can study. On the whole, social science has suffered from too little rather than too much getting about (except to conventions). Anthropologists are great people to get around, but only lately have they begun to study the larger and more confused settings where races meet and where new nations are being made. The racially mixed locations and cities of Africa are places where the former subjects of the anthropologists are facing the favorite problems of the sociologist. In fact, sociologists and anthropologists are meeting there, too. In those cities, native prophets and evangelists preach half-Christian, half-tribal gospels and predict great events in which God's black people will come into their own while the white malefactors will be destroyed or driven back to their own land. Such prophets enjoin their people to make themselves pure and ready for their glorious future by a return to some idealized form of the ways of the past. One thinks of the Pharisees tithing mint and rue as part of their program of getting rid of Greek and Roman.

In the Times of New York or of London, one can follow from day to day the crises of a dozen interracial or intercultural conflicts; in most of them Europeans are reluctantly and bit by bit giving up political, economic, and social power over others. The underdog group is in most cases undergoing revolutionary changes in its culture and social structure and is awakening to a new group-consciousness on larger scale than in the past; it is usually rewriting its history, not because of Carbon 14 or new archaeological finds but because people with a new sense of unity and a new vision of the future seem always to need a new past different both from their traditional ones and from that given them by their foreign masters. Every rewriting of history—especially our own—is grist for the sociologist's mill. Racial and cultural frontiers are but one problem which can be understood only by wide-ranging about the world of the present, either in the flesh or in the mind's eye, and about the past, through the eyes of historians and through the works of art and literature in which men have expressed their hopes, hates, and aspirations.

A basic assumption of the study of mankind—hence of individual branches of study such as that called sociology—is that it is impor tant and fascinating to find out what things do and what things do not repeat themselves in human history. Sociologists work rather more on those which are repeated. They assume that although the people of any race, culture, time, or place inherently merit study as much as those of any others, still each historic social time and place may show some special feature which may make it an especially fit laboratory for study of some problem or process of human society. Part of the adventure of the study of human society is the seeking out of the most intriguing living laboratory, prepared by the fortunes of history, for study of the problems we are especially interested in, for use of our particular skills, and for catering to our particular tastes, curiosities, and preoccupations. Our choices may spring from a sense of political and moral urgency, from a desire to advance knowledge for man's good, from some ill-defined identification with all that is human, or from some aesthetic sense.

Some of the students of man's doings should be creatures ready to invade the territory of others, both figuratively and literally, and to compare anything with anything else without shock or apology. It is a friction-generating and improper pursuit. Any social situation is in some measure dear to those in it. To compare it with others is to seem to dull the poignancy of the wrongs of the underdogs, and to detract from the merits of those who have the better place in it. Comparison may violate the canons of status and prestige, as when one compares the code of secrecy of the gentleman's gentleman with that of the lord chamberlain. Comparison of religion with religion appears to reduce the claim of each to a monopoly of truth. Such invasion is also dangerous and improper on the academic front, for any series of human events, any social time and place, and most of man's institutions are each thought to be the game preserve of one of the learned professions. Shoving over scholarly line-fences is even more dangerous than shifting boundary stones in Vermont.

Most perilous and improper of all is it to compare the academic disciplines with one another by pointing out that each is an historical entity which had a beginning and which will probably be superseded by others in the future. If we study man and his institutions with broad-sweeping curiosity, with the sharpest tools of observation and analysis which we can devise, if we are deterred from no comparison by the fallacy which assumes that some people and peoples are more human than others, if we do not allow loyalty to truth to take second place to department or academic guild, we will all be proper students of man. And when we become too respectable, too much bound to past methods, whenever our means show signs of becoming ends, may we all—even the sociologists—be succeeded by people to whom *nihil humanum alienum est.*

7

POLITICS

A New Look at Leviathan

by Peter H. Odegard

THERE is a new look in the study of politics; an increasing awareness of the baffling complexity of what since Aristotle has been called the queen of sciences—the science of politics. No longer a hostage to history, and freed at last from its bondage to the lawyers as well as from the arid schematism of the political taxonomists, political science is in the process of becoming one of the central unifying forces for understanding why we behave like human beings. As the dominant mood of the interwar period was one of specialization and isolation among the major disciplines, so the mood of this postwar generation is one of specialization and integration.

The process of fission which a generation or so ago gave political science its independence from moral philosophy and political economy was not arrested at the borders of the new discipline but continued into its own nucleus with devastating results. Public Finance broke away to join economics; Public Administration cut loose and set up shop with its own institutes and schools and its own Society of Public Administration; International Relations began to assert itself as a separate domain; and students of Political Behavior and Public Opinion grew restive under the formalistic restraints of traditional political science. Comprehensive treatises on *Principles of Political Science* or *The State*, after the manner of Aristotle and

Hobbes, disappeared. Specialists and empiricists, calling themselves scientists, replaced the generalists and the philosophers as the central figures on the scene. The change was reflected in a greater concern for methodology, as speculation about basic principles and values gave way to empirical, quantitative studies of movements and trends. Preoccupation with methods of quantitative analysis in some circles reached a point where the meaning or significance of what was being measured or counted became of only incidental interest and the triumph of technique over purpose was complete. But apart from these aberrations political science shifted its emphasis from structure and statics to political dynamics. The search for a single body of eternal values or first principles yielded to a search for pragmatic solutions to real and insistent problems in what was judged to be a pluralistic universe.

At the same time, however, there is a growing demand for closer coordination and sharing of methods and insights of the specialists, not only within political science itself but also with other social sciences. This demand for integration has at least temporarily arrested the trend toward separatism and disintegration that characterized the earlier period. Allowing for local variants, political science in the United States today may be said to focus on *political behavior* in the widest sense of the term. And this is true in varying degree of all contemporary political scientists, whatever their own specialized field may be—Political Theory, International Relations, Public Administration, Public Opinion, Political Parties and Pressure Groups, Comparative Government, or Public Law.

This emphasis on political behavior is reflected in impressive recent studies on administrative behavior, legislative behavior, judicial behavior, and voting behavior, as distinguished from studies in which the law, organization, and formal procedures of government were emphasized. It has also led political scientists to take a fresh look at many cherished cliches and slogans. "Freedom," "Policy vs. Administration," "Public Opinion," "Decision Making," to name but a few, have been subjected to searching analysis not only by a new school of political positivists, but by a small and growing army of empiricists as well. Moreover, the increasing recognition of demographic, psychological, cultural, and economic factors affecting political behavior has forced the political scientist into friendly collaboration with other social science and humanistic disciplines. And this collaboration has been evident not only in scientific research, but also in the day-by-day conduct of public affairs. Even diplomacy has become less a field for cookie-pushers in striped pants than for political scientists, working with cultural anthropologists, sociologists, psychologists, economists, and even artists, poets, and musicians. In short, contemporary political science has become but one specialized branch of an increasingly unified body of disciplines engaged in a comprehensive and objective inquiry into the nature, forms, and dynamics of human behavior in all its complex and fascinating variety.

The political scientists' special preoccupation is with those aspects of human behavior having to do with the exercise of political power as a means of social control. As Harold Lasswell says, "The study of politics is the study of influence and the influential. . . . The influential are those who get the most of what there is to get." What there is to get is power and the fruits of power—"income, deference, and safety." It is therefore with the nature, basis, structure, scope, and dynamics of political power that the political scientist is mainly, although not entirely, concerned.

Any individual or group able to command and control the behavior of other individuals or groups has power. Obviously, in this broad sense, power is widely diffused in society. The trade union leader, the business executive, the teacher, the priest, any group leader—even the father in the family—has power. For all, in varying degrees, may command and control the behavior of others. Yet none of these can be said to have *political* power. For the distinctive quality of *political* power is the right to use force to enforce commands.

The working man who violates the commands of his trade union may be fined or suspended or expelled from the union. The child who disobeys the commands of his father may be punished by penalties of varying severity. But in none of these cases may those who disobey be punished by imprisonment or death. Only *political* power carries with it the supreme sanction of force—of life or death.

And since the State alone claims a monopoly of force, it alone has a monopoly of *political* power. Indeed, it is this that distinguishes political power from other forms of power in society—and the State from other associations. It is this that makes control of the State of such transcendent importance.

As Thomas Hobbes long ago observed, it is only by giving up the private exercise of violence to the State that we can insure peace, security, and freedom. "During the time," he wrote, "men live without a common Power to keep them all in awe, they are in that condition which is called War . . . and such a war as is of every man against every man. . . . In such condition, there is no place for industry, because the fruit therof is uncertain. And consequently, no culture of the Earth, no navigation nor use of the commodities that may be imported by sea; no commodious building . . . no knowledge of the face of the Earth . . . no account of Time; no Arts; no Letters; no Society; and which is worst of all, continual fear and danger of violent death; and the life of man is solitary, poor, nasty, brutish, and short."

Politics is not merely a game which one may or may not choose to play, but a condition of survival. As Aristotle observed, man is by nature a political animal, and whether as subject or as sovereign he is a *state's man*. And the terms on which political power is held and the goals for which it is used indicate, as clearly as anything can, the quality of a civilization.

When we describe the State as an organized monopoly of coercive force, we are only at the beginning of our problem. For compliance with the commands of the State requires the use of force only in rare instances. Whether in the organization of public services, application of the criminal code, or in making provision for external security, voluntary compliance is the rule. Indeed *political* disobedience is probably less frequent than disobedience to other forms of social control—in the family, the trade union, or the church. In all this, habit, custom, and tradition play prominent roles, and become, therefore, relevant for any realistic study of political behavior. Since force is more often implied than explicit, we are led to inquire into other factors that induce compliance.

What, for example, is the relation of *political power* to *influence*, and to *authority*? Influence has been defined as encompassing all motivations inducing *voluntary* compliance; power as compliance motivated by *sanctions*; and authority as compliance motivated by attitudes toward *legitimacy*. We are coming to see that to understand political behavior we must understand the relation of power, authority, and influence to the general problem of inducing or compelling compliance with the commands of the State.

How far, for example, are the "formal" attributes of power—the pomp and pageantry of kings—essential to the exercise of political power? The mace and scepter, the orb and crown, according to Walter Bagehot, are more than the childish baubles of kings—they are the essential symbols of the State, the visible and outward signs of sovereign power, without which government becomes a mean and common thing, ripe for disobedience and rebellion. They sheath the sword of power with *authority* and make compliance palatable and even pleasant.

Governments which fail in one way or another to invest power with these symbols of authority tend to be weak. For the loyalty that makes for greatness in a state, that evokes not sullen obedience nor indifferent compliance but service beyond the call of duty, this loyalty is not won by force but by enlisting the mind and heart of the citizen in the service of the state. In the long run, it is not force but will that is the only stable and enduring basis for political power. The political scientist has therefore come to ponder the role of symbols as a major political instrument.

How the sanction of force as the unique attribute of political power is to be restricted or transformed into will, and/or reason, is one of the major problems confronting both the student of government and the practicing politician. To invest political power with authority, that is, to make it legitimate, is essential to the development of stable political institutions. For without authority political power lies exposed as naked force without support in reason, sentiment, or will.

Except for a few primitives, no government or ruler has been willing to rest its claim to power on force alone. Natural Law, Divine Right, Popular Consent, have at various times served as rationalization for the exercise of political power. Even Mussolini and Hitler, Stalin and Mao Tse Tung have sought authority for their power in "the people."

This notion of government "of the people" or by "consent of the people," however, is easier to repeat as a slogan than to understand as an operating principle of political power. Government by what people—or with whose consent? The simple answer of course is to say by the consent of qualified voters who vote. Yet only recently has "the people" in this sense included women, and in many parts of our country the term still, in effect, excludes Negroes. In Georgia, where most Negroes are barred by various illicit means, eighteen-year-old white residents are included. And in any case, voting behavior is but the end product of multiple and complex antecedent factors found both in the individual voter and in society. In probing such matters the political scientist becomes very like a sociologist.

And how are "the people" to govern? How shall they give their consent? What are the forms or channels through which power is thus invested with the authority of "the people"? Obviously, the right to vote is vital to this process. So, too, is the right to seek office, to write and speak one's mind on the goals and objectives for which power is to be employed and on the manner of its exercise, and to join with others in such activities. So it is that political parties and pressure groups of almost infinite variety emerge as the formal channels through which consent or dissent is mobilized and directed.

In its outer reaches, the study of consent thus cuts a wide swath, involving not only the whole complex pattern of voting behavior but also the structure of government (whether parliamentary or presidential, unitary, confederal or federal), legal and administrative provisions relating to the suffrage, elections, and party organization; legislative, executive, and judicial organization, the apportionment of representation, and rules governing the civil service. All provide the formal structure of power within which political parties, pressure groups, and others seek to manipulate and mobilize consent.

Equally important with these legal and institutional arrangements are demographic factors—the size, composition, distribution, and mobility of the population. The politics of the South, for example, generally revolve around the position of the Negro. Similarly varying ethnic and religious patterns in other areas significantly affect the pattern of political behavior—the Scandinavians in the Red River Valley, Puerto Ricans, Negroes, Jews, and Irish in New York, Germans in Wisconsin, and the Irish in Boston, of which city an immigrant from San Francisco once remarked "Boston is ruled by a 90 per cent majority with all the psychoses of an oppressed minority."

The problem for students of American politics is further complicated by the extreme mobility of our population and the relative absence of any rigid pattern of social stratification. The American people have been a people on the march, not only from the Old World to the New, from East to West, and South to North, and from farm to city, but up and down the social ladder. These mass migrations have had an almost lethal effect upon party organization and political traditions and habits, but the social processes involved are only beginning to be understood.

Stuart Rice, in a pioneer study on *Quantitative Methods in the Study of Politics*, found a significant correlation between urban or rural populations and differential voting behavior. The development of the modern metropolitan complex, the emergence of Suburbia as a national phenomenon, and the urbanization of rural life introduce new factors in this picture and new problems for the student of politics. Rural constituencies in many states are controlled not by horny-handed sons of the soil but by large industrial farmers or urban interests having their political base in the country and their financial home in the city. The simple distinction between urban and rural interests and attributes is breaking down, although the representative system in state legislatures and the national Congress continues to be weighted in favor of the countryside and against the city. In California, for example, the four largest urban counties with 60 per cent of the state's population elect only 10 per cent of the state senators. Connecticut's ten largest cities with nearly 50 per cent of the state's population have only 7 per cent of the representatives in the lower house. Similar conditions of malrepresentation are to be found in two-thirds of the states and in the Congress at Washington. Denied their full share of representation in the legislative branch, urban voters are turning more and more toward executive officers elected on a statewide basis where urban votes count heavily. The governor for the state level and the president for the nation are coming more to represent urban as against rural interests and thus find themselves increasingly in conflict with legislatures.

Political behavior is a function of still other variables, including national income and its distribution, employment and unemployment, wage and price levels, the cost of living, occupational distribution as among industry, agriculture, trade, commerce, and the professions.

Patterns of economic organization in business, agriculture, labor, and the professions may be as important as patterns of formal political organization. The CIO and AFL, now combined in a unified labor movement, the Farm Bureau Federation, American Legion, American Medical Association, and the National Association of Manufacturers—all reaching into nearly every state and county—share the molding and the mobilization of consent. Political scientists no longer approach this phenomenon as moralists condemning pressure politics as invisible government and hence irreconcilable with pure representative democracy. On the contrary, there has been a return to the more realistic analysis of James Madison and a frank recognition and acceptance of a group theory of politics. Consequently, much greater attention is being given not only to the role of groups in the political process but to the internal composition, structure, and governance of groups themselves. The so-called "iron law of oligarchy" set forth by Roberto Michels has been subjected to closer analysis not merely in empirical studies of group dynamics but in a systematic search for a general theory of organization.

Certainly the importance of so-called pressure groups in American politics can no longer be gainsaid. In 1951 the officially reported political expenditures of the American Medical Association alone exceeded $1.5 million; and those of the Farm Bureau, a similar amount. Over a period of three years those groups which file reports in Washington reported total expenditures of approximately $75 million—a sum much greater than political party expenditures except in presidential elections.

These large outlays represent expenditures not only for professional lobbyists, but for space and time in the major media of mass communications. The development of radio and TV, growth of newspaper and periodical criculation, and consolidation of ownership of these media have posed new and difficult problems.

The effect of mass media on political behavior remains largely a mystery, and has increasingly concerned students of politics. Is it true, as one hears frequently these days, that elections are won or lost not by the precinct worker checking precinct lists, ringing doorbells, and getting voters to the polls, but by saturating the press, radio, TV, and other mass media with political propaganda? The comparatively recent emergence of professional hucksters as campaign managers, and the lavish expenditure of funds on mass media, seem to suggest that this may be true.

If it is true, what are its implications for government based on consent of the governed? The road to power might then be through control of the mass media rather than through party organizations which enlist the active participation of millions of citizens. The citizen will then become more an observer and less a participant in the process of government. As control of the media becomes more and more centralized, the implications of this development for responsible democratic government could be serious. One characteristic of the authoritarian personality seems to be a willingness to prefer the role of observer, whose mind is made up for him by others, to that of the active participant who makes up his own mind.

One characteristic of the totalitarian state is the monopoly which it enjoys over the channels of communication. Notwithstanding Democratic Liberal-Labor complaints, Western democracies are still a long way from one-party monopoly of mass communications media. But we need to be alert to current trends toward concentration, consolidation, and systematic bias in the reporting of political news.

It is for these reasons among others that students of government are concerned with the control, content, circulation, and effect of mass media. Although many studies—some of them highly significant—have been made of control, content, and circulation, little progress has been made in the measurement of "effect." A recent study of television during the 1952 campaign in Iowa shows no "reliable difference either in voting turnout or in the percentage of the vote cast for the Republican candidate between High Television Density and other areas." If, however, any reasonable inference can be drawn that volume of coverage and/or systematic bias in content does affect voting behavior, recent charges that the American daily press has become a "one-party press" deserve a better reply than they have thus far received. A recent study of four California newspapers (San Francisco Examiner, San Francisco Chronicle, San Francisco News, and The Oakland Tribune) during the 1954 campaign for Governor and U. S. Senator reveals conclusive evidence of flagrant bias in the reporting of political news.

We need also a thorough reexamination of campaign financing. Most informed scholars today take a dim view of the traditional practice of imposing limits on expenditures. To insist that a candidate may not spend more than $10,000 in a campaign that every layman knows cannot be financed for ten times as much is not only unrealistic but promotes deception and hypocrisy. Some affirmative measures will be necessary if we are to insure that "equitable access" to the voters by rival parties upon which our democratic system depends. Making campaign contributions—within reasonable limits — deductible for income tax purposes, extending the franking privilege to rival candidates, publishing and distributing at public expense campaign bulletins, and even contributing to campaign funds from public revenues are some proposals now seriously discussed. If, through poverty, political parties or duly qualified candidates for office are denied equitable access to the voters through the communications media, opportunity of the voters in turn to choose among alternative candidates, parties, or issues will be restricted or even denied.

This opportunity for citizens as voters to choose among meaningful alternatives—parties, candidates, or policies—together with the opportunity for minorities, through organization, education, or agitation to strive to become majorities—is central to the whole theory of the modern democratic state. It is important, threfore, that the alternatives among which the voters may choose be meaningful and significant. To have one's choice limited to Tweedledum and Tweedledee is to be denied the opportunity for making a real choice.

One of the standard criticisms of the American party system lies precisely here. The Republican and Democratic parties, it is argued, are for all practical purposes indistinguishable—labels on empty bottles. This, it is said, is one reason why we have always had a spate of minor parties on the ballot. Liberty, Free Soil, Granger, Populist, Socialist, Communist, Prohibition, Progressive—their name is legion, arising from the failure of the major parties to face up to the real issues that trouble the voters. When the Democrats and Whigs failed to provide any real choice on the issue of slavery, the Liberty, Free Soil and, finally, Republican parties were born. When the Republican party failed to recognize some of the problems arising from American industrial growth in the nineteenth and early twentieth centuries, the Populist, Socialist, and Bull-Moose Progressive parties helped to force the issue.

No student of American politics, I believe, would deny the important role played by these minor parties. What needs more careful study is the notion that the Republican and Democratic parties are empty bottles.

Innumerable studies can be cited to show that on literally hun-

dreds of issues these major parties either agree or are so divided
within themselves as to make any differences between them as parties
invisible to the naked eye. But obviously the significant question is
not to ask "On what issues do Republicans and Democrats agree?"
but rather, "On what significant issues do they clearly disagree?" Examination of the characteristics of Democratic and Republican
voters, party platforms, speeches of Republican and Democratic
candidates for office, messages of Republican and Democratic gov-
ernors to state legislatures, of Republican and Democratic presidents
to Congress, and votes of Republican and Democratic members of
state and national legislative bodies tend to show that differences between Republicans and Democrats are not only fairly numerous, but
significant.

"Today," wrote Paul Lazarsfeld in 1944, "in most sections of the
country, the politician can count on the banker, the business man-
ager, the independent farmer, the bishop (of the Episcopal Church),
and a good many of his flock, to vote Republican. In the same way,
he knows that the immigrant, the working man, the [Catholic]
priest and most of his parishioners, particularly in cities, constitute
the mainstay of the Democratic Party outside the South." And to
these, we should add the Negro.

The features which differentiate Republican and Democrat, then,
seem to be economic status, religion, residence, occupation, and possible age—with youth favoring the Democrats. Yet this pattern itself
is subject to change and there is evidence to show that explanations
of political behavior in terms of social stratification are extremely
hazardous under conditions of crisis. Moreover, generalizations applicable to a national sample may be most unreliable if applied to
smaller segments of that sample. And the reverse is also true. It is
interesting to note, for example, that according to a study by Law-
rence Fuchs the Boston Jewish voters represent behavior sharply at
variance with what one might expect in terms of the generally accepted pattern set forth in Lazarsfeld's *The People's Choice*.
Whereas normally voters with low income and low educational background are correlated with a *Democratic* vote, among the Boston

Jews, the opposite was true—i.e., those with high income and high educational rating were more Democratic than their low income and less well educated co-religionists.

In general, however, it seems that as a voter's economic and social status improves in the community, and his educational level goes up, as he moves from urban to suburban and rural areas, and from Catholic to Protestant communities, the chances of his being a Republican increase. If his economic and social status are low, if he lives in the heart of the city, if he is a Negro, Jew, or Catholic, he's likely to be a Democrat.

Equally significant was an effort to classify voters in the 1952 election as (1) candidate-oriented, (2) party-oriented, or (3) issue-oriented. The high degree of party orientation is indicated by the fact that some two-thirds of those who voted in 1952 said they had always voted for the same party, with Democrats having a two-to-one advantage among these party regulars. So strong is this tradition of party loyalty even among those Democrats who voted for Eisenhower in 1952, that nearly 45 per cent justified their defection by saying that Mr. Eisenhower wasn't a real Republican anyway. How far this notion extended is indicated by the fact that no less than 31 per cent of the Republican regulars expressed a similar doubt. To many old-line Republicans Eisenhower must have appeared as a sheep in wolf's clothes—as, to many a Democrat, he looked like a wolf in the skin of a sheep. Only this kind of doubt could explain Mr. Eisenhower's decisive victory at an election where, on the congressional level, the Democrats polled nearly 500,000 more votes than the Republicans.

If, on the basis of Republican and Democratic attitudes not only among the voters but in legislative bodies, one were to construct a model of these parties, it might look something like this:

Democrats as a rule take an affirmative view of government, Republicans, a negative view. Democrats talk about what government ought to do. Republicans about what government ought not to do. To the Democrat, government ought to provide for old age and survivor's insurance, unemployment compensation, education, child care centers, school lunches, public health, and even medical care. To the faithful Republican, government ought not to do most of these things. Its proper functions should be limited to national defense, internal police, the maintenance of law and order, the protection of property, and the encouragement of business enterprise—mainly by not doing the things Democrats want done.

Democrats take a sentimental view of foreign relations, tending to favor free trade, international cooperation, the League of Nations, Union Now, and the United Nations with all its specialized agencies; and Republicans are more likely to take what they call a "realistic" view of world affairs and to favor protective tariffs, noninvolvement in international organizations, and a minimum of participation, if any, in such bodies as the United Nations. Like most models this one does not provide for the many deviants who do not conform to the general pattern.

If one could extend this analysis to the equivalent of the psychoanalyst's couch, even more significant differences between the regulars of our major parties might emerge—differences on the role of influence, authority, and power in society, and on the role of reason in public affairs and on force or persuasion in international relations, on progress and poverty, on permanence and change, on liberty and law, security and freedom, war and peace, and even on human nature. One is reminded of the contrasting views of Alexander Hamilton and Thomas Jefferson concerning government by the people. To Hamilton, the people were a "great beast"; to Jefferson, the best repository of political power.

To be a Republican or a Democrat, as Gilbert and Sullivan observed of Liberals and Conservatives, may be associated with more fundamental personality traits than we have been willing to admit. It increasingly appears that the differences between the Republican and Democratic parties in America are as great or greater than the differences between the Conservative and Labour parties of Great Britain, although less than between some of the parties of Continental Europe. When, therefore, they appeal to the American people in soliciting their consent to control the state, they offer a real choice between meaningful and significant alternatives.

This is not to say that political scientists are satisfied with the prevailing patterns of political organization through which consent is mobilized and the State invested with the authority of "the people." A special committee of the American Political Science Association, after several years of study, recently offered a plan for radical revision of party organization, calculated to insure much tighter internal control and closer integration of the party with its representatives in Congress.

In their preoccupation with political behavior, contemporary political scientists are not neglecting the important problems involved in the formal structure of political power. For behavior is related to political structure as physiology is related to anatomy, and neither can be understood without the other.

Every student of political parties, for example, recognizes the integral relation between the forms of party organization and the formal structure of government which parties seek to control, and through which they must operate. A parliamentary system with an integrated legislative-executive structure presents different problems and different patterns of control and consent than a presidential system characterized by a separation of powers. Similarly varying electoral systems—universal versus limited suffrage—and differing systems of representation—single member districts versus proportional representation, for example—will affect voting behavior. The political scientist is only beginning to understand the nature and extent of these factors in differential voting behavior.

But studies of the structure and organization of political power have wider significance than their relation to voting behavior. They involve a continuing inquiry into ways and means for improving governmental organization to meet the needs and aspirations of the people. Take, for example, the over-all structure of government in the United States. Recent estimates indicate a total of some 110,000 different government units in this country. Of these, the national government in Washington is but one. In addition, there are 48 state governments, 3000 counties, 17,000 incorporated municipalities, 17,000 towns and townships, over 60,000 school districts, and nearly 12,000 other special districts. How can this complex political mechanism be organized to best serve the American people? Do we need a unit of government for every 1200 or 1500 people?

At least one important group—the Council of State Governments —suggests some radical surgery on the complex body of American local government. All separate school districts would be abolished, special and ad hoc districts would be eliminated, townships in the Middle Western and Middle Atlantic states would disappear, the less populous towns of New England would be consolidated, and consolidated city-county units would be established wherever feasible to administer city, county, and school district functions; in rural or semiurban areas the county would remain as the main unit for performing local services and services of statewide importance. If adopted, such a plan of reorganization would reduce the number of independent governmental units from the present 110,000 to less than a fifth of that number.

Such problems of over-all organization are matched by others involving the internal structure of government at every level, whether federal, state, or local. They relate to familiar management problems of personnel administration, span of control, morale, optimum size of governmental units, intergovernmental relations, and bureaucratic responsibility. Even here the political scientist must acquire the insights of the social psychologist.

More than 1800 departments, bureaus, divisions, and authorities make up the federal government. How can this vast machine be organized to avoid the dilemma of "creating a manageable number of unmanageable departments or an unmanageable number of manageable ones"? The growth of the federal government is said to illustrate not only spontaneous generation (Pasteur to the contrary notwithstanding) but also nuclear fission long before it was achieved in physics. Divisions grow into bureaus and bureaus into departments and departments in turn spawn bureaus and divisions. And once born, few agencies ever die. "The nearest approach to immortality on earth," said Jimmy Byrnes, "is a government bureau." And the functions assigned to them are often as much the result of accident and pressure as of administrative logic. Mr. Hoover once noted that brown bears came under Agriculture, grizzly bears under Treasury, and polar bears under Commerce.

One of the great inventions for which we as a nation may take credit is the federal system of government. The growing interest in the federal principle as the basis for regional and world organization emphasizes the importance of systematic study of federalism and its corollary, intergovernmental relations.

Federal systems, it has been said, inevitably succumb to one of two fatal maladies. Either they dissolve into a number of separate and independent states, or they evolve into centralized unitary states that remain federal only in name. Is this true? How can we conserve the advantages in such a system and avoid the disadvantages and dangers? Is it possible to identify and in some measure control the centrifugal and centripetal forces that operate to destroy a federal system? Since the Civil War the centripetal forces have been in the ascendant with an increasing tendency to expand the powers and responsibilities of the national government. This is reflected, for example, by the fact that, whereas until recent times from two-thirds to three-fourths of all taxes collected went into state and local treasuries and only one-fourth to one-third to Uncle Sam, the situation is now reversed and Washington collects from two-thirds to three-fourths of the total. Numerous studies have been made to seek ways and means for redressing the balance.

Is it true, as W. Y. Elliott of Harvard once said, that "the states as at present geographically constituted have lost all reality as economic or political units"? Do the states in fact serve as experimental laboratories in government, or do the major problems of government in the mid-twentieth century transcend state lines and call for action on a regional, national, or even international basis? Have we discovered in the Tennessee Valley and other regional authorities a new pattern of government, a new source of strength for our federal system?

Among the well-established myths of American government is the notion that local government is more democratic and responsible, more efficient and economical than government at higher levels extending over wider areas. The village store and the New England town meeting as the prototypes of a vibrant democracy are part of our folklore. How do these notions look in the cold light of objective analysis? What about the relation of size—in terms of population or area—to economy and efficiency, morale and responsibility? The problem of scale or optimum size is a familiar one in science and industry. Only recently has it become a concern of serious scientific research for political scientists and psychologists.

Within the region and the state, there are other vital problems of intergovernmental relations. The fact, for example, that some twenty-seven cities have larger budgets than the states whose "creatures" they are makes one wonder how long they will permit the tail to wag the dog. The fact, also, that many of our great metropolitan areas spill over state boundaries poses another problem of federal-state-city relations. A recent study of California city government points out how "obsolete governmental boundaries severely hinder area-wide planning. As population has increased and industry has grown, many California cities have become surrounded by unincorporated fringe areas that are beyond their control. Yet these fringes draw upon the city for numerous services and frequently contribute to the decline of adjacent urban areas." With their offices or places of business in the city and their homes and hearts in Suburbia, the residents of these areas have been described as urban carpetbaggers.

These problems of structure inevitably merge with all the complex patterns of behavior involved in the process of governmental decision-making and administration. We used to think we had boxed this process when we had described the formal legal structure of legislative bodies, and the executive and judicial establishment. But the frontiers of both politics and administration have been pushed far beyond these relatively simple concepts. Research in the dynamics of power today requires the multiple skills not only of the political scientists, but of the lawyer, sociologist, economist, and social psychologist.

Since political power involves as its *ultima ratio* the use of force to insure compliance, the question inevitably arises as to how far it should extend. The anarchists would banish it altogether and rely upon voluntary compliance in what they call a cooperative commonwealth. The totalitarians would wipe out the distinction between State and Society altogether and extend the power of the State to every conceivable aspect of human life. Education, marriage, recreation, the total economy, communication, even religion would, under this view, be subject to the coercive power of the State.

Democratic political theory, while admitting the legitimacy of political power, has sought to restrict the jurisdiction within which it may apply. This theory of limited government is reflected in the adoption, formally or informally, of constitutions in which·the metes and bounds of political power are set forth. It is reflected in the American theory of delegated and reserved power, and in the adoption of Bills of Rights to restrain political intervention in certain areas.

But it is easier to state the principle than to apply it in practice. The terms themselves are ambiguous. What is meant by a law respecting an establishment of religion as forbidden in the First Amendment? Is it legitimate for New Jersey to pay the bus fare of students in parochial schools? Is "released time" for religious instruction in the public schools a breach of the Constitution? How far may Congress and the State go in imposing limits on the press or speech or public meetings? What is meant by "due process of law," "equal protection of the law," "bills of attainder"? What, if any, are the constitutional limits of the congressional power to investigate—and may congressional committees disregard all formal safeguards otherwise available to protect the citizen from abuse by those invested with political power and authority? Many of the answers will be found in the decisions of courts in particular cases. But the student cannot stop at the law reports. Basic to this problem are the ideas, social forces, traditions, and rules that mold the minds and inform the judgment of the courts. If we had more briefs prepared by social scientists in such cases, the decisions of the courts might be less confused and more consonant with common sense and democratic theory.

The recent unanimous decision of the Supreme Court (in Brown vs. Board of Education) holding that racial segregation in public schools violates the "equal protection" clause of the Fourteenth Amendment, illustrates how a scholarly brief can assist the Court. By marshaling the best scientific evidence from political science, sociology, psychology, and education—rather than relying on a parrot-like recital of legal precedents—counsel in these cases persuaded the Court to sweep away nearly sixty years of confusion and contradiction on this point.

But study of the scope of political power extends beyond problems associated with Bills of Rights to nearly every aspect of public policy. The expansion of government is a matter of common knowledge. In the United States, for example, while population has multiplied by some thirty times since 1790, the number of civilian employees of the U. S. Government has multiplied over 3000 times, tax revenues over 1500 times, and debt by over 3000 times. Although not so spectacular, the rate of expansion of state and local government has exceeded the rate of population growth.

The political state has moved far beyond the days when its functions were confined to defense, policy, and the administration of justice. Today it is involved at all levels with education and social welfare, economic planning and control, conservation, management and development of natural resources, public health, recreation, sanitation, and a hundred other aspects of modern life.

Where is state intervention to end? Is the present trend immutable and irreversible? What are its underlying causes? Which of these can be controlled? Are there any objective scientific canons in terms of which existing and proposed governmental activities can be analyzed and evaluated?

These are a few of the questions with which political science is currently concerned. Beyond them lie the vast and important fields of International Relations, Comparative Government, and Area Studies, in which exciting research is being done. In these fields as elsewhere, the new emphasis is dynamic, behavioristic, empirical rather than normative—concerned more with what *is* than with what *ought* to be.

More recently, new voices have begun to reassert an interest in values and value theory. Whatever the radical empiricists may say, the study of politics involves inescapably the study of morals and ethics. Save for the moral idiots of society, political power is not an end in itself but a means to an end. Aristotle thought this end to be a good life. Plato thought it to be justice; Hobbes, peace and security.

To John Locke, political power was a means to secure life, liberty, and property; and the author of the Declaration of Independence saw its purpose as being life, liberty, and happiness. The framers of the Constitution were fearful of political power save as it was used to "form a more perfect union, establish justice, insure domestic tranquility, provide for the common defense, promote the general welfare, and secure the blessings of liberty. . . ."

If every exercise of political power involves a value judgment, no matter how selfish or depraved, the study of politics must perforce include ethics. It was no accident that Aristotle's *Politics* was but the second part of a larger work of which the first part was the *Ethics*, that Hobbe's *Leviathan* began with an essay "On Man," that Adam Smith wrote his theory of the *Moral Sentiments* before he composed the *Wealth of Nations*, or that Bentham called his great work a study of *Morals and Legislation*. The ethical basis of political power and the moral or ethical ends for which it may legitimately be used, has been the constant preoccupation of the great students of politics in the past, and must continue to be now and henceforth.

To be concerned with ethics does not mean that the student of politics must abandon the objectivity of the scientist, yield to wishful thinking, or substitute rationalization and revelation for objective observation, measurement, and analysis. It does mean that he cannot be indifferent to the ends for which political power is to be used.

It was when political science became an independent discipline, cut off from natural and moral philosophy, that its dependence on psychology and sociology, not to mention economics and philosophy, became obscure. It has required something of a revolution to think of political science again as but one special aspect of the broader study of human behavior.

8

GEOGRAPHY

Expanding Horizons in a Shrinking World

by George H. T. Kimble

GEOGRAPHY isn't what it used to be. This, perhaps, is just as well, since for many of us the word merely conjures up painful memories of childhood hours spent wrestling with the tributaries of the Mississippi and

> . . . alle the havenes, as they were,
> From Gootlond to the Cape of Fynystere,
> And every cryke in Britaigne and in Spayne.

However, even in Chaucer's time there was much more to geography than dexterity with place names. The geographers of his day were men of broad-gauge minds, skilled in the arts of navigation and mapping, and well versed in history, theology, and natural lore. The known world was their parish and they strode across it in seven-league boots, describing volcanic activity here, social customs there, and climatic influences elsewhere, and citing authorities at every step. Frequently they overshot their borders and marched off into *terra incognita* about which they were inclined to write with equal enthusiasm, if fewer footnotes. But they did most of their marching within the four walls of classroom and cloister; their exploration was largely intellectual.

With the progressive subdivision of the field of knowledge in later times, geographers moved out of doors, bequeathing to other and more competent hands the manipulation of their body of physical fact into systems of thought. From the Great Age of Discovery down to the turn of the present century, their main concern was with the exploration, the systematic description and mapping of places.

Today the position is different. There are few places in the world that have not been the subject of such scrutiny. Even Antarctica is better known than West Africa was four hundred years ago, and there are far more maps of the Canadian Arctic and Amazonia than there were then of the Mediterranean. There is scarcely a peak that has not been scaled, or a tribe that has not been filmed and pyschoanalyzed.

With the change of circumstances there has come a change of concern. The dominant interest of the mid-twentieth century geographer is the areal differentiation of places, and its causes and consequences. His "world" may have shrunk, but not his horizons. On the contrary. Places are complicated things, compacted of many diverse elements, sensitive to internal disorders, and in these days of ever-growing ease of communication, capable of exerting an enormous influence beyond their borders. Those who would learn their meaning must also be endowed with broad-gauge minds and acquainted with many arts. For every place has position (the precise determination of which demands a knowledge of geodesy and mathematics), form (for the understanding of which some acquaintance with geology, geomorphology, physics, and meteorology is prerequisite), vitality (no proper appraisal of which is possible without the insights of economist, sociologist, psychologist, and historian), and what, for want of a better word, we might call direction (which we are unlikely to apprehend apart from anthropology, political science, and religion).

It should not be supposed on this account, however, that modern geography simply consists in collating, scissors-and-paste fashion, the more "geographical" parts of other men's disciplines. In point of fact, none of them is geographical enough for the geographer. Consider, for instance, the matter of rain. The physicist's interest in rain may be said to end the moment he has solved the question of how it is produced. The geographer, on the other hand, wants to know why it falls where it does when it does. That is, he is interested in the factors governing its areal and temporal distribution, and he is equally interested in finding out what it does in a given place and time to the plants, animals and men living there. Or take the subject of land forms. To the geomorphologist, it is the mode of origin and evolution of the present-day configuration of a mountain or valley that is important. To the geographer what matters most is the location of the mountain or valley and its influence on the siting of towns and villages, and on the lives of people living there.

Because the subject of modern geographical study is global in scope and complex in nature, two things follow. First, there are many kinds of geographers or, to put it another way, geographers are interested in many kinds of things: they tend to specialize in one or another of the fields that furnish them with their basic materials— thus, there are physical geographers, political geographers, social geographers, and so on. Second, there is great need of serviceable generalization: without it geography would be no more than "a thing of shreds and patches," and geographers no more than purveyors of unassorted trifles. To reduce to order the one million and one facts that make up the geographer's world and to find meaning in the likenesses and differences that characterize them, he must define categories of associations and study them in their areal contexts.

This being so, the geographer tends to think in distances and areas, distributions and densities; that is, in maps—much as the musician does in keys and clefs, chords and intervals; that is, in scores. Ideally his statements should be capable of expression in cartographic form. If they aren't he might well stop to question the legitimacy of his work. For maps provide the geographer with the only really satisfactory way of looking at things which are unequal areally (and most things in life are—from atmospheric disturbances and alluvial deposits to a nation's voting habits and xenophobia) and of getting the measure of the inequalities.

It is this habit of thinking areally—of the incidence of flood in the Mississippi Lowlands, of the distribution of Eskimo settlements in the Canadian Arctic, of the migrations of Fulani cattlemen in the Western Sudan, and of the location of industry in Chicago—that identifies the modern geographer. Without the touchstone of place studies, physical geography quickly becomes indistinguishable from geology, oceanography, and meteorology; biogeography from botany and zoology; economic geography from economics; and social geography from sociology.* And physical geography and the other constituent branches of the subject tend to become ends in themselves, specialisms which recognize no disciplinary bonds and possess little or no cultural purpose.

The trouble, of course, is that reality has a habit of eluding the grasp of the classifier. The world of man can be more easily "unpicked" than knit together again: it is much greater than the sum of its measurable and classifiable parts. We may plot the distribution of droughts and floods, but our maps will tell us nothing of what drought and flood do to the people subject to them. We may likewise plot the distribution of airfields, industries, and unemployment but, again, our maps tell us nothing of the impact these things make upon the lives of the communities concerned. The ideas produced by airfields, industries, and unemployment cannot be card-indexed, let alone localized and measured, yet it is ideas that largely determine the vitality and direction of places—even their very form. An engineer conceives a plan, the upshot of which is the Tennessee Valley Authority, that alters the whole areal pattern, from drainage schemes to settlement, and at the same time fires the imagination of engineers living in Israel, India, Australia, and a dozen other problem areas. Or to take another instance: when the Italians moved out of Cyrenaica, the Arabs moved in. Today they live in the same houses, farm

* Needless to say, geographers are not the only people who think "areally," just as historians are not the only people who think temporally. Many anthropologists, economists, sociologists, political scientists, etc., do so habitually; in so doing, they are thinking geographically—which to our jaundiced eye makes them a lot more interesting!

the same land, raise the same crops, travel the same roads, buy and sell the same goods, as did their Fascist predecessors. But Arab Cyrenaica is a different "place" from Italian Cyrenaica. The Italians were intruders: they were in the country, but not of it; they were there to sell an alien idea, not to learn the ways of the inhabitants or live as equals with them. The Arabs, on the other hand, "belong." Today, in spite of its Italian framework, Cyrenaica is, in cultures and loyalties, just another part of Islam.

All of which makes the task of the modern geographer different from that, let us say, of the physical scientist. The latter has before him myriads of repetitions of given phenomena. He can abstract irrelevant aspects and isolate relevant ones, and infer a law which will enable him to foretell, and in suitable cases produce, given results from given causes. The geographer, on the other hand, has to try to decipher the meaning of a "one-of-a-kind" world. For him there can be no question of law in the physical sense, since there are no other worlds where, as yet at any rate, he can test out the validity of concepts and generalizations based on his study of our planet: geography no more repeats itself than does history. There is consequently a strongly interim quality about all geographical work. Even as the student plots his distributions, men are shifting their animals and breaking new ground, floods are altering contours and soil profiles, and new social pressures are changing the demographic map, thereby compromising his exploratory findings and impairing the utility of any measures he may propose on the basis of those findings. Because of this constant improvisation, the most the geographer can ever claim to possess is a partial view of an imperfectly understood process which is under no compulsion to continue as it began.

At the same time, inability to peddle prescriptions and cures—let alone predict the map of tomorrow—is no reason for not broadening the factual basis on which economic, social, and political programs are devised. In these disjointed times, periodic areal analyses of the material circumstances of a place, be it township, county, or nation, are, so we contend, as essential to the continued viability of that place as are accurate, frequently revised maps of terrain, roads, railways, power lines, airfields, and ports to the furtherance of a military campaign. Before now the absence of such analyses, or, what amounts to the same thing, the absence of data on which such analyses can be made, has had ruinous consequences. In no small measure it was for lack of such maps that one farm in every three in the dry belt of Southern Alberta was abandoned between 1921 and 1926. Attempts to mass-produce peanuts in Tanganyika in the late forties were thwarted for not dissimilar reasons. Those who planned the brave project simply did not know enough about the climatic peculiarities of the place, the lay of the land to be cultivated, the nature of the soil, and the local labor force. It is no exaggeration to say that because there were no maps—good maps, that is—the project perished and the British taxpayer lost more than £30 million and a much-needed fat supply. On the other hand, it is not too much to say that because of the detailed land classification maps produced in the 1930's by the Land Utilization Survey of Britain, that country was able to expand its plow land acreage in the early days of World War II by 60 per cent, and to double its output of essential foodstuffs.

But the modern geographer is able to do more than make maps: with experience, he can interpret the significance of the areal differences which his maps reveal. In so doing he is sometimes able to identify areas of maladjusted economy and stress points which threaten cultural stability and to indicate the location of other areas offering greater possibilities for development. The Canadian prairies have provided examples in plenty of such maladjustments and stress points. To the early settler the prairies of Southern Saskatchewan looked much the same as those of the Red River of Southern Manitoba, and for a while they yielded so well that even the farmer saw no reason to doubt the evidence of his eyes. By the mid-thirties his children knew otherwise: whereas the Red River Valley was still yielding tolerably well, even in the face of subnormal rainfalls, Southern Saskatchewan was now the scene of a mass emigration. Today that country is better understood; more ample data are available concerning its water-table levels, its soil profiles and precipitation regime, as a result of which much of the erstwhile derelict land is now being put to productive use as cattle pastures, wood lots, shelter belts and irrigated truck land. Some of the reclaimed country is already supporting a denser rural population at a higher standard of living than it did in the "wheat-mining" era. By understanding the true nature of this region, man has, in effect, changed its nature.

Nor should infirmity in the field of prescription and long-range forecast deter the good student from exposing the limitations of others in the same field. Granted that it is much easier to mark the mote in another's eye than remove the beam in one's own; still, no geographer can view the territorial arrangements which are made from time to time between nations, and within nations, without feeling that in many instances far too little importance has been attached to the "place" factor. Thus it is difficult to see how Japan, shorn of all the possessions she came by after 1894 when she had a population of less than 30 million, and denied any major population outlets, is going to satisfy the legitimate needs of its nearly 90 million people. It is hardly less difficult to see how Pakistan can maintain itself in economic health, divided as it is into two widely separated and unequal parts. In few areas of the world are the geographical arguments for political fusion so clearly drawn as in the Indo-Gangetic plain with its complete absence of natural barriers to communication, its master streams demanding unified control if their power and irrigation potentialities are to be properly exploited, and its unequal distribution of fertile soils, mineral resources, and rainfall.

The most important thing the geographer can do, needless to say, is to remove the beam from his own eye. And this he is seeking to do. As his awareness of the intricacies, uncertainties, and inequalities of the world increases, so does his awareness that no "world" problems are greatly illuminated by putting large dots on small maps, or by making small tours of large areas. Consequently he is turning to more modest and, it is hoped, more useful tasks, notably to the systematic study of single phenomena and significant combinations of phenomena that are differentiated areally, and to the intensive study of the "working parts" of areas small enough and sufficiently well defined to be amenable to scholarly analysis.

High on the list of such studies is that of land use. And it would be hard to name a subject more pertinent for geographical investigation, for until we know how the totality of the world's land is used and how badly or how well it is used in relation to its intrinsic merits, nobody can make more than the roughest approximation of the population-sustaining power of the lands already producing, to say nothing of those that are as yet unproductive. And until we know what there is to be developed and where it is, the investment of good American (or any other country's) money in the "backward areas" is bound to be fraught with needless hazard. There is this further to be said for such a study, namely that until the present use of land in the backward areas is better known and understood, development schemes for these areas are almost sure to cut across the existing economic and social structure in such a way as to cause more harm than good. Not the least of the administrator's problems in "colonial" territories like Kenya, Uganda, and the Belgian Congo spring from the fact that the ordinary African still does not share the European's notions of land use and finds it hard to believe that the continuous cultivation of a single four-acre field can possibly serve him better than the periodic cultivation of forty half-acre plots scattered over almost as many square miles. It is primarily for these reasons that the International Geographical Union has recently embarked on the heavy task of mapping the land use of the world.

Equally exciting to many geographers is the application of their field and laboratory skills to the subject of disease. In 1948 the American Geographical Society established a department of medical geography in the belief that the mapping of the incidence of diseases and the vectors of disease throughout the world together with the study of their environmental correlatives, would provide new techniques and perhaps new clues with which to prosecute this most pressing of all human problems. True, some diseases seem to exist almost everywhere, but even syphilis produces a much higher incidence of cutaneous lesions among Mediterranean peoples and those inhabiting the tropics than elsewhere, and tuberculosis, another of the "global" diseases, proves more deadly to Africans than to Europeans. How significant may be the areal differences which these maps reveal it is not for the geographer to say—particularly in view of the limited and imperfect data on which most of them are based: but so long as the real nature of poliomyelitis, cancer, influenza, heart disease, multiple sclerosis, and the like remains a mystery, can anyone say that the beginning of wisdom may not lie in plotting what is known and correlating the results with other areally differentiated variables?

Less wide in its territorial scope, but no less relevant to the times, is the Arid Zone Program of UNESCO in which geographers, plant and animal ecologists, and geographically-minded physicists, engineers, geologists, and meteorologists are playing a prominent part. Among other variables significant in desert life that are being studied in several areal contexts are wind velocities (which take on a special interest in terrain bedeviled by sand and low water tables), surface cover, evaporation rates, alkalinity, and homo-climates (that is, areas whose characteristic weather conditions are recognizably as well as statistically similar).

The list of work of this kind now being done could be greatly lengthened. The list of work to be done is practically endless, for until recently almost the only systematic studies undertaken by geographers were in the fields of geomorphology, climatology, and plant and soil distributions: the possibilities on the human side were well nigh untapped. However, the postwar years have seen a steady increase in the attention paid to such "human" themes as town and country planning (the areal aspects of which concern the geographer quite as much as the sanitary aspects concern the engineer), resource conservation, environmental change (in which man is already a potent factor and yearly becoming more so), and, among the more genetically minded, the development of cultural climaxes and successions.

And what may the geographer learn from such studies about the nature of his "world" and the people whose cultures differentiate it?

First, that it is a remarkably strong and fruitful world. In spite of all the manhandling it has had and all the abuse, it still yields its increase in due season, and it can still bring forth abundantly. Further, it continues to show a surprising resilience to the blows and bluster of unruly men, and to the buffetings of storm and flood. Within two years of the bloodiest war in history, the countryside of Western Europe not only had hidden its scars but had garnered a harvest second to none in its long agricultural record. After yielding a crop of wheat every year for the past hundred and more, the Broadbalk at Rothamsted in southern England still gives annually between ten and twelve bushels to the acre. Over large parts of India and China two crops are regularly taken off the same piece of ground in the course of a twelvemonth, and it is not exceptional for farmers in the Lower Nile and Ganges Valleys to raise three separate and sizable crops on their irrigated land over the same period. In the English fenlands and Dutch polders, a wheat crop averaging less than fifty bushels an acre is considered indifferent: even yields of sixty to seventy bushels call for no comment. Nor are these especially favored parts of the earth. The grainlands of Flanders face the perennial hazard of too little sun and too much rain. Uncontrolled, the waters of the Nile and Ganges are more of a liability than an asset. And as for the fenlands and polders, were they not won from the sea, and, by equally arduous toil, drained and sweetened?

Some parts, we readily acknowledge, are stronger and more fruitful than others. At the same time, it would not be hard to show that even the deserts of the world are far from weak and barren. Thus, without the deserts of the Arctic the climates of the Eastern States would be much less satisfactory for agriculture, and much less stimulating to mind and body. And one does not have to be an Arnold Toynbee to discern that the warm deserts of the world have played a monumental role in the evolution of those cultures from which our highest moral and spiritual standards have sprung, or to see that the present division of the earth into dry land and water, high land and low, woodland and waste, would take some improving upon.

Second, that this very diversity of the world's surface has been one of man's greatest sources of enrichment throughout his long schooling in the art of living. It is easy, we know, to get sentimental about the feeling of unsophisticated peoples for native materials and for landscape. Yet the fact is that sensitivity to differences of environmental conditions and the ability to use them for aesthetic as well as more purely utilitarian ends has been one of the more conspicuous features of human history. Though none would have called themselves artists, the men who built the roads and villages of the English downlands five hundred and more years ago possessed skills in the working of chalk, flint and thatching straw, and an understanding of the needs and resources of their locality that enabled them to endow every hill and vale with the stamp of uncontrived beauty. Though none would call themselves scientists, the vinegrowers of France learned centuries ago to exploit the micro-differences of their land, the nuances of soil, of contour, exposure, light and shade, rainfall and drainage. To the unaccustomed eye, there might seem to be no ecological difference between one slope and the next: to the vigneron's there is all the difference between a vintage wine and vin ordinaire. The same sensitive molding of life to land, of work to place, characterizes the pristine economy of a thousand cultures and has been a continuing inspiration to artists, musicians, and men of letters. True, in these days many regional discriminations are in danger of being blurred under the glacier-like creep of prefabricated culture—whether it comes in the guise of mass-produced foods and drinks, dwelling places, or dances—but they are not likely to be obliterated. Even that great leveler, the bull-dozer, is weak in the presence of a mountain; not even the hydrogen bomb can do much about a hurricane; and no alchemist has yet succeeded in synthesizing vintage French wines.

Third, that fruitful and agreeable as the world is, it has some sizable limitations. Consider, for instance, its shortages. Many people have long known about these. The Chinese have been managing to live on garden-sized plots for generations. Since the time of the Pharaohs the Egyptian *fellah* has known that his life hung by a thread. Luckily that thread—the Nile—has never broken, but it has nonetheless bound him to a life of constant effort and frugality. The Hollander has long been habituated to living within narrow walls, one of which might, almost without warning, collapse about his head. However, this idea of shortage, of restricted opportunity, to say nothing of decreasing opportunity, is still strange doctrine to North American ears. It is not less valid for all that. Already it is clear that there is not going to be enough of everything for everybody. "All God's chillun" may get shoes some day, but all of them are most unlikely to get six-roomed houses complete with automobile, refrigerator, TV set, and garden. For one thing, there is not enough material to make them. If the steel output of the world were to rise to the American (per capita) level, it would exceed the present estimated 250 million tons by 1500 per cent, an output that would exhaust the known iron ore resources of the world in less than twenty years. If the copper output of the world were to rise to the existing American level, the known copper resources would not last more than six years. And for another thing, there is not enough land for them. At the present time there are less than five acres of habitable land for each person in the world; by the end of the present century, when the population curve is expected to have flattened off, there will be even less—perhaps not more than two acres; by the time a part of this has been set aside for food growing, another part for roads, airfields, public buildings, factories, etc., there is not much left for houses and gardens. This does not mean to say that anybody need go hungry, or unclothed, but it does mean to say that it is high time we started to take stock of our dwindling assets and, perhaps more important, to school ourselves in the almost forgotten art of saying "No."

Or, again, consider the world's contrariness. Things have a remarkable aptitude for *not* running true to form. "When God wills, it can rain with any wind"—and make a mockery of the best weather forecasts. And man can be every bit as "cussed" as Nature. How often, for example, have the French tried to persuade their Berber wards in the Atlas Mountains of Algeria to broaden the basis of their slender economy, only to find that the seed grain and potatoes distributed for the purpose were added as a relish to the evening dish of couscous! (In defending this habit the Berbers are wont to argue that if Allah had wished them to cultivate such crops, he would have made them indigenous to the country.) And why should the Eskimo prefer to live in an environment that is always difficult and demanding to the point of rewarding the sluggard with death, when he could easily migrate southward to more genial lands?

At the same time, there is no reason to suppose that all these limitations are inexorable. Many men see in shortage only a challenge to invention. Thus, during the past war the people of Sweden, shorn of almost all their overseas food supplies, discovered that they could practically live off their trees. Not the least of their achievements was the manufacture of one million tons of a cellulose cattle feed and the popularizing of broiled cellulose hamburgers (said to be "highly comestible"), thanks in no small part to both of which the Swedes managed to keep themselves and their animals in fine shape throughout the war years. Likewise, much contrariness can be, and is being, cured by exposing the sufferer to the expulsive power of new infections. Thus, the desire for more goods, more security, and more leisure is beginning to make even the "quite contrary" Babingas—pygmies—of French Equatorial Africa and the diehard cattle-keeping Wakamba of Kenya respond to the blandishments of the Western entrepreneur, educator, and traveling salesman.

Which brings us to the final thing we learn from our studies, namely, that the record of man in his places is such as to encourage the belief that he can go on adjusting himself to their caprice and changefulness, and to their metes and bounds. For equivocal as some of the evidence may be, it is hard to deny the capacity of society to withstand hard knocks, to carry on in the face of recurring calamity, to take action against its enemies and counsel with its friends, and to acclimatize itself to strange new political and economic atmospheres.

Consider, for instance, the peoples of Greece and Israel. There are few things they cannot do and do well, if the necessity arises, and they have been faced with plenty of necessities in their time. The Children of Israel are first disclosed to us as cattle-breeding, tent-dwelling Bedouins. Once across the Jordan, in Canaan, they turned farmers, planting vineyards and olive groves and raising grain. In exile, whether in Babylon, Benghazi, or Boston, they turned middlemen and manufacturers. Now, back in the land of their fathers, they are all these things, and more besides. The Greeks are no whit less versatile. They, too, began as wanderers; later they plied the arts of husbandry to such good effect that they found themselves with surplus wares and surplus people. Taking to the sea in search of land and custom, they established a Mediterranean-wide network of trade routes, a string of city-states on three continents and a reputation for being able to turn almost any physical situation to good commercial account, a reputation that the lapse of time has done little or nothing to dim. For, like the Jews, the Greeks continue to get around. As Sir Winston Churchill has put it, with his characteristic vigor: "The passage of several thousand years sees no change in their characteristics and no diminution of their trials or of their vitality. . . . Centuries of foreign rule and indescribable, endless oppressions leave them still living, active communities and forces in the modern world. . . ."

And this "capacity for survival," as Sir Winston calls it, is not confined to the Greeks and Jews. It is found in a hundred other peoples, from the Fuzzy-wuzzies, who have been pitchforked from a Stone-Age eternity into a world of time clocks, motor traffic, and trusteeship, to the Finns, who since 1944 have effected, quite peacefully and with scarcely a word of dissent, a redistribution of their farmlands to accommodate half a million refugees from territory ceded to Russia and to give half as many again the chance of a better living.

Modern geography, then, is concerned with the changing relationships between men and their places: with the ways in which, and the reasons for which, men have fashioned and refashioned those places to suit their comfort and convenience. That is, the geographer is concerned as much with man's changing conceptions of what a place should be like as what it is like: he is as interested in the voting habits of a community as in its use of the land (which may well be influenced by government policy) and in the occurrence of race prejudice as in the distribution of factories (which, in the Union of South Africa, at least, is becoming more and more a "racial" matter). In other words, he is inclined to believe that the most potent geographical factors in the world are not climate, or soil, or location, or overcrowding, or undernourishment, or any other objective "environmental" circumstance, but rather the shape these circumstances assume in the mind's eye and the willingness of the mind to do something about them.

In so saying, the geographer claims, not to be able to offer a selfcontained system of explanations for the terrestrial distribution of man and his works, but to provide a vantage point from which to regard such things. His role is rather like that of the viewer of a silent film. The film, by its very nature, is a record of things seen from one angle, with all the highlights and shadows, the limitations and advantages peculiar to that point of view. At the same time, the film shows all there is to see from that angle, which is usually a great deal more than the untrained eye can see, as anybody knows who has watched a prize fight and subsequently seen it in slow motion on the screen. But being silent, the film leaves very much to the imagination of the viewer: at best he can only guess what the characters in the story are saying and why they are acting as they do. All the same, he can usually get the gist of the plot without the aid of either captions or conversation.

So with the geographer: he sees what there is to see of the visible relationships between men and their places and between place and place, and with time and training he can usually get the gist of what he sees. For the fuller understanding of the action, however, he needs the assistance of other students of humanity. He needs the historian's "silent backward tracings" that enable him to view the matrix in which the present relationships have their roots; he needs the economist's assessment of the role of capital, labor, and trade policies in influencing the use men make of their resources; the anthropologist's and sociologist's perceptions of the manner in which relationships between men and their places may be molded by custom, social institutions, and group experiences. And, not least, he needs the preacher's reminder that a man's life does not consist entirely in the abundance of things that can be measured, mapped, and related.

9

ECONOMICS

The Taming of Mammon

by Kenneth E. Boulding

It is not the noisy revolutions of politics but the silent revolutions of skill that change the course of man's destiny. The rudder and the horse collar were mightier than Caeşar, and the turnip and steam between them changed the face of the earth more than Napoleon. When historians of the future turn back to the twentieth century, it will not be the public turmoil and wars which will attract their main attention. Hitler and Stalin will be seen as disturbances, mere pimples on the changing countenance of time. The great movement of this century will be seen as a continuation of that fabulous increase in human skill which constitutes the scientific and technological revolution, a continuation furthermore not only toward new material skills, as in the atomic revolution, but toward new skills of organization and of society.

The economist is participating fully in this revolutionary increase of skill. The skill of the economist is not so spectacular as that of the physicist or the engineer. Here again, however, it is the silent revolution which may echo longest. There has been a Great Change in economics, a mutation which took place almost entirely in the period between the two World Wars. And this Great Change may have much more effect on the future history of man than the wars which serve to date it. Evidence for this change is found not only in the text book and the lecture room: it is written in the contrasting histories of the postwar periods. World War I was followed by a deep, though short, depression in 1919-20, a period of unsteady prosperity in the United States, catastrophic inflation in Germany, and a long depression in England even before the collapse of 1929-32. After the much worse catastrophe of World War II there was no postwar depression, no German inflation—indeed, a spectacular economic recovery of devastated Europe—no depression in England, and to date, ten years of postwar full employment in the United States. If we get through the next ten years without war and without serious depression we may confidently proclaim a New Era. Until then, those who remember the collapse of an earlier New Era in 1929 may be excused a little skepticism. It may be claimed also with some justification that the economic success of the past ten years has not been the result of wise and conscious economic policy but has been largely an accident—due, among other things, to the cold war and the high level of armaments.

Nevertheless, a professional economist cannot doubt the Great Change in economics. It has three aspects, all closely related. It is a change in theory, a change in information, and a change in policy. The change in theory is associated above all with the name of the late Lord Keynes. The change in information concerns the development of adequate statistics of national income and its components. The change in policy consists of the acceptance of responsibility by governments for the maintenance of full employment and economic stability.

I shall never forget the excitement, as an undergraduate, of reading Keynes' Treatise on Money in 1931. It is a clumsy, hastily written book and much of its theoretical apparatus has now been discarded. But to its youthful readers it was a peak in Darien, opening up vistas of uncharted seas—"Great was it in that dawn to be alive, and to be young was very heaven!" Imagine, therefore, the expectancy with which the General Theory of Employment, Interest, and Money was received in 1936—an expectancy baffled at first by the obscurity of much of the writing, gradually yielding to the realization that a great step forward had been made as the obscurities were resolved, the inconsistencies cleared up, and the meaning made clear by successive commentators.

To understand the nature of this advance it is necessary to take a look at the state of economics in, say, the 1920's.

On the practical side there was an obsession with the problems of international trade almost to the exclusion of domestic economic problems, and a striking lack of concern for the problems either of unemployment or of inflation. The restoration of the Gold Standard and "back to normalcy" represent the peak of practical economic wisdom.

On the theoretical side the basic model was that of a price-profit equilibrium: given resources are supposed to be divided among different industries and occupations in such a way that profits and wages in all industries tend to equality, subject to adjustments for nonmonetary rewards and immobility. Market prices are those which "clear the market," that is, which do not leave any unsatisfied buyers or sellers. Market prices determine the actual rewards accruing to resources in different industries, and hence always tend to move toward "equilibrium"—a set of "normal" values at which no further transfer of resources between occupations takes place. Unemployment is regarded as an essentially temporary disequilibrium, soon to be remedied by appropriate adjustments of prices and wages. Saving and investment are brought into equilibrium by the rate of interest —"too much saving" immediately results in a fall in interest rates, which stimulates investment and discourages savings.

This is an ingenious and admirable system, and was first stated essentially by Adam Smith in 1776. It throws a lot of light on the major forces that determine the system of relative prices. If, for instance, a pound of butter usually costs four or five times as much as a pound of bread, the reason is that if it were not so, the "natural" forces of self-interest and mobility would soon change the situation. If a pound of butter was worth ten pounds of bread, butter production would be profitable, bread production not so profitable by comparison, butter production would increase, bread production diminish, and this would lower the price of butter and raise the price of bread until the "normal" ratio was restored. What the system does *not* do is to give an adequate account of what determines the over-all or aggregate output, price, income, or employment levels of the system. It became frighteningly clear in the 20's, and especially in the 30's, that unemployment could not be regarded as a "temporary disequilibrium" but was a deplorably stable element of the system. The great achievement of the Keynesian economics was to show that simple theoretical models could be constructed which dealt with the *whole* economic system in terms of a few large aggregated quantities—total output, total consumption, total investment—and that this theoretical model under certain circumstances could show an *underemployment equilibrium*. Unemployment was then seen not as a temporary divergence from equilibrium to be dealt with by patiently waiting for the economy to turn a corner, but as a deep-seated equilibrium property of the system which could only be dealt with by deliberate government policy.

The basic notions of the Keynesian theory are so simple that once they are grasped it is difficult to realize the desperate intellectual struggle by which they were evolved. The basic concept is that of the Gross National Product—the total value, measured in constant prices, of all goods and services produced. The basic idea is that the national product must be "disposed of" in some way. Four broad ways of disposal may be distinguished. The product can be taken by households (consumption). It can be taken by government. It can be shipped abroad (the foreign balance). What is not used up by these three methods must still be around somewhere in the hands of businesses. What is "still around somewhere" is the addition to the real capital of businesses, and is called "investment" or "accumulation." Just to simplify the argument, let us suppose that we lump the first three items together under the head of "consumption," and suppose further that total consumption *depends* on the national product itself—that is, for each value of the national product there is a given value of consumption habits, assuming that institutions, policies, etc., are held constant. Then for each possible level of the national product there is only one possible level of *actual* accumulation.

To take an example: suppose consumption were always 80 per cent of aggregate production. Then if production were 300, consumption would be 240, and aggregate accumulation would have to be 60. Now suppose that people are not willing to add 60 to their holdings of goods. Actual accumulation is greater than desired. Stockpiles of all sorts of things would then be piling up at a rate faster than their owners wanted. Two things might happen. People might try to get rid of their stockpiles of goods by offering to sell them at lower prices, and prices might fall until people became willing to buy the existing stocks. Or the producers of goods would simply cut back production, thus creating unemployment, hoping that excessive stocks would thereby be reduced. Under a "sticky" price and wage system the latter is more likely to happen. Unemployment is thus seen as a result of a deficiency in "aggregate demand"—that is, an ability or unwillingness of people to consume and accumulate as much as they can produce at full capacity. If such is the case, and if the society is operating at full capacity, there will be unwanted accumulations. The attempt to get rid of these reduces output and employment down to the point where accumulation is small enough to be absorbed voluntarily. Especially in a rich society the decline in output and employment may have to go a long way before accumulation is sufficiently reduced, because each reduction in output also reduces consumption; output chases consumption, trying to reduce the distance between them (accumulation), but consumption flees as output pursues; only as output finally succeeds in gaining on consumption does accumulation decline.

It is not necessary to go into the details of the Keynesian system. It is, of course, an oversimplified theory. It is bulldozer economics, designed to push large problems around, not scalpel economics designed for fine operations. There are still important theoretical problems unresolved, especially in the area of time lags between causes and effects. Nevertheless this system, simple as it is, makes the difference between being hopelessly at sea when faced with the problem of unemployment and having a faint light by which to steer. We know now what we did not know clearly in 1929, that a developed market economy is subject to the possibility of serious and meaningless fluctuations in aggregate output and in the level of employment, and that in order to prevent ups and downs positive action must sometimes be taken by government. We know moreover the direction that these actions should take. We know at least that when faced with unemployment we should not raise taxes, balance the budget, and stiffen interest rates. We know that when faced with inflation we should not lower taxes, increase the budget deficit, or lower interest rates.

This change in theoretical viewpoint, which it is not unfair to call the Keynesian Revolution, has been paralleled and supported by an important development in economic information in the form of the collection of National Income statistics. This revolution in the collection and presentation of economic information has had an impact on economic thought and knowledge at least comparable with that of the revolution in theory. It dates essentially from 1929, when the U. S. Department of Commerce first began to issue annual estimates of aggregate income, output, consumption, investment, and government purchases for the United States. Estimates are available back to 1919, but they are not reliable. For more than twenty-five years now, however, we have records of the major aggregate magnitudes of the American and of several other important national economic systems.

This information, covering as it does by now a major cycle in economic activity and a World War, has had a profound effect on economic thought. The late Professor Schumpeter of Harvard, one of the wisest and most learned economists of the last generation, once said in a jocular vein "How nice economics was before anybody knew anything!"—meaning that the steady growth of information about the real world is constantly limiting the free play of the economist's speculative imagination. There are still great gaps in the economic information system. We know little about the composition and distribution of assets—stocks of goods, money, and securities—though this gap is closing .We know still less about the more stable psychological factors which affect economic life—people's hopes and fears and expectations, though this gap, too, is beginning to be filled. Compared with the pre-1929 economist, however, the economist of today moves in a world in which all the large outlines of the economic landscape are visible. We know from quarter to quarter not only the over-all size of national income, but its components (consumption, investment, government purchases, foreign balance) and its distribution as between wages, profits, interest, rents. By contrast the pre-1929 economist operated in a dense fog in which only scattered lights and noises, like price data and foreign trade statistics, gave much indication of what lay about him.

The revolution both in the theoretical position of the economist and in the information available to him has had a profound effect on the political attitudes and policy recommendations of economists. This change has taken place so slowly and subtly that it has not received much attention, but it may easily be the most significant result of the movement in economics of the past twenty-five years. In the old days economists could be classified easily along the radical-conservative or socialist-liberal spectrum. There were Marxists at one end, social-democrats in the middle, and laissez-faire economists at the other end. Now all this is changed, and it has become hard to tell a liberal from a conservative. One can regard the "new economics" as in some sense a Hegelian synthesis of the old quarrel between the two apparent extremes of socialism and capitalism, making that dispute curiously obsolete and irrelevant. The orthodox Marxist and the orthodox laissez-faire man are today stranded on their little self-contained islands while the great commerce of discourse has swept to other shores. Keynes has drawn the sting of the Marxist scorpion by showing that the instability of capitalism—its tendency to intermittent periods of underemployment—is a real defect which is capable of remedy by fairly simple means. The position of the conservatives who maintain that there is no defect in an unregulated market economy was made untenable by the Great Depression.

Thus we emerge with a genuine Political Economy. Government has certain economic functions and responsibilities which it cannot dismiss. Its main function is not to "take over" the operation of the economic system, but to act as a "governor"—to throw forces into the system which will counteract the tendency of unregulated systems of private enterprise and free markets to spiral into unnecessary depressions or inflations. Just as the governor of an engine speeds it up when it is going too slow or slows it down when it is going too fast, or a thermostat turns on the heat when the house is too cold and turns it off when the house is too hot, so government must be inflationary when the private economy is deflating and deflationary when the private economy is inflating.

There is almost universal agreement also among economists that by far the most powerful instrument of government stabilization is the system of public finance, and especially the tax system. Banking policy and other indirect controls have their place, but it is a secondary one. The shift from regarding the tax system simply as a method for raising money for government to spend to the view of taxes as an instrument of stabilizing the whole economy is perhaps the most fundamental change in policy outlook of this period.

This rather optimistic picture is not, of course, the whole story and it is time for a few academic hems and haws. It is still a moot question, for instance, whether a vigorous full employment policy does not land us in a long-run rise in the general level of money prices. If government overdoes its counterbalancing role, and especially if it displays too much inflationary ardor in a time of threatened depression, remitting too many taxes, running too large a deficit, making borrowing too easy, the result will be an aggregate demand in excess of what can be satisfied at current prices even at full employment, and prices will rise. Once they have risen it may be hard to get them down again, for whereas an overdose of inflationary government action will raise prices, deflationary government action may merely create unemployment if prices are "sticky." Hence we get what has been called a "ratchet effect," and what goes up doesn't come down as much as it went up. It may be, of course, that the thing to do with long-run inflation is to learn to live with it, and there are many signs that we are adjusting our institutions in this direction—for example, pension plans based on stocks rather than bonds, or with cost of living adjustments in them, and so on. On the other hand, the example of countries which have had a long inflation, like Brazil, is not wholly encouraging, and there may be long-run problems in this connection which will only emerge over the decades.

Another problem of great importance which is yet unsolved is that of the distribution of income and wealth. We have moved noticeably in the direction of greater equality of incomes in the past fifty years, mainly through the instrument of the graduated income tax. Nothing like clarity and unity has emerged in the field of distribution, however, either in theory or in policy, by comparison with the field of stabilization. There is still much dispute even about what ultimately determines the distributional shares, especially as between wages and profits. One fact of importance emerges from the national income figures—that the rise of the labor movement has been much less important in affecting the over-all distributional shares than is popularly supposed. Indeed, the percentage of national income going to wages actually *fell* from 74 per cent in 1933 to 62 per cent in 1942, at a time when trade union membership was rising from under four million to about fifteen million—the effects of full employment and inflation effectively masked small influences such as the Wagner Act and the rise of the C.I.O.! Even our economic information in this crucial area is incomplete: we do not know for sure, for instance, whether rent control made incomes more or less equal. Furthermore, many of our policies which are ostensibly directed towards removing inequalities or injustices actually have the reverse effect. Much of American agricultural policy, for instance, probably benefits rich farmers much more than it does poor ones.

Another area with many unsolved problems is that of economic progress (more fashionably called "development," "progress" being a word of deplorably nineteenth-century connotations). Here is a field where, oddly enough, the classical economists from Adam Smith to J. S. Mill still have important' things to say, and where no modern economist has arisen to weld the insights of the classics into a coherent system. The difficulty here may lie in the limitations of the economist's abstractions—economic development is merely one aspect of the larger problem of cultural change. Economic progress is something which we take almost for granted in our own society. The study of other societies, however, indicates that there is no necessity about progress, and that it has roots deep in the religious, domestic, educational, and political institutions of society as well as in economic life.

Thus many periods of economic development are associated with profound changes in religious outlook—for instance, the rise of the monastic movement in early medieval times had something to do with the economic developments of the tenth and eleventh centuries, the rise of Islam certainly had something to do with the amazing development of Arab civilization, and the Protestant and Evangelical reformations are intimately connected with the so-called Industrial Revolution. Sometimes political revolutions have set off economic growth, as in modern Turkey or nineteenth-century Japan. The land grant college had a profound effect on American economic life through its impact on agriculture. There is much work to be done here: the Keynesian economics throws a lot of light on the forces which sometimes make for stagnation, but not much on those which make for growth.

Although the Keynesian Revolution is unquestionably the Great Change in economics, it must not be thought that it is the only change. The interwar period also saw important developments in price theory, in "welfare economics," and in the theory of economic behavior. These, too, have had important consequences for economic policy. In price theory we have seen the development of a theory of "imperfect competition." Before 1930 economists generally worked with two models: a theory of perfect competition on the one hand, and a theory of monopoly on the other. Competition was "good," monopoly "bad," and if monopoly threatened to raise its head, the thing to do was to restore competition by breaking the monopolistic firm into competing parts. This is, rather crudely, the philosophy of the Sherman Anti-Trust act of 1888.

Criticism was raised from many quarters at the end of the last century that this view of affairs did not correspond very well to reality. It was not, however, until the 1930's that a theory of imperfect competition was developed which explicitly recognized that the great bulk of the economic system operated neither under perfect competition nor under monopoly' but under various intermediate forms of market behavior and interaction. It cannot be claimed that at the present time this part of economics is in good shape, and in regard, for instance, to antimonopoly policy it may be that the new theoretical developments have merely confused the issues. The anti-trust division of the Department of Justice sometimes reminds one of the knight who jumped on his great white horse and rode off in all directions. It can at least be said, however, that much of the unreality which flavored the old theory based on perfect competition has gone, and that economics can today take account of a wide variety of market conditions.

Another important, though again rather frustrating, development in economics goes under the name of "welfare economics." The name is apt to give the layman a false impression, as welfare economics has nothing to do with social work or welfare agencies, but is an abstract mathematical discipline which has attempted to answer the question, "When is one set of conditions or circumstances economically 'better' than another?" The conclusion seems to be finally that we can never be sure that one set of economic conditions is better than another unless we have some way of ordering the various possibilities on a scale of "better or worse," and this ordering cannot be found within the formal framework of economics itself. In spite of this rather negative ultimate conclusion, however, the struggle to make clear what we mean when we say that one set of conditions is "economically" better than another has been a valuable one. It at least saves us from the error of invoking scientific authority to support our personal preferences—an error to which other social scientists, and especially the psychologists, are unusually prone. It has done more than this, however; it has led to a clarification of some *objectives* of economic policy, its influence can be traced in some actual policies, and it has made an important contribution to the controversy about socialism.

An attempt was made, for instance, to erect guides for economic policy on the theory that we could be sure that a policy was good if it made some people better off and nobody worse off. This led to the "compensation principle"—that a change was worth making if the people who benefited from it could compensate the people who were injured by it, and still leave themselves better off than before. Another important conclusion is that people will be better off if they are allowed to trade freely than if they are not. None of these conclusions can be maintained absolutely, for reasonable exceptions can be envisaged. Rascals, for instance, should presumably not be compensated for their rascality, nor should vested interests be vested for ever. Nevertheless, it is not a bad thing to suggest that sometimes things can be done which make everybody better off, even at the cost of buying off a few rascals. The consequences of these developments for economic policy have been to develop a greater respect for individual freedom of choice, even among socialists and planners. An example of a wartime policy which would almost certainly not have developed without the influence of the economists is "point" rationing. Instead of trying to allot scarce goods to people according to their supposed "needs," a "price system" in terms of ration points was developed which would permit a certain amount of individual choice. The scarcer items were given higher "point prices," which meant that only the people who wanted these things very badly would sacrifice their ration points for them. Thus there was some tendency for scarce items to go to people who wanted them the most, instead of being distributed according to some administrator's fancy.

Closely related to the above developments is the rapidly expanding field of "decision theory," or the theory of "rational behavior," or "economic behavior." The problem here is akin to that of welfare economics. When we think of "rational" behavior—as opposed, perhaps, to instinctive, compulsive, or purely mechanical or habitual behavior—we envisage a situation in which the actor confronts a number of possible choices and selects one of them. This implies knowledge of the alternatives which are open to the actor, an ability to rank these alternatives on a scale of "better or worse," and the further ability to detect which alternative stands highest on the scale. The selection of the "highest" or "best" alternative is known as "maximization"—hence this type of behavior is known as "maximizing behavior." An elaborate and rather beautiful theory has been worked out around this notion, especially in the simple case of the business firm, which, it is supposed, maximizes "profit." That is, it selects those prices, selling activities, outputs, and other quantities under its control which will yield it the highest profit.

The practical impact of this theory on business has not been great except perhaps in the direction of arousing the interest of accountants in what they call "incremental" and what economists call "marginal" cost—the addition to cost produced by a unit addition to output, a figure which must be known if profits are to be maximized. There has also been a good deal of criticism of the theory from economists themselves—not all of it well considered, but having in the mass a certain force. It is argued, for instance, that people simply do not behave in the way supposed—that their behavior is influenced by all sorts of irrational, impulsive, or compulsive considerations and that we do not usually calmly survey the field of choice and pick out the finest plum on the tree. The criticism is not without point, and yet it can be argued in defence of rational behavior that these irrational elements can be regarded as chance disturbances, that people do not consistently choose the worse rather than the better alternative, and that almost all behavior, even at animal levels, involves some kind of selective process out of a field of alternative choices. There is important support for this view coming out of recent biological and psychological theories—the view, for instance, that even in simple perception we perceive the world the way we do because it "pays" us to see it that way!

A more important criticism of simple maximization theory which has led to an extensive new theoretical development, is that it does not take into account the fact that information about possible alternatives is limited and uncertain. What do we mean by "rational" behavior when we do not know, or at least know only very imperfectly, the consequences of our acts and therefore the real nature of the choice we are making? Practically all choices are actually made under conditions of ignorance and uncertainty. We invest, we buy a car, we marry, we take a job, we build a factory, or we go into a war in desperate ignorance of the consequences. Investments go bad, cars turn out to be lemons, marriages break up, jobs and factories alike turn out badly, wars are lost, yet everyone goes into these enterprises in hope of gain. It is hope and faith that guide poor old economic man, and maybe charity that helps him to bear the constant weight of disappointment. But what becomes of "rationality" when hope and faith rule the field of choice?

One answer to this question has been sought in the "Theory of Games"—a relatively new development dating only from 1947. This seeks to answer two questions: what is rational behavior for a single person operating under uncertainty as to the consequences of his decisions, and can there be a coordinated and consistent system of rational behavior for a number of persons when the decisions of each one affect the consequences of the decisions of the others? A number of "rational" persons interacting according to definite rules is what the mathematicians mean by a "game," which may, of course, be a game of cards, a war, or economic competition. One interesting rule emerges from this highly abstract mathematical theory—act so that you will make the best of it if the worst happens. Every action is thought of as having not a single consequence but a range of possible consequences: spread out in your mind the worst of these, and pick the best of this bunch, rather than thinking only of the most favorable possibilities. Marry the girl who will be a good wife even in adversity, not one who will be wonderful but only if things go smoothly.

Another important recent development arises out of the reflection that decisions are generally made by organizations rather than by individuals, and that even the individual himself is a kind of internal committee. Interesting work is under way on the problem of how organizations should be structured, and especially how information should be gathered and circulated, in order to give the best chance of the right decisions. This recognizes that all decisions are a result of a political process of compromise, and at this point economics finds itself veering toward a union with political science and sociology.

It is in this area of decision-making that we may perhaps look for the most important developments of the next few years—developments which may have great importance for the practical conduct of affairs as well as for pure theory. Up to now the decision-making process, in government, in war, in business, in marriage, in the conduct of a household, in fact in all human affairs, has been a matter of "feel"—an almost subconscious weighing of alternatives in the dim light of uncertain information and a decision formed we know not how. It is as unlikely as it would be undesirable that we will eliminate this element of subconscious "judgment" and have all our decisions made for us by electronic calculators. We are facing an age, however, in which minor decisions will become more and more a matter of conscious calculation, and the area of subconscious judgment will be pushed back to more fundamental and momentous decisions. A fascinating possibility is emerging, for instance, that we will begin to know something about the circumstances under which ignorance is bliss—one can have too much, as well as too little information for successful decision-making, and we see in the making today a much more self-conscious control of their own information systems on the part of the decision-makers. This has frightening as well as desirable aspects—the "Brave New World" of endless manipulation and machination in the interest of nothing much in particular is too close around the corner for comfort.

Looking towards the next twenty-five years in economics, it may perhaps be doubted whether they will be quite as exciting as the past twenty-five. As far as the Keynesian economics is concerned we appear at the moment to be in the time of the disciples, not of the master—a period of clarification and consolidation rather than of great new ideas. To be sure, a new genius may appear next month. But genius apart, within the present boundaries of economics there are still important problems which demand attention. We have already noticed the unsatisfactory state of the theory of monopoly and competition, of the theory of distribution and income, and of the theory of economic development. There are great opportunities here for the pioneers.

It also seems probable, however, that the next period will be one in which economics will grow towards many other disciplines, and in which the most exciting areas of advance will be those which lie somewhere between the regularly established disciplines. Even in the present generation, for instance, there has been an enormous increase in the use of sophisticated mathematics in economics. The amount of formal mathematical training used by economists has been steadily increasing, from zero at the time of the classical economists, to simple geometry, algebra, and calculus by 1900, to matrix algebra, set theory, symbolic logic, and the theory of games at the present day. This is not to say that economists must be familiar with these more erudite branches of communication. There are still many economists who plod along usefully with simple apparatus, and there is still and always will be a great deal of "not-mathematics"—good judgment, sensitivity to empirical reality, knowledge of affairs, and so on—necessary in the skill of the economist. The sharper the tools the easier it is to cut oneself with them, and there have been sad cases of mathematical economists grinding out nonsense because it happened to come out of their equations. Nevertheless, as the economist ventures into the handling of more and more variables, both in theory and in empirical work, more and more powerful mathematical tools have to be devised to deal with the complexities involved. Mathematics is a set of tools, and just because tools may be misused or used for improper purposes does not mean that they should be thrown away. At the frontiers of economics today therefore will be found many able young men working away at complex problems with complex equipment, and if no great simplicities have emerged as yet from all this complexity, bases are being established from which any further advance must set forth.

It may be objected that mathematical economics is not really an "interdisciplinary" development, mathematics being a language or a tool rather than a "science." However that may be, there are many signs that economics is stretching out towards other sciences. There are signs, for instance, of what is perhaps a new discipline of economic sociology, which will generalize the economist's abstraction of exchange to the more universal notion of a "transaction," and will study economic organizations and their interaction in a less abstract way and with more variables than has been done in economics proper. The field of industrial relations pioneered this sort of thing. There are indications now of a genuine integration of economics and politics, in the study of the political aspects of decision-making processes in "economic" organizations such as firms, and in the study of rational decision-making in political organizations like governments. Much needs to be done to bring economics and anthropology together; this, however, is being forced on both by the development of the specialized study of economic development and cultural change. Even stranger rapprochements may be in the making. Economics has contacts with biology at many points. In theory, the biologist's view of the organism has many relevant similarities to the economist's view of a firm or a household, and the biologist's notion of an "eco-system" of interacting biological populations has much in common with the economist's idea of an economic system. Even in the realm of economic policy, however, the problem of conservation requires the concept of man as an agent in the biosphere, and it is wise for man not to forget his biological base.

Professor Pigou, the grand old man of British economics, is reported to have defended his existence as an economist by saying, "We do economics because it is fun." The remark may arouse derisive laughter from those whose memories are confined to a dreary textbook in Introductory Ec. Nevertheless, for those who have been in the game economics in the past twenty-five years has been fun, and more than fun. There has been a sense of intellectual excitement, of living through a "classic" period. There has also been a sense of urgency, a feeling that time was short, that great problems of vital importance for human welfare had to be solved and solved quickly. This sense of urgency is perhaps less today than it was in the grim days of the 1930's—the urgent problem now is not depression and economic collapse, but war and total collapse! The time may even come, as Keynes himself suggested, when the technical problems of economics will not be interesting because they will have been solved, and man can go on to the real business of life without all this fussing about the organization of scarce resources. That time, however, is not yet. Mammon is not yet tamed. Depressions may still break out; inflations may still plague us; progress may lag; injustice may wax; organizations may get out of hand; poverty lingers with us; fecundity and ferocity may still dash the cup of plenty from our lips; and we still have a long way to go before we establish securely in the organization of society that Hidden Hand which transmutes the dross of Self-Interest into the gold of General Welfare. But the taming is under way, and Mammon-taming is a fine career.

10

HISTORY OF SCIENCE

The Imagination of Nature

by I. Bernard Cohen

THE HISTORIAN of science considers science to be more than a collection of instruments, techniques, exact data, laws, and theories. For him science is a creative activity, the fruit of human imagination applied to consideration of the universe and all it contains. Recognizing that the basic scientific concepts are inventions of the mind, he is naturally interested in their creators. In nature, for example, there are no such things as forces, and the concept of force has been devised in order to explain the observed behavior of matter under conditions of strain and of motion. The historian of science, recognizing this aspect of scientific concepts, asks how such an idea as a force came into being. What did people consider "force" to be at different times? How did they employ the notion of "force"? Why, at the end of the nineteenth century, was there an attempt to write a physics without "forces"?

Unlike the scientists, therefore, historians of science study science in all its aspects: its origins, its effects, and its growth, and also the conditions under which notable changes have occurred. The practicing scientist generally has no need of such historical considerations. Applying Newtonian dynamics, the physicist does not waste a moment's consideration as to whether the principles he is using were discovered in the seventeenth century, the nineteenth century, the Middle Ages, or Classical Antiquity. How different this seems from humanistic studies! Could we even begin to understand Milton's *Paradise Lost* or Dante's *Purgatorio* without a knowledge of the period and place of their composition and the character or personality of their author? To the degree that the scientist needs only to ask of a system such as Newton's dynamics "Does it yield verifiable results?" his efforts may be called objective.

The historian of science, however, takes an opposing point of view. He holds that the discoverer and the modes and conditions of discovery are of as fundamental interest as the thing discovered. Behind each advance in science he sees the men responsible for it and the human culture which was its context. He is aware, as the scientist is not, that such a great system of the world as Newton proposed could not possibly have arisen in the Middle Ages or in Classical Antiquity. The form of Newton's ideas reflects in some way Newton's unique personality, his education, and his reaction to the main currents of thought of his age.

The historian of science believes that the astronomer is as significant as the galaxies he explores, the biologist as important as the concepts of gene and species which he invents. His aim is to understand that explosive reaction between the scientific imagination and the data of experiment and observation it confronts. Exploring the interaction between the creative scientific mind and the matrix of culture in which its owner and his ideas are imbedded, the historian of science studies not only the origins of scientific ideas and techniques of investigation, but the diffusion and influence of such ideas and techniques. This inquiry is not limited to effects on other scientists, but on all thinking and feeling men and women, and it reveals the impact of scientific ideas on the general cultural environment and the social changes that result from the applications of such ideas.

Because today the fruits of scientific knowledge have so vastly altered our technological and medical practices, we tend to think of science as itself a practical rather than a creative activity. History shows that until recently science was considered, like philosophy, a part of the liberal arts and it is still characterized by that affection for the impractical which is the essence of the contrast between the contemplative and the active life. In the past the natural sciences were more closely associated than at present with humanistic activity. It would be meaningless to try to disengage Aristotle the scientist from Aristotle the philosopher or Leonardo the artist from Leonardo the scientist. The greatest philosophers of the past— men like Democritos, Plato, Aristotle, Lucretius, Averroes, Thomas Aquinas, Spinoza, Descartes, Leibniz, Hume, Kant, and Comte— were either scientists in their own right or were vitally concerned with the science of their day, which they knew well and integrated into their general systems of thought. This has changed today. In contrast to the past, those who now call themselves philosophers apparently cannot help but be largely ignorant of contemporary science: relativity and quantum mechanics, or mathematical genetics and biochemistry. Many of our major scientists are philosophically minded and the designation of humanist may still be applied to such men as Einstein, Bohr, Planck, Weyl, de Broglie, Born, Sherrington and Ramón y Cajal. Yet our poets, painters, and philosophers no longer follow them in their explorations of life and matter as did their predecessors in Antiquity, in the Middle Ages, in the Renaissance, and even in the seventeenth and eighteenth centuries.

Dr. James B. Conant has recently called attention to the fact that the most fruitful activity in the philosophy of science has taken a form of mathematics, symbolic logic, which is as far removed from ordinary comprehension as any other kind of higher mathematics. The history of science, however, with a strong appeal to all students of culture and to philosophers, remains a focal point for the humanistic study of science. Humanistic activity, whether in the arts or in literature or in philosophy, has always as its subject matter the records of human activity, whether tangible objects or written records. The scientist, as Professor Panofsky has shown, "deals with human records, namely with the work of his predecessors. But he deals with them not as something to be investigated, but as something which helps him to investigate. In other words, he is interested in records not in so far as they emerge from the stream of time, but in so far as they are absorbed in it. If a modern scientist reads Newton or Leonardo da Vinci in the original, he does so not as a scientist, but as a man interested in the history of science and therefore of human civilization in general. In other words, he does it as a *humanist*, for whom the works of Newton or Leonardo da Vinci have an autonomous meaning and a lasting value. From the humanistic point of view, human records do not age."

Especially in an era like ours, when we are apt to equate science with its applications, the history of science bids us keep in mind the humanistic component of the scientific adventure. This study emphasizes the daring quality of the creative act of imagination which enables the scientist to prove the worth of his concepts by predictions which must be verifiable in the experimental realm. Science itself preserves only the useful records, the successful theories, and the great advances. The history of science tells of useless experiments, misleading data, false theories and outmoded concepts. We learn of courage and of heroism in the face of opposition to new ideas, but also of cowardice and knuckling under.

History shows us that scientists have their flounderings and failures, and that like other creative men and women their imaginations are imprisoned by their culture. We see a Galileo revolutionizing the concepts of mechanics and rejecting Aristotle and Ptolemy for the new world of Copernicus. But even a Galileo could not accept the radical suggestion of Kepler that the traditional circles be discarded in favor of ellipses for the representation of planetary orbits. By restoring to this creative activity the name and personality of each creator, the history of science shows how scientific discovery and invention have the humane dimensions of all creative activity. Thus it helps to compensate for the at times forbidding aspect of abstraction which is the very nature of science.

We may now understand why the combination of historical method and scientific subject matter creates a discipline apparently founded in contradiction. The historian's task is to study documents, monuments, and other artifacts which reveal the activities of man in previous ages, so that the paths whereby we have reached our present estate may be clarified or so that the workings of human minds and hearts may be comprehended. The scientist is interested in bygone experiments, observations, and theories only to the extent that they provide a basis for future research. His aim is always to uncover new mysteries and to produce theories which will enable him to discard or revise our present ideas about the universe and all it contains. The study of Chinese astronomical records, for instance, is important to the historian because it reveals the state of knowledge and the kind of interests that prevailed in that culture. The astronomer finds such a study valuable only if it provides information he may use in his research. Thus eclipse and cometary records help him to fill a gap in his data. Equally useful is the oriental record of a supernova of July 4, 1054, A.D., whose wreckage we see as the Crab Nebula in Taurus. Scientists revere the great men of the past, of course, and piously celebrate their anniversaries, but they do not read the works of Archimedes, Harvey, and Lavoisier in the way that their literary colleagues read and reread the *Iliad*, *Don Quixote*, or *Macbeth*. The humanist who admires and studies the writings of Homer, Cervantes, or Shakespeare is well aware that these writers had an insight into human nature and character far more profound than have most of our contemporary writers, and a gift for imagery and expression that makes many of today's best writers seem puny by comparison. The scientist, however, would find little point in devoting his creative time to an analysis of past achievements when so many of nature's secrets remain hidden, when innumerable great new discoveries still lie before us at the interface between knowledge and ignorance. It is plainly evident that the men of science in our day are the equals if not the superiors of the scientists of the past, if not in genius, at least in methods or research, vastness of conception, and plain ordinary possession of information.

Every historian of ideas knows that Newton's book, the *Mathematical Principles of Natural Philosophy*, usually abbreviated in the single Latin word of its title, *Principia*, is one of the most majestic works ever composed by man. In it Newton set forth the laws of motion and the principle of universal gravitation, thus explaining for the first time how the planets move in regular orbits about the sun, and the moon about the earth, under the force of gravity; how sun and moon can jointly produce the tides; and in general how bodies move on and near the earth. Newton showed how a single principle of gravitation, and three fundamental axioms, could account for practically all the motions that we see in the heavens and on earth. This book of Newton's is one of the greatest monuments of the creative imagination—but it has been treated in a shabby fashion. There are "variorum" editions of Shakespeare and splendid scholarly editions of Homer, but there has never been a critical edition of the *Principia*. No one has ever taken the pains to collate the three editions which Newton produced to find out how he refined the original conceptions. For that matter, although the book has been many times reprinted, and translated into many languages, no edition has ever appeared with a complete table of contents or a usable index.

To understand the present state of the history of science, it is important to know that scientists do not deplore the lack of a decent edition of one of their greatest books, and that almost all scientists are unaware that none exists.

The reasons are not hard to find. The scientists will say that all of Newton's valid results are contained in every modern textbook or treatise and that, therefore, scientists have no need of consulting the original work. This is the very basis of the "accumulative" quality of science. All of the useful work of the past is incorporated in every present treatise, so that the original work may be dispensed with. While few physical scientists have ever read Newton's actual words, there is not one physical scientist who is ignorant of Newton's law of gravitation, his three axioms of motion, and the way in which they were and are still applied to account for the phenomena of the external world. Moreover, should some intrepid physicist take up a copy of Newton's masterpiece he would quickly find that the modern way of presenting Newton's work is simpler and vastly easier to comprehend, and in this sense is a real improvement on the original. Conceive a similar improvement on Homer or Thucydides, on Aristotle or Plato, or Hume or Gibbon or Flaubert!

Today one has little difficulty in reading the works of Newton's contemporary, John Locke. Yet not only the physicist but even the historian of science finds it almost impossible to read the *Principia*—which indicates the absurdity of including Newton's masterpiece in a "great books" program. Fully to grasp Newton's *Principia* requires a knowledge not only of physics and astronomy, but also of the science of the seventeenth century. Furthermore the *Principia* is written in the language of mathematics and this language has undergone notable changes since Newton's day. The language appropriate to a description of the very laws and phenomena which concerned Newton is the differential and integral calculus, an invention of Newton himself. Yet Newton did not choose to write his book in the new language he had devised, but preferred to base it on the models of Classical Antiquity, the compositions of great Greek mathematicians, Euclid and Apollonios. Hence to understand what Newton wrote, the reader must prepare himself—as Newton advised a correspondent who wished to study his book—by reading the classics of Greek mathematics.

To appreciate the magnitude of what Newton did, the reader must know wherein Newton's contemporaries and predecessors had failed. And to understand the mind of Newton he must explore Newton's errors and his failures and not merely those successful portions of his work which have been incorporated into the living stream of science. It is thus easy to see why most scientists say that for them the history of science, studied as a discipline in itself, is an investigation of the mistakes and the discarded theories of previous ages, while all that is useful from the past is available in the modern books. For the practicing scientist, research in the history of science appears a useless effort.

Only half the paradox of the new discipline of the history of science is that its subject matter is science, and that the advance and application of science do not depend upon historical studies. Historians now recognize that the growth of science has important vital bearings on history. They are, therefore, anxious to incorporate the results of research in this field into their own presentation of the growth of man and his works. Yet most historians have little if any advanced training in the sciences, and as a result cannot read the great scientific classics. They must depend on the interpretive commentaries of other scholars, save in questions of the influence and effect of scientific progress on nonscientific men—artists, writers, theologians, philosophers, political and social scientists. Since the content of the history of science places this subject outside the range of competence of the general historian while the historical point of view appears to make this subject of little real worth to the creative scientist, one can understand why the history of science has been but little cultivated. It is a new discipline, pursued by a small but ardent band of scholars whose training in the sciences enables them to work with the primary documents, but who have added—as a result of self-education or technical study—the tools to become historians.

At the present time, there are only four universities in America having full-scale programs leading to higher degrees in the history of science. Although the number of professional historians of science is small, it is constantly increasing. There is active recruitment from the ranks of younger scientists, especially those who have a philosophical turn of mind or who have a keen social awareness. The growth of interest in the history of science is due, in large measure, to the impressive results of scholarship to date. The historian of science, however, is still apt to be regarded by scientists as a "refugee from the laboratory," and the worth of his studies finds appreciation primarily among historians and philosophers.

The reason that the historian is most interested in the history of science is that it has altered his perspective and has provided a new dimension to the whole historical experience. It is influencing our historical judgment and our judgment of human nature.

Take, for example, the "miracle of Greek science." A hallowed tradition has impressed upon all students of thought the miraculous birth of science in the sixth century B.C. along the coasts of Asia

Minor and on the islands nearby. The Ionian "nature-philosophers," sometimes called the pre-Socratics, are said to have originated such notions as that the universe can be explained by the use of man's reason, that there are general laws or principles governing all phenomena, and that mathematics may be constructed by logic. We are all aware of the "Pythagorean theorem," supposedly discovered by Pythagoras, which states a general property of all right triangles: the sum of the squares on the two sides is equal to the square on the hypotenuse. And we have been told that among the discoveries of Thales of Miletos is the general theorem that an angle inscribed in half a circle is a right angle. These are aspects of the Greek "miracle," the beginnings of scientific principles where none had existed before.

The pre-Greek civilization that we know best is that of ancient Egypt, which has a strong romantic appeal as the source of all wisdom and the center of the origin of civilization. In the eighteenth century especially, the veneration for the mysterious wisdom of the East centered on Egypt. The reverse of the Great Seal of the United States—designed soon after the founding of the Republic, and reproduced on every one-dollar bill today—bears the famous pyramid with the watching eye in the top of it. A considerable research has shown conclusively that the mathematical knowledge of the ancient Egyptians was rudimentary, thus emphasizing the Greek "miracle."

In recent times, however, further study has uncovered the methods used in mathematics and astronomy by the peoples who lived in Mesopotamia at about the same time as the Egyptians. The discoveries have been so astonishing as to surpass belief: we now know that the mathematical techniques of the Babylonians—long before the first Greek philosopher-scientists—were of a highly developed order. They could solve many kinds of simultaneous equations, could compute compound interest, and could even solve quadratic equations and those of higher order in certain forms. The great discoveries in mathematics attributed to the men of the sixth century B.C., such as the angle inscribed in a semicircle being a right angle and the theorem ascribed to Pythagoras, were known and used by the Mesopotamian mathematicians at least a thousand years before the Greek "miracle" occurred. Thus research in the earliest history of science, notably astronomy and mathematics, has pushed back the recorded beginnings of man's intellectual activity in the exact sciences half again and more in time than the whole span of such activity was considered to be until recently. The events of the sixth century B.C. may thus be seen as the culmination of a long tradition, rather than a creation de novo of a small band of men concerning whose actual lives and actual achievements we know next to nothing. We become aware of our great debt to nameless minds in ages past and only dimly envisioned, and we see that the beginnings of exact knowledge lie in a long series of semimiraculous advances rather than a single bold leap from nothingness.

Or what has the history of science begun to tell us about the "Dark Ages"? It has long been customary to treat the intellectual history of man from the fall of Rome to sometime in the fifteenth century (the "Renaissance"), as a period in which a cloud descended on man's intellectual activities, and in which there was no progress or interest in science. This point of view derived largely from the fact that when ancient science reached its zenith in Alexandria, during the four centuries from roughly 200 B.C. to 200 A.D., it was not continued in Europe.

The Alexandrian achievements were themselves astonishing. The distance from the earth to the moon was accurately computed by Hipparchos to be about sixty earth radii, while Eratosthenes (a librarian and playwright as well as geographer) accurately estimated the size of the earth. A reasonable if somewhat small value was obtained for the relative distance of sun and moon from the earth, and consequently, their relative sizes. Catalogues of the stars were made, and a beautiful system was devised to predict the positions of the planets, sun, and moon. In biology, such men as Herophilos and Erasistratos studied anatomy and physiology and made such profound discoveries as the difference between the motor and sensory nerves in the animal body. Experimental studies were made of phenomena of refraction, and brilliant contributions were made to various aspects of mechanics.

The "darkness" that followed was a darkness over Europe only. The fact is that, even during the four centuries of its flourishing, the achievements of Alexandrian science had never taken root on European soil. When the center of science was transferred from Athens to Alexandria, soon after the time of Aristotle, there began a movement of science eastward, and Europe did not partake of it. The Romans were not interested in pure science, and Cicero expressed a rather general opinion when he scorned the abstractions of the ancients and praised his Roman countrymen for being more practical. We remember Rome for its literature, its law, and its engineering—but there were no original contributions made to science by Romans, nor does history record a truly original Roman philosopher.

Science moved eastward, carried in the later period largely by members of heretical Christian sects such as the Nestorians and the Monophysites. After the rise of Islam, the Greek scientific writings were translated into Arabic and were cherished and improved. Typical of this process is the Muslim development in arithmetic following the introduction of the Hindu numerals, today often mistakenly called Arabic numerals. In medicine, physics (notably optics and mechanics), mathematics, astronomy, and biology, science continued to develop in the world dominated by Islam, where many of the leading scientific figures were Christians and other non-Mohammedans.

From the second to the twelfth centuries of the Christian era, there was darkness from the point of view of science in Europe, but there was surely light in the East, and it became especially brilliant in Islam. Thus the history of science shows the need of having a world view in order to comprehend a continuous history of the human mind. Our perspective is distorted if we limit ourselves to the European continent.

And what about the "Renaissance"? Cultural historians have often viewed the "Renaissance" or rebirth of knowledge as a phenomenon of the fifteenth and sixteenth centuries. From the point of view of the history of science, we would place any such renaissance earlier, preferring to accept what the late Charles Homer Haskins called the "twelfth-century Renaissance," a period in which a frantic activity on the part of European scholars made available the classics of Greek science with their Arabic emendations. Perhaps the word renaissance is misleading here, because this may—in a genuine sense—be accounted the birth of science on the European continent rather than a rebirth. The history of science has shown not only the preservation of Greek science in the Islamic world and the changes that occurred there in the individual fields of scientific activity, but also the eventual dissemination of this knowledge in Europe. Symptoms of this influence are such Arabic words in our technical language as algebra, algorithm, alkali, elixir, or the star names Algol and Aldebaran.

The thirteenth and fourteenth centuries are usually considered to be a period in which the influence of Aristotle waxed and imprisoned men's minds within strict scholastic canons. But now we are finding that during the thirteenth and fourteenth centuries many of the Aristotelian principles of mechanics were discussed, found inadequate, challenged, and improved upon. The study of the so-called "latitude of forms," long thought to be nothing but a sad example of the complexity of scholastic classification, has now been found to contain the germs of the great scientific revolution associated with the name of Galileo. We have learned that during this period the roles of reason and experience, or of induction and deduction, were carefully discussed, and many of the foundations of the methods of science characterizing the revolution in the seventeenth century were laid down. Above all, the mathematical laws of changing phenomena were set forth clearly, and principles of uniform change, and of uniform and nonuniform acceleration, were expounded in words and with diagrams that appear again almost word for word in the writings of Galileo. The history of science has shown that the medieval schoolmen, far from being examples of the shackling of men's minds by the abuse of reason, were actually laying down some of the foundations of modern science. No human activity, it seems, can be fully understood in isolation from what occurred in neighboring ages. The "new science" which blossomed forth in the sixteenth and seventeenth centuries was preceded by the preparatory work of the fourteenth century which teemed with the new philosophical conceptions of the *moderni*.

One of the most impressive subjects of research in the history of science is the relation between the "Scientific Revolution" of the seventeenth century and the imagination. A great moment in the development of science, a moment for which there is nothing comparable in the whole development of scientific thought, occurred in 1609 when Galileo pointed a telescope at the heavens. Until then, there had been discussions of the nature and movement of the stars and other heavenly objects, and speculations upon the nature of world systems and the character and qualities of heavenly objects. When Copernicus had stated that the earth is just another planet, in his famous book *On the Revolutions of the Celestial Spheres*, this statement had little meaning because naked-eye observations of the heavens do not reveal any similarities between the earth and stars. To say that some stars, called planets, move in the heavens with respect to others, sometimes moving forward and sometimes backward, is hardly the ground for belief that they are like the earth. Most people had thought of the stars as some kind of perfect, unchangeable, pure bodies, in contrast to the earth on which there is generation and corruption, birth, life and death, and change of all sorts. Thus the physical characteristics of the earth could account for its unique position at the center of the universe, a fitting abode for man who himself was impure, sinful, corrupted. But when Galileo turned his telescope to the heavens, he saw for the first time what the heavens are like. The moon he found to have mountains and valleys and to look like a miniature earth, except that it was dead and not alive. The earth was found to reflect sunlight so as to illuminate the moon, thus making clear that the earth did shine like the other planets and would appear as the planets appear to us if an observer could stand and look at the earth on Mars or Venus. Venus showed phases like the moon, and the earth presumably did so, too, and also the other planets. Jupiter was found to have four moons, thus removing another feature of uniqueness of the earth, until then thought to be the only body which had a companion.

Galileo's discoveries indicated that the Copernican view of the universe could be treated as more than a mathematical abstraction, more than only a device for computing the future positions of planets and moon. It was no longer absurd to think of the earth as a planet, since the earth and planets had so many features in common as revealed by the new telescope. Plainly, when Galileo published an account of some of these discoveries in his *Sidereal Messenger* of 1610, the effect was explosive. Now scientists and theologians had to consider the consequences of man's abode on earth being set in motion and relegated to a minor position in the solar system rather than the center of the universe. At the same time poets and playwrights and philosophers found challenges to their imaginations in the possibilities of a vast hitherto unknown universe at last revealed to man. The stars, the planets, the Milky Way, the sun itself, and nebulae had presumably been out in space since the time when God had created the world, but man had never known about them until Galileo pointed his telescope at the heavens.

A complete catalogue of those influenced by Galileo's discoveries would include almost every creative writer of the seventeenth century. John Donne, who had evinced little interest in scientific matters prior to 1610, now wrote about problems in astronomy. He discussed Galileo's book and the discoveries it contains in *Ignatius His Conclave*, and summed up his bewilderment about the "new philosophy" which "calls all in doubt," and which "arrests the sunne, and bids the passive earth about it runne." "So wee have dull'd our minde," he concluded; the sun, "is lost, and th'earth, and no man's wit can well direct him where to looke for it." Another who quickly appreciated the significance of Galileo's discoveries was Ben Jonson, who wrote two masques referring to the telescope, one appropriately entitled *Newes from the New World*. In Milton's *Paradise Lost*, a mere listing of the astronomical reference makes a ready catalogue of the discoveries of Galileo, the "Tuscan artist" whose "optic glass" uncovered the mysteries of the bodies out in space.

The period in which the influences of science on the development of ideas of philosophy, society, government, and theology are best known is the eighteenth century, the Age of the Enlightenment. Newton's great synthesis of celestial and terrestrial mechanics aroused wide interest among educated people of all sorts. Significantly, the first popular exposition of the Newtonian philosophy, as the science associated with Newton's name was called, took place in a pair of sermons delivered at about the opening of the eighteenth century by Richard Bentley. We are not surprised, then, to discover that the concept of Deism, associated with a universe that could run mechanically once the Creator had built it, and without His continual intervention, was influenced by scientific work in the field of mechanics.

The first general account of Newtonian science for the layman—still one of the best guides to the subject, even after a passage of two hundred years—was made by Voltaire, who had learned about the importance of what Newton had done while in England. Books about the meaning of the Newtonian philosophy were written for all classes of reader, and there was even a special version of *Newtonianism for the Ladies* which—despite its title—turns out to be a rather good presentation of the subject. At the Constitutional Convention held in Philadelphia in 1789 no one was surprised to hear the lawyer John Adams use arguments from Newtonian mechanics to defend his notion about the need for two houses of Congress.

In the seventeenth century, both Bacon and Descartes had expressed their belief that in time the new experimental sciences would alter men's daily lives. The Royal Society of London, the oldest existing scientific society, founded in the seventeenth century, had included among its aims the improvement of technology. However, it is difficult to think of any scientific discovery made before the nineteenth century which radically altered man's diet, his health, his means of production, his transportation and communication, or even his methods of warfare. Today we are aware that the applications of new discoveries about the nature of the universe will be tomorrow the source of a new fabric, a new military weapon for offense or defense, a new means of controlling or preventing disease, or of founding an industry. Every major corporation in the United States now supports great research establishments; and the constant stream of new products and devices emphasizes the fecundating power of abstract science and its applications in altering the world. Yet this aspect of science is a characteristic of the last one hundred years only. Not until the middle of the nineteenth century did the applications of science begin to make themselves felt. Indeed, the organized research laboratory as a part of industry is hardly half a century old. Much of our bewilderment at the world in which we live may arise from the novelty of the revolutionary century at whose end we stand, and which itself was altered at its midpoint, about fifty years ago. The history of science helps our understanding of social and cultural change. In our day, it provides a bridge between the sciences and the humanities, as philosophy used to. But the history of science, stressing as it does the changing aspects of science and the role of the creative imagination, has yet another purpose: to clarify the nature of science and to elucidate the role of the scientific enterprise in human experience.

If today we fear the awesome destructive potentialities of a science-based technology, the record of history speaks to us of the enlargement of our view of the universe as well as of the growth of our control of it. In the mysteries that still face us—of distant galaxies, of matter and energy, of the nature and origin of life—there is history to be made in the discoveries of the future. If history gives any guide we may predict that man's quest into the unknown will not be stifled and that some future historian of science may say of us, as Newton said of himself, that we were merely playing with pebbles on the seashore while great oceans of discoveries lay before us.

11

MUSICOLOGY

The Anatomy
of a Temporal Art

by Manfred F. Bukofzer

IF ONE SCANS the books presenting a cultural synopsis of an age, of a country, or of Western civilization as a whole, one will find that they show—and often brilliantly—the relations between social history and the arts but either leave out music altogether or deal with it in a few perfunctory paragraphs. The reason why music should so often be treated as the ugly duckling is its peculiar mode of existence. The masterworks of literature and of the fine arts are readily accessible; they are there for everybody to see and read, especially in our age of magnificent color reproductions. An edition of a musical score on the other hand is mute and almost meaningless to the larger public. It needs an interpreter who, in the literal sense of the word, translates the musical symbols into sound, and only through this second step does music become an artistic experience. Thus musical monuments always remain once removed from direct access. Unlike a painting or a novel they cannot "speak for themselves."

Music is the John Alden of the arts and this dependence on an interpreter creates peculiar difficulties. When we perform a masterwork of Renaissance music, we do it with the instruments, voices, and the unconscious musical habits of the twentieth century, and unavoidably add something that is not found in the original. Indeed, what *is* the original if the musical monument needs interpretation and changes character in the process? A piece of performed music is a composite of old and new: we strive to be as faithful as we can, but there is the constant danger that a performance may give a distorted picture, as though we were looking at a painting through colored glasses which cancel out certain colors completely.

Music, then, by its very nature is not directly comparable with the other arts. It is a temporal art; it must always be recreated in time. But the need for re-creation is only one of the reasons for the peculiar position of music. More important is what may be called the "cultural lag" between music and the other arts. Look, for example, at the masterworks of medieval architecture. Cathedrals have become one of the major attractions of the traveler who, in the course of his tours, is proud to have learned to distinguish between Romanesque and Gothic styles. Now, let us assume that, while reverently glancing up the lofty pillars of the nave, he is confronted with the music of the time; he would turn away in horror or confusion.

The music sung in the Middles Ages in Notre Dame of Paris or in the Duomo of Florence has actually been preserved. In its own way it is as overwhelming and significant as the architecture, yet the average listener will not think so, certainly not after one hearing. He cannot perceive or "see" the beauty of the music as readily as that of the architecture and will jump to one of two conclusions: either that he is forever excluded from the circle of the elect because he is not "musical" enough; or he will say "I do not know anything about music, but I know what I like" and dismiss the case by not liking the music.

These two attitudes sum up much of the public sentiment about music, but common as they are they are nevertheless misleading. The idea that one must have that special and mysterious gift called "musicality" in order to recognize the charms of music is an exaggeration of a truism. However, to deny that the average listener can learn intelligent listening even without having a high innate endowment would be tantamount to saying that he need really not bother learning how to read because he is no poet. Just as literacy can be acquired by those who are not writers so it can be acquired in the field of music by those who are not composers. In either case literacy is the condition for the understanding of the masterworks. It is well to remember that only a few generations ago the word "Gothic" was used only in a derogatory sense. Indeed, with regard to Gothic style in the visual arts we have become literate only rather recently. In music we have not yet reached this state. Music is lagging behind and creates the cultural lag between it and the other arts. The "I-know-what-I-like" attitude accepts this lag as inevitable and eternal and tacitly rejects the idea of musical literacy. This complacent and defeatist attitude condemns music to the level of shallow entertainment. As a natural consequence persons professionally devoted to music are regarded essentially as entertainers, some of whom may be more "long-haired" than others but entertainers all the same.

In short, while we have reached a stage of literacy in literature and the fine arts, we have not yet fully grown up in music and this is why it has not yet become an integral part of the humanities. Although it is agreed in theory that music belongs to the family, it has in practice had the status of a poor relation. Indeed, some have seriously doubted that music, because of its special nature, could ever become a proper subject of humanistic study. However, a wider and more enlightened conception of music, which releases music from its position of Cinderella, is now gaining ground. The Prince Charming who has come to her rescue goes by the name of Musicology.

Musicology, the scholarly study of music, is a newcomer among the humanistic disciplines. It takes music seriously as one of the liberal arts and sees it in its cultural context in a way which contributes to a fuller understanding both of music and of that context. There have been learned disquisitions on composers in the past but the emphasis is now shifting to the music itself. Every work of art makes tacit assumptions which were understood as a matter of course in their own time but which no longer hold today. The reason why there are scholars specializing in Shakespeare, Michelangelo, or Byzantine Art is precisely that a discerning appreciation of art is not an automatic response but the result of a directed effort. We have come to recognize this in literature and the fine arts, and now we are beginning to do the same in music, which has its specialists not only for the well-known masters but also for Monteverdi, Josquin, Machaut, and Perotin of Notre Dame.

The purely intuitive "I-know-what-I-like" approach to music perpetuates the rift which has become so glaring today between the esoteric circle of professionals who are "in the know" and the lay public. One will find that the "intuition" which this approach calls for is just another and more pretentious name for the standards and prejudices unconsciously taken over from our grandparents and from the music of yesteryear with which we have become familiar by habit. The application of such standards has led to the dangerous isolation of those two immense bodies of music which lie outside of the current repertory: the music composed before Bach and modern music.

If Gothic music does not at present find general acceptance it is not for the lack of innate musicality but for the fact that the untutored listener listens with an unconscious bias. He anticipates the familiar and is disappointed when his expectation is not fulfilled. He does not know what to listen for and concentrates on nonessentials while the essentials pass by unnoticed. This is not a matter of subtle details but one of broad principles. Gothic music and "classic" music rest on principles as different as those between Gothic and eighteenth-century architecture. It is one of the most fascinating tasks of musicology to study and describe the underlying assumptions in the music of different ages.

Just as we have learned to "see" things in unfamiliar styles, so we are learning to "hear" as the result of the musicological approach. Through understanding, an understanding that involves not just a favorable emotional response but also the mind, music becomes a more intense aesthetic experience. Music is an art that appeals to the senses as well as to the mind, more particularly through the senses to the mind. The two keys that open the doors to a more profound understanding of music are *structure* and *style*, two concepts that are closely interrelated. Those who believe that a composition comes into being because a composer by some mysterious instinct is driven to pour out his heart on ruled paper, do not know that composition is a creation of the composer's mind. It embodies a definite conception of beauty in sound which is characteristic of its own age. It has an inner structure which must be understood like any other form of artistic communication. If one listens to the *Haydn Variations* by Brahms without being aware that the whole is a set of variations in which the theme is modified by successive steps, one misses the main point of the work. One misses the delight that comes from comparing the original statement with the variation, misses the surprise that an imaginative departure from the theme brings, misses the unifying ideas that tie the whole together. In short, one misses structure. It is true that the variations do not become completely meaningless—one could still enjoy the composition as a series of seemingly unrelated but pleasurable episodes—but it would be a dim musical experience, like attending a dramatic production in a language one does not understand. One could still enjoy the rudiments of the plot, the acting and staging, but this is a poor substitute for the real thing, the drama. In music the structure is even more important because there are, as a rule, no words to tell the listener what is going on. Tutored ears can easily grasp the elements of structure. While professionals can go to any lengths in analytical listening, the average intelligent listener needs no more than the rudiments, but these are indispensable. The elementary grasp of musical structure is not a matter of taste, but one of musical literacy, which is the condition for the formation of taste.

The second key, musical style, sets music in an historical perspective. The conceptions of musical beauty change with each age and these changes reflect changes of mental attitude. Take, for example, the Masses by a medieval composer, by Josquin des Prez or Palestrina, Bach's B-minor *Mass*, Beethoven's *Missa Solemnis*,

Stravinsky's *Mass*. In all of these works the words and the liturgical function of the music are the same, but the compositions themselves are as different as night and day. Each age approaches the identical words with different assumptions, and Bach sums up the conception of the Baroque Era as clearly as Beethoven does that of the early nineteenth century. These differences can be shown in the structural changes which are circumscribed by musical style. Style is the projection of structure into the historical dimension.

Not all musical means are possible at all times or ages. Musicology has studied the inner development of historical styles and shown that a style emphasizing harmony, for example, must necessarily neglect certain forms of rhythm, and vice versa. Musical style is a distinctive configuration of all elements of musical structure available at any given period which produce the inner unity and coherence of the music. Once we have understood the style we have understood also the principles of the music. No longer can Gothic music be dismissed as crude or primitive if it is recognized that it has a consistency of its own, as developed and indeed as sophisticated as the architectural style of the period. And what is true of this period is equally true of the Renaissance, the Baroque, and other periods.

The study of musical styles is the central task of musicology; it goes to the very heart of the musical matter. It operates in a strictly historical context because the stylistic changes in music have been found to occur at the same time as the cultural changes in the history of man. Thus the periods of human civilization become palpable to the humanist in a new medium: the stylistic periods of music history. For example, the idea of evolution, the magic slogan of the nineteenth century, finds an early expression also in music. It appears as one of the innovations in Beethoven. He likes to let the listener witness the genesis of his musical ideas by evolving them from smallest motives. The beginning of the *Ninth Symphony* gives a concise example of this method. Thus Beethoven, though he could know nothing yet of Darwin, belongs to the Age of Evolution. Examples could be multiplied to show that the history of musical styles is in the last analysis a history of ideas.

The decisive contribution of musicology to the humanistic disciplines is not any particular discovery in the field of music—though these are numerous and certainly remarkable—but to have brought about a new conception of music which really makes it part of the humanities and the history of ideas. Thus the scholarly study of music has made it a proper subject for the "proper study of mankind."

The fundamental change in the conception of music provides the general background to the other contributions of musicology to the musical life. The musicologist is interested in all types of music from all periods as manifestations of the human mind. An immense amount of the newly gathered musical knowledge can be turned directly to practical purposes, even though utilitarian application is not necessarily the driving motive of the musicologist. The practical goals of musicology change with the times and what at one time may seem farfetched and esoteric may become commonplace at another. When the works of Bach were published for the first time in a complete edition during the nineteenth century, the editors never dreamed that these unwieldy tomes would revolutionize musical practice. The edition was planned as a monument with about as much practical value as a Bach statue, yet it laid the foundation for the revival and the present popularity of Bach's music. In musicology, as in theoretical physics, certain activities thought of originally as unrelated to practical application may suddenly become practical.

How musicology is expanding the range of musical experience can be seen very clearly in the amazing upsurge of LP recordings—completely unforeseen by the recording industry. Works which up to recently had not even the remotest chance of ever being recorded, the composers of which were virtually unknown to the general public and even to musicians, are now available on records, and the supply cannot keep pace with the demand. Especially noteworthy are the recordings of large-scale works by such masters as Berlioz, rarely performed in complete form, the earliest operas by Verdi and

Mozart, and the once famous but now forgotten works of lesser composers. In addition, we have complete recordings of Baroque operas by Lully, Rameau, Scarlatti, and Monteverdi—all masters of the first rank—of some of the greatest Masses from the Renaissance, and a good sampling of medieval music. It is indeed a new and unusual situation when the recording companies begin to scan musicological publications in search of new material.

The advance of musicology has its effect also on the attitude toward modern music. The anomalous position of modern music in our musical life—it is the music of our time yet it has not gained a sure foothold in the concert hall—is due to the fact that its stylistic principles are only vaguely understood. Modern music does not differ in this respect from medieval music or, to take an extreme example, from oriental music. It is one of the immensely practical sides of musicology to elucidate the grammar and syntax of each style and to show that the methods of composition have their own consistency. The often-heard criticism of modern music that the increased use of dissonance seems arbitrary and forced could be made also to some extent of medieval music. Certain methods of medieval composition have reappeared in modern music, so that the study of the one will give us an insight into the other. It is therefore not just a freakish accident that a composer like Hindemith has taken an interest in the music of Guillaume de Machaut, the leading French composer of the fourteenth century.

Like all humanistic disciplines, musicology, too, is a child of its own time and it would be difficult to say whether the heightened interest in medieval music today is the result or the cause of the new developments in modern music. It is most probably result as well as cause. By a subtle process of mutual influence, dissonance has become one of the most timely questions in both the scholarly and creative spheres of music. At the risk of sounding paradoxical, one can say that by pursuing the study of medieval music, musicology serves at the same time the needs of the day.

Hand in hand with the expansion of musicology and its influence on our musical life goes a notable broadening of its own basis and the development of new methods in the use of material. With the serious interest in older musical styles it was inevitable that the question should arise of how this music was performed and on what instruments. A generation ago hardly anybody dared to suggest that Bach or Scarlatti would come off best on a Baroque organ or harpsichord. These instruments were generally considered "obsolete"—a polite synonym for "inferior." Today we have recognized that they are neither technically nor artistically inferior; they are merely different, but in their crisp and clear sonorities artistically better suited for Baroque music than their modern equivalents. To play Chopin on a harpsichord would be as senseless as to play Scarlatti on a piano. Here again the numerous LP recordings of recitals for Baroque organ or harpsichord show that they are being accepted today as an artistic advance.

The proper styles of singing, the combinations of instrumental and vocal ensembles, present tricky problems that still await solution. Paintings of the time are being studied for what they show us with regard to musical ensembles. Where the old scores are ambiguous a painting or miniature may be able to settle the point. Thus the fine arts may serve as valuable documentation for music history. Similarly, works of literature of all ages contain countless references to music, some vague, some extremely precise, actually giving titles or performers, as found for example in Rabelais. They often tell us more about the position of music in society than many a learned treatise of the period. But also treatises on special aspects of music provide valuable information beyond the actual subject-matter discussed. A book on counterpoint or harmony, for example, must be read not merely for what it says about the rules of composition but also for what it implies between the lines. The tacit assumption of the author, the weight he gives to one topic, his silence about others, allow us to extract the general principles of the age which were taken for granted. The results of such interlinear interpretation, if cautiously pursued, give us valuable and new musical insights. This oblique method of reading music books cannot be dismissed as "subjective"; it is as valid as examining the paintings of the past for what they reveal about the religious ideas of the time.

The example just mentioned is only one of many showing how closely musicology is allied with other humanistic disciplines. Indeed, to watch the growth of interdisciplinary relations and the emergence of a large unified field of humanistic studies is one of the most stimulating experiences of the humanist today and is comparable only to the joy an artist experiences in the process of creation. There is hardly an aspect of musicology that does not in one way or another have a bearing on nonmusical matters. Language and music are two entirely different media which ought not to be confused, but they may be happily joined together in artistic form, as they are in opera and especially in song. Whenever they co-exist—as they do all over the world—they become the subject of musicological as well as literary study. In the past such studies have been carried out with little or no cross-fertilization, but more and more we recognize that such forms cannot be treated intelligently from the musical or literary standpoint alone.

The historian is interested in music as part of general history. But aside from his general interest there exist compositions for political occasions from the Middle Ages to the present, songs of protest and censure, music for propaganda, and so forth which are directly linked with political history. Also church history and the history of liturgy are intimately connected with music. On the other hand, acoustics, physiology of hearing, and musical psychology bridge over to the natural sciences.

Another important branch of musicology is the study of oriental and "primitive" music, in short, of all types of music outside of the orbit of Western civilization. The traditional humanistic disciplines have shown until quite recently a determined and self-conscious limitation to the pattern of European thought from antiquity to the present. The high cultures of the Orient and the lower and primitive civilizations of the rest of the world have not yet been fully integrated into the general conception of man. Too often the "proper study of mankind" has been not man, but Western man. With the shift of interest to Asian problems these limitations have become abundantly clear. The modern view of the humanities transcends the self-centered interest in Western civilization and includes all cultures, high and low, in order to arrive at an understanding of human behavior.

Being a young discipline, musicology has shared the traditional limitations to a lesser degree. A few musicologists have been interested in non-Western music right from the start. The Second World War and recent political shifts in the Pacific area have suddenly brought into focus the immense practical importance even of musical studies. Our broadcasts have tried to reach the masses of the Orient in an effort to further intercultural understanding. But one has found that a symphony program has a limited appeal to a Chinese peasant, and that our popular music, on the other hand, tends to supplant and destroy the native music. Adverse propagandists have been quick to denounce this as "American imperialism" in the cultural sphere. It is actually nothing of the sort, but merely documents the grim fact that Gresham's Law applies also to cultural commodities.

The study of non-Western music is faced with much the same problems as anthropology. We are dealing here mainly with living cultures many of which lack written historical documents. The problems become especially acute in non-Western music because it defies the traditional forms of Western notation which are suitable only for our kind of music. Our notation cannot accurately record in writing shades of rhythm, subtle inflections of pitch, tone color, and style of performance, and these are precisely the most important characteristics of non-Western music. Recording by tape or disc is the only accurate way of putting this music literally "on the record." These recordings are the primary evidence, although they are not documents in the traditional sense. If we transcribe the music into Western notation the result is a musical "document," but one lacking some of the really essential evidence. Thus non-Western musicology must develop specific research methods that can successfully resolve the paradox of "evidence without documents" and "documents without evidence." An additional difficulty is the fact that the basic musical concepts of the Orient have almost nothing in common with those of the West and, as a result, Westerners cannot directly understand the music of the East and vice versa. It is no exaggeration to say that we shall have fully understood Oriental mentality only when we have understood Oriental music. The collection of the various musics of the globe is the first step in this direction. The comparison of Western and non-Western musical concepts will ultimately give musicology a truly worldwide perspective.

The knowledge of man's material culture is not enough if we want to understand his mind and emotions. Music reveals to us man's inner life and emotions, and its scholarly study contributes to that understanding of man which is the goal of all humanities. This goal is in itself timeless, although it is realized in each age in a different way. The new methods of musicology, especially the analysis of style, have made it possible to observe historical change also in the musical medium. Thus the study of music has added a new dimension to the history of the human mind.

12

ART HISTORY

Victory Without Trumpet

by Alfred Neumeyer

For generations students of archaeology had to look at pictures of the famous Nike of Samothrace in a reconstruction which showed her with a long trumpet in her outstretched hand, blowing a fanfare of triumph. This attempt to complete the image of the armless statue was based on a Hellenistic coin which shows a similar Victory, trumpet in hand. To the modern eye, educated by the sculptural aesthetics of Maillol and Henry Moore, the thin accessory looked decidedly unpleasant.

Digging in 1948 on the native island of the statue, Samothrace, American archaeologists discovered parts of the missing hand in the fountain basin in front of the original sanctuary. From these incomplete fragments it became evident that the reconstruction with the trumpet had been erroneous. Later when the excavators visited the Archaeological Museum in Vienna, which had sponsored the original excavations in the 1870's, they found the missing portions of the hand and thus were enabled to offer a completely new reconstruction of the statue. The hand had been empty and open, the arm raised in a gesture which we know today as the Fascist salute. Thus the disquietude of the modern spectator had been justified: there never was a "Victorian" Victory of Samothrace. The story shows all the features that enter into the life of scholarship: the searching mind asking the right question, *Fortuna*—good luck, power of observation, pertinacity, exactitude, reasonableness combined with imagination.

What has been the pattern of art history in America? In leafing through volumes of the *Art Bulletin*, today the leading journal in the field, from 1913 through 1948, one notices during the first ten years a strict limitation to art education. With two exceptions all the articles deal with such subjects as "How to arrange a curriculum in the Fine Arts," indicating that art appreciation courses preceded those on the history of art. Only a few islands of archaeological research emerge, surrounded by a sea of educational essays.

Yet by 1923 the situation had changed completely and America had begun to rise to the level of Europe, where art history had been established for generations. Of the approximately 430 essays listed in the thirty-five-year period, we discover 96 studies dedicated to the medieval period between 1100 and 1400 (1500 in the North of Europe), 90 to the Renaissance, followed by 62 on the Early Christian and Byzantine epoch and 53 on iconography including a few on general aesthetics. Then follows the Baroque with 38, the modern epoch since 1800 with 32, Antiquity with 30, the Near and Middle East with 29, American art with 27 and the Far East with 22. If one realizes that a great number of the iconographical studies are also concerned with the Early Christian, Byzantine, and medieval epochs, then the fact stands out that about half of the investigations deal with the pre-Renaissance history of European art.

To this must be added the geographical distribution which also is indicative of America's special interests. Of the articles, 110 deal with Italy, 46 with France, 44 with Spain, followed in considerable distance by Germany with 28, England with 15 and Holland with 13. Joining the two groups of figures we get a clear picture of the overwhelming concern with the Mediterranean world, particularly in the Early Christian, Byzantine, Medieval and Renaissance periods. One notices especially the relatively large number of Spanish studies as compared to research in the arts of Northern Europe. The picture differs considerably from that of a similar journal in Europe. There the arts of Central Europe (especially Holland, Belgium, Germany,

Austria, and England) would prevail while the Oriental countries and Antiquity would be relegated to specialized periodicals. As to periods, the later epochs, especially the Baroque, would be more strongly represented.

In seeking to discover why research in the United States should differ so markedly from that in Europe we arrive not so much at ideological causes as at personal ones: the influence of a few great scholars who gave momentum to a slowly growing field of learning and direction to succeeding generations.

At Harvard under the leadership of a great teacher, Charles Eliot Norton (active as a lecturer between 1873 and 1897), a "medievalist" atmosphere developed toward the end of the last century. From it emerged Bernard Berenson's interpretation of Italian art, too modern to be appreciated by Norton himself. Berenson has influenced the collecting activities of museums and private individuals more than anyone in our time, and from his library a host of critical essays, books, and *catalogues raisonnées*, full of wisdom, wit, and anger have emanated.

If Berenson directed our attention to Italy, Henry Adams, man of letters and member of a presidential family, turned the interest of a wider audience to medieval France. His *Mont St. Michel and Chartres* (1905) is written with a fine sense for the use of literature, theology, and the visual arts in conjuring up the peculiar spirit of time and place. In him the Puritan reserve toward the Catholic and feudal aspects of the Middle Ages yielded to aesthetic admiration. Another ten years and the fruits of the medieval interest would begin to show and to make America one of the centers of medieval research in the world. In 1923 Kingsley Porter's *Romanesque Sculpture of the Pilgrimage Roads* appeared in ten volumes in which he traced the spread of medieval sculpture from the heart of France to westernmost Spain in Santiago de Compostela. We follow the actual expansion of a style, its modification on the way from the center, and its absorption into another artistic idiom.

Investigation of individual monuments in order to explain the larger context was a method favored also by Charles Rufus Morey who gave to research in Early Christian and Byzantine art a permanent home in Princeton. His quest for the origins of the art of the Early Church, which he found in three main' currents (Rome, Constantinople, Alexandria), his concern for book illumination and objects of the minor arts, have given scope and direction to this field. The peculiar interest in Spanish art which gained impetus from the work of Kingsley Porter was taken up by Chandler R. Post, who gave us his eleven volume corpus of the *History of Spanish Painting* (ending with the Renaissance) and by Walter Cook, who instigated the study of medieval Spanish sculpture on a broad basis.

Such investigations centering upon Europe were amplified by research in Oriental art, as the fifty or so articles in the *Art Bulletin* make duly clear. America's location between Asia and Europe permits and even demands such a global view. In general, the study of Chinese bronzes and of Far Eastern ceramics (with some neglect of the later periods) absorbs the main interest of our scholars, while in painting, attention has turned to the Ming and Ch'ing and to the importance of literary sources. The art of India, especially considered for its philosophical and religious symbolism, has added its jungle wealth of forms and meanings to our awareness. The frontier sections of Chinese Turkestan and Afghanistan have directed interest to the great caravan roads of artistic exchange between the Mediterranean world and China.

This account of the specific features of American scholarship would remain incomplete without mention of the contribution to art history which German, Austrian, French, Italian, and Spanish displaced scholars who found a new home in American colleges and universities have made. It is through some of the members of this group that another feature of art-historical research, namely iconography, has taken a significant position in America. Yet today iconography no longer is concerned merely with the investigation of attributes of mythological figures and saints but has turned into an interpretation of the intrinsic meanings which lie behind these images. Every chosen image appears now as an action of memory drawn from the storehouse of accumulated traditional meanings.

The transformations of the classical gods and goddesses from the idealized humanity of their Graeco-Roman origin to star constellations in the Arabic world, to their ominous place as sorcerers and witches in medieval lore, and their triumphant return to the art of Italy during the fifteenth century, reflect exactly such accumulation of the most diversified meanings in one symbolic image. Venus landing on the shores of Greece had to throw off her Asiatic fertility attributes and accept Greek manners and mores. With the rise of Christianity and later of Islam her nudity became sinfulness and the goddess was banished to the starry sky whence she radiated her astrological spell. Could she be anything but a sorceress since she bewitched Tannhäuser in the Mount of Venus? Only at the moment when "modern" individualism during the Renaissance had taken a positive view of the realm of human passions could Venus be restored to her original good conscience. Yet how surprised Praxiteles' Venus of Knidos would have been to meet her gentle, Christianized descendent in Botticelli's painting of the seaborn goddess!

Thus iconography has become a key to the symbolism which every story, attitude, or attribute is carrying on its long passage through history. It reveals the migration of such motif-images as a process in which every single detail has a necessary place within a total historical context. One objection to the present preponderance of iconographical studies in the narrow sense of the word is that it disregards the spontaneous and semi-free creative act which expresses itself primarily in the form and in the style of the art work. It is at this point that we have to widen the circle of our observation beyond the United States.

Just as the handwriting of a person is expressive of individual traits, of communal habits, and of cultural traditions, so the form of every art work is shaped by the visual concepts of an epoch, a country, and a personality. It is with these aspects that European art history, beginning with the biographical compilations by Renaissance artists and developing into the analytical observations of connoisseurs, is primarily concerned. With the Hegelian age of *Universalgeschichte* these observations on the "handwriting" of individual artists have expanded into a description of the style of entire epochs;

for as Aldous Huxley has written, "At any given epoch there is only one prevailing style of art, in terms of which painters and sculptors treat of a strictly limited number of subjects. Art may be defined, in this context, as a process of selection and transformation whereby an unimaginable multiplicity is reduced to a semblance of unity."

And if art selects and transforms, so does the historian. He eliminates what he considers nontypical and he emphasizes what he finds meaningful to bring order into the complexity and the contradictions of reality. Such a selective act is, for instance, the raising of the Gothic period by the Romanticists from the neglect in which it had been held in the previous centuries. There followed the discovery of a "Renaissance," which previously had not been isolated as an epoch; Jakob Burckhardt's research and masterful literary presentation will forever be connected with this concept.

In the 1880's the concept of the "Baroque" crystallized, while the idea of "Mannerism" (1520-1600) emerged in the 1920's. Seen from the vantage point of today the appearance of each of these styles is not simply the discovery of new phenomena such as an improved magnifying glass might yield, but is to some extent a subjective creation endowed with all that seems desirable to the historical conjurer. Thus the "Gothic" gave chivalry and religion to its Romantic discoverers who, opposed to the spirit of the French Revolution, wanted chivalry and religion. The "Renaissance"—as formulated by Burckhardt—was in some ways a creation of the liberal opposition against the reactionary "medievalism" of the conservative powers ruling Europe after the Congress of Vienna. The "Baroque" provided the Rubensian opulence for a late Victorian and Wilhelminian society with its expansive but undifferentiated tastes, and "Mannerism" presented a spiritualized and "abstract" art to the antinaturalistic tendencies of contemporary creation. However, within the framework of such visions sober rational investigation has taken place, has assembled and organized the material, has shown the peculiar pattern of time-and-space, has determined artifacts, until at length the accumulated facts and a new attitude begin again to question the correctness of the vision.

This concept of autonomous style-epochs such as the Renaissance has been attacked from two sides: first by those who believe that many qualities assigned as original to the Renaissance had already been present in the Middle Ages, at least since Giotto, and second by those who do not accept such collective phenomena and see in them errors of historical perspective and fashionable products of ideological couturiers. The latter was the position of the Italian philosopher Benedetto Croce, who exalted "individual intention" beyond collective formal compulsions. But also from the point of view of empiricism, English and American scholars have shown resistance against such constructed entities. Is it surprising that in the country of William James and John Dewey empirical approaches are preferred to a search for a priori laws in the realm of art?

Not only has the existence of styles as, in a sense, living beings with their own evolutionary laws been debated, but also the peculiarly national characteristics of artistic phenomena have been questioned as a result of the ever growing revelation of artistic interaction between the various nations and cultural areas. We know today, for instance, how much of the Germanic animal ornament of the migration period (400-800 A.D.) is really Central Asiatic. Or we may recall the "International style" in Gothic painting of around 1400 A.D. which often makes national localization a guessing game. And who has not been struck by the truly international character of contemporary abstract art? While national characteristics and modifications of foreign "imports" by national traits do exist, forming by their manifoldness the orchestration of a world art, these national features can always be transgressed or transformed by the spontaneous creation of genius, of which the earmarks are anticipation and consummation. Today the complex interaction between individual and collective traits is generally recognized and notions of isolated historical units may be relegated to a mythological past.

Yet transgression and interaction do not eliminate the fact that there exist national styles and period styles. Their characteristic way of expression raises the question whether these "handwritings" of entire epochs do not point—just as in human beings—to conscious intentions, inherent ideas, and subconscious meanings. In the light of such a question, a work of art becomes raised to the status of a symbol and art history conceives of itself as a history of ideas. It assigns to the art work its place within the context of literature and philosophy of its time, all of which are taken as expressions of a common spirit of an epoch without sacrificing minute observation of detail to universals. Art is to be regarded as expressive of the innermost drives for man's orientation in the universe. The art work as a reflection of active spiritual forces cast into symbolic images has, for instance, guided Erwin Panofsky to choose perspective as such a symbolic form and to use it for demonstration of the meaning of the great spiritual revolution of the Renaissance. All these investigations have in common a "philosophy of symbolic forms" whose chief exponent, Ernst Cassirer writes: "Cognition as well as language, myth and art, all act not only as mirrors which reflect the images of outer and inner existence, but—far from being such indifferent media—they are primarily the original sources of light; they are the conditions of seeing as well as the fountain heads of all creations." Art history as a history of ideas deals with the "conditions of seeing" in a given culture as they are expressed in works of art.

In all the approaches we have discussed so far, the aesthetic aspect of the art work has been the most important. However, the art work is, to some extent, also the expression of the social and economic forces that have determined the needs and the ideals of the artist and his epoch. The source material directly related to art, such as contemporary biographies, guild laws, ecclesiastic records, building instructions, memoranda, letters and instructions of patrons, are the material from which a fruitful contribution to a social history of the arts can be expected. One has only to read the letters of Germany's greatest master, Albrecht Dürer, to Jakob Heller, a wealthy cloth merchant from Frankfurt who had ordered an altar panel from him, to understand the importance of material and economic factors in the execution of a painting. In paying a higher price the patron is assured of the fact that every part will be executed by the master's own hand while reduction of the price would involve the execution of parts by apprentices after the design of the painter. Even in

Michelangelo's struggle for the execution of the tomb of Pope Julius the Second, the legal and financial aspects played their part in "the tragedy of the Julius Tomb" of which, due to inner and external conflicts, only sorry fragments could be carried out by the artist.

Explanation of artistic creation from a strictly Marxian social history, on the other hand, has led to grotesque distortions of the semi-autonomous character of the art work. It is rather in the widening of the field of vision, in the inclusion of areas until recently passed over as "folklore," that the social history of the arts can gain. The lower and simpler strata of artistic creation represent not only what a former definition of folk art had described as "debased cultural goods of the upper classes": they also can contain the essences of human experience and the basic principles of representation. It is for this reason that contemporary art has received a vital stimulus. from a mere "Sunday painter," the French toll collector Henri Rousseau. The child-like frontality of his figures, his admiring denotation of each detail with equal exactitude, his naive distortion of space, in short his "magic" intensification of the world, have—according to their own testimony—influenced great modern artists like Fernand Léger and Max Beckmann in their search of a pictorial reality independent of merely optical sensations.

Vast as the field of art history has grown, from iconography to the social aspects of creation, there are still two areas of scholarship that have not sufficiently been absorbed into it. One is anthropology. The study of man's habitat on earth had by necessity to examine the way in which artifacts are related to the life processes of man. But anthropologists in classifying and describing form and ornament have made, in general, all too little use of the interpretive methods developed by art history. On the other hand an art historian, George Kubler of Yale, in his Mexican Architecture of the Sixteenth Century has fused demography (population analysis) and other approaches worked out by anthropology with the form analysis of art history in a method beautifully fitted to the mixed Indian-European setting of this culture. His work points the road to future researches.

Much, likewise, can still be done to draw from contemporary psychology for the interpretation of the history of artistic creation. While it is true that admirable biographies of artists have been written which contain a great deal of psychological insight, the results of modern methods of scientific psychology are rarely used. Since the beginning of our century the interest of the psychologists has been directed toward the field of cultural creation as a symbolic expression of man's dreams, drives, and memories. In general, the approach of the psychoanalysts has suffered from the unhistorical and materialistic trend of thought of the analyzers. Yet such a fusion of art history and psychoanalysis has also given us historically valid and psychologically convincing interpretations of important aspects of Oriental and Occidental art. In recognition of such pioneering work, Thomas Mann dedicated his Hindu legend *The Transported Heads* to Heinrich Zimmer, a scholar who, with a deep understanding of the context of myth and art in India, has worked towards such a fruitful fusion. We have gained in insight by psychoanalytically trained art historians who interpreted the appearance, since the second part of the eighteenth century, of physiognomical studies of "abnormal cases" in sculptures and paintings. The art of the insane and of prisoners, but most of all the creative work of children, has been examined in the light of such research and has given us access to a deeper understanding of the creative process. The very fact that such combinations of disciplines have been worked out successfully and have provided us with clues to the nature of myth, of obsessions, and of formal habits must be taken as an incentive for a much wider mutual stimulation.

What have been the major results to date of art history? Probably the most apparent is the gradual emergence of the continuity in man's creative history. There gradually has risen the picture of a continuous and universal practice of the arts from Peking to Quito and from Cheops to Chagall. While the recent deciphering of the Minoan script as a Greek idiom has pushed the beginnings of Greek history back to the flowering culture of Crete in 1500 B.C., other

modern discoveries have widened the orbit of Greek art from Gandhara on the Indian frontier to Burgundy in France. Only recently
the excavation of the tomb of a Celtic chieftain in Vix in Burgundy
yielded magnificent Greek (or Etruscan) bronze vessels from about
500 B.C. which owe their existence on this remote spot to the barter
of Mediterranean artistic goods for the tin which was transported
down from Cornwall to this distant trading place on the "tin road."
Moreover, the appearance of Hellenistic acanthus foliage in Chinese
pottery of the Sung period, the Apollo-like features of the Buddha
statues from Gandhara (N. W. Pakistan and Afghanistan), or the
discovery of Chinese silks in Near Eastern and Roman tombs and
of Central Asiatic animal designs in Germanic metal art, reveal
continuous cross-fertilizations, with the Graeco-Roman world as a
focal point for the give-and-take along the caravan roads and rivers
from China to Scandinavia.

While Graeco-Roman art has humanized, the Orient has
supremely spiritualized the world of images. This spiritualization
occurred at the time when Christianity, an Oriental mystery religion
of salvation, began to replace the Olympian gods. One of the most
puzzling questions facing art history in the past has been where
to look for the Oriental style from which the early Christian Syrian
and Egyptian artisans and their European disciples developed
their semi-primitive, half-abstract and magic art. The solution came
in connection with British military actions at the conclusion of
World War I when the sand covered desert city of Dura-Europos
was discovered at the middle Euphrates. It revealed itself to subsequent excavations by French and American expeditions as one of
the most important archaeological sites since Pompeii came to light
in the middle of the eighteenth century. Here all the great civilizations of Antiquity met on the caravan route to Persia and left
their traces in the sand. Temples founded by the Army of Alexander
the Great and by the Roman legion from Palmyra introduced European religion and art into the heart of the Middle East. In their
shrines Persians and legionnaires worshipped the hero-God Mithras,
of whom another temple was recently discovered near St. Paul's

in London; Syrians adored the great Baal of Hebrew defamation; Jews erected their synagogue which they covered—against the Mosaic law—with pictures of Old Testament stories; and finally, some time before the destruction of the city by the Persians in 256 A.D., the Christians built a baptistry with some of the earliest painted representations of New Testament scenes. Not only was a melting pot of immeasurable interest for the history of religion discovered, but here in the murals of the Temple of Baal (80 A.D.) one encountered an artistic style of magic frontality which clearly revealed itself as the Oriental antecedent of the early Byzantine mosaics on the walls of the churches of Ravenna. Due to this discovery, the unknown Oriental sources of the style of early Christian art could be established in at least one major example whose existence, so far, had been only a postulate. In the light of this new discovery early Christian and Byzantine art can now be understood as a dramatic dialogue between the hieratic style of the Orient, as it was handed down in the East since 3000 B.C., and the naturalistic style of Graeco-Roman tradition.

While the excavation at Dura brought light to the "Dark Ages" of Christian art, the discovery of the murals of Castelseprio illuminated another period between the Byzantine and the Medieval epoch. This little country church in Lombardy lost its whitewash in 1944 and revealed a series of Biblical frescoes painted in the liveliest late Antique manner such as hitherto was known only in copies of Byzantine book illuminations of the fifth century executed another five hundred years later. If the assigned date of about 700 A.D. (which has been contested) is correct, a missing link has been inserted between the art of dying Roman naturalism and that lively flowering of the arts at the court of Charlemagne and his sons (800-850 A.D.) which is known under the name of the Carolingian Renaissance. We might be hesitant to entrust to a single and small monument such far-reaching conclusions, were it not for the fact that the discovery of Castelseprio is not an isolated incident. Within the last twenty years new discoveries have pushed the history of medieval mural painting back to the ninth and tenth centuries. Muenster in the Grisons of Switzerland, and the West of France have yielded totally unexpected murals, while Northern Greece and Yugoslavia have shown the extension of the Byzantine style in magnificent mural cycles from the twelfth to the fifteenth century. Clearly then, we can make out in the Byzantine realms and within the confines of the former Roman empire an unbroken continuity of Christian art from the days of Constantine (320 A.D.) to those of Giotto and Dante (1300 A.D.).

By contrast to the approach in the United States, medieval research in the various European countries has put its supreme effort into isolating the national characteristics of art in the soil of the Middle Ages. Together with a continuous analysis of individual monuments, the establishment of typically French, German, or Italian artistic languages became a main endeavor of continental scholars.

After decades of research on the great cathedral sculpture of the twelfth and thirteenth centuries, the emphasis now seems to swing to church architecture, to stained glass and the decorative arts. Through this preoccupation with the history and the aesthetics of glass and metal, a deeper insight into the spirit of an era has been gained, in which artistic expression did not concentrate so much on representation as on symbolization and decoration. Accordingly, color, light, transparency, and opaqueness have been discovered as instruments of meanings and carriers of concepts of beauty which changed at the end of the Middle Ages.

With the realization that the Renaissance was the period of the great artist-individuals, the saints of a beauty-worshiping age, modern scholarship, equipped with a refined science of attribution and purified of Romantic exaltation, has given a new status to the art of the monograph. Comprehensive presentations of Dürer, Leonardo, and Michelangelo have been undertaken, with a tendency to favor a critical evalution of the works over a traditional biographical approach. For the Baroque age Caravaggio, a favorite of contemporary scholarship, has received not less than four monographs in as many years, while Rembrandt at last has been given his first scholarly biography in English. Thus the biographical approach with which art history first made its appearance in Vasari's *Lives of the Painters, Sculptors and Architects* (1550) appears as a natural literary form for the interpretation of the age of rising individualism.

Interest in the post-Renaissance extension of Europe overseas is reflected in the emergence of a new field of scholarship: Latin American studies, investigating the artistic heritage of the Iberian realms on American soil embodied in thousands of churches, statues, and paintings which have added a so-far totally unconsidered province to the art-geographical map of the world. Thus an unknown chapter of the Gothic style in the New World, lingering on for over a century after its disappearance in Europe, has come to light. The wonderful Mestizo Baroque of Mexico, the Portuguese Rococo wonders of church architecture in the Brazilian mining province of Minas Gerais, have enriched our outlook on the creative achievements of the New World. The woodcarvers' "retablo" style impressed its ornate and flat carving manner upon the church facades of Mexico and created an intriguing decorative style of ornamentation in the remote churches of the Lake Titicaca region in Peru and Bolivia. One of the most fascinating folk arts of the world here has conquered a monumental architecture imported from Spain. And, of course, the chapter on modern architecture can never be written again without consideration of North America's contribution in this field.

This brings us to the modern epoch. Slowly the sense of historical continuum begins to include our own period and its antecedents in the nineteenth century. In architecture the stylistic garments of the eclectic ages such as the Neo-Gothic, the Victorian, and Neo-Baroque architecture are beginning to be examined. As a result one can now detect beneath the pseudo-historical costumes of the nineteenth century a new interest in structure as a generator of form: the open ground plan, the curtain wall, the asymmetrical balance, the use of steel and glass anticipated twentieth-century architecture first in such subarchitectural areas as the cheap "balloon frame" house, the prefabricated cottage, the cast-iron commercial structures of Chicago, the Crystal Palace, and the Eiffel Tower.

In the field of nineteenth- and twentieth-century painting and sculpture, "close-up" biographical sketches, supported by the recording eye of the camera which can juxtapose the actuality of the motif next to its pictorial interpretation, have given us so intimate a contact with some of the great artists that we seem to be witnesses to their studio and alfresco experiences.

A high standard of workmanship has been set by the catalogues in book form which Alfred Barr has introduced at the Museum of Modern Art in New York and which so far remain unsurpassed. Some of the great artists of our own era as well as some of the main currents of contemporary art have been given such careful biographical, bibliographical, and interpretative examination as previously only Old Masters had deserved. However, the interpretation of the last and of our own century owes much to the great non-professional essayists: Roger Fry and Sir Herbert Read in England, Karl Scheffler and Julius Meier-Graefe in Germany, Paul Valéry and André Malraux in France, José Ortega y Gasset in Spain. Here historical writing becomes in itself an aesthetic achievement.

And more; the history of the nineteenth century is being rewritten in the twentieth as an act of historical justice. Never before had there been such a discrepancy between the "official" taste and the judgment of posterity. Juries, acquisition committees, and critics crowned works which we today have banished to basements, and rejected true masters like Courbet, Manet, Cézanne, Gauguin, and Van Gogh, who had to wait for their resurrection in our own century. While Titian, Michelangelo, Poussin, or Rubens were recognized in their own lifetimes as the leaders in their field, the French Revolution and the Industrial Revolution brought the dissociation between the creator and the patron which resulted in the popular success of conservative or sentimental artists whom an unsophisticated, new middle-class public could follow. In this sense art history has not only reconstructed the past but has created the artistic actuality of the nineteenth century as it was unknown to its own contemporaries.

Modern art history's scope extends from the investigation and material analysis of facts to the lofty structures of systematic interpretations of the meaning of artistic creation. It has opened a vista of a battlefield of conquering and declining cultures expressing their creeds and dreams in carved gods and painted idols. What was cherished or feared, hoped for or newly discovered took form in a world of images. This world of images revealed itself as governed by formal expressions which showed unity of style combined with infinite variety of individual traits. In restless but not senseless motion these styles seem to have an evolutionary life of their own. Within them art was revealed, as Heinrich Schnaase wrote a hundred years ago, as "the surest awareness of a people and the embodied judgment of the values of things."

The history of art dissolves the static art work again into a state of becoming, and makes it a living part of today. This polarity of approach reflects the very nature of life itself, because, as Ortega y Gasset has said, "Life is continuation, is survival into the moment which will arrive after now. Life, therefore, suffers under an inevitable imperative of realization."

Cézanne liked to speak about "realization" as the essence of his heroic struggle with his subjects. This "inevitable imperative of realization" is the very stuff of art history.

In these terms we can perhaps understand better the meaning of the restoration of our "Victory without Trumpet." Not satisfied with the chance-given appearance of a mutilated statue, historical investigation has suggested the most probable solution and by it has transformed a seemingly definite status of "being" into an open situation of "becoming." It has exposed the sediments of past life to the growth processes of the present mind, to its store of knowledge and its perceptive sensibility. Without the trumpet sound of poetic inspiration it won a quiet victory. Thus as an interpreter of man's creative self-realization, art history gradually realizes itself.

Truth, Fiction, and Reality

by Howard Mumford Jones

THE HIGHER study of literature is a branch of learning, and must be distinguished from book reviewing, "appreciation," "reading good books," "reading as a worthy leisure-time occupation," much teaching, popular lectures by authors on themselves or other authors, and other modes of genteel amusement. As a branch of learning, literary study is ancient. In the Western world its foundations were laid in Greece and, like other branches of learning descending to us from antiquity, it has as its formal aim the disinterested pursuit of truth. It is one of the humanities, and in modern America it is probably the most conspicuous branch of humane study.

All the parts of learning are subjected to pressure from outside the academic environment which is their common home, but this pressure varies from subject to subject, from situation to situation, and from age to age. Thus the "pure" mathematician, the astronomer, the Sanskrit scholar, and the student of Greek epigraphy are commonly free from political and social pressures except the continual reproach that their subjects are not of immediate utility. Some scientists—for example, botanists—enjoy qua experts a relative freedom from outside meddling. At the other end of the spectrum economists, historians, political scientists, and professors of education never know when they may arouse popular fury. The historian may be accused of unpatriotic bias when, as a matter of theory, he is supposed to have no bias at all, and his books may be thrown out of libraries and schools. The economist may be charged with introducing "creeping socialism," the political scientist with being favorable to some unpopular political group or hostile nation, and the educationist with being "anti-intellectual."

Literary study in one sense lies between these extremes, and in another sense is subjected to more pressures from "outside" than is almost any other branch of learning. Inasmuch as the literary scholar is commonly regarded as a person of vast erudition that is at once reputable and useless, the populace—even the enlightened populace—does not worry about his views unless he openly violates one or more of the prominent taboos. Hence, the assertion that literary study is subject to outside pressures may seem odd. But literature takes nothing less than the universe for its province, inasmuch as it may deal with human beings, it may deal with animals, it may deal with nature, it may deal with any branch of learning, and it may deal with God. The literary student is concerned with the motives of authors, with motives imputed to their characters, with philosophies, with ethical judgments, and with religious (or non-religious) points of view. Inevitably, therefore, even though he may not know it, the scholar yields in greater or less degree to pressures of opinion and practice that have only a secondary relation to the disinterested pursuit of truth.

For example, inasmuch as literary study is supposed per se to make for both cultural and ethical improvement, emphasis is given to masterpieces commonly held to be somehow improving. Works "wholesome" in intent are unconsciously upgraded as art, whereas works thought to be "decadent" are downgraded. Philosophical idealism expressed or imputed to literary works is, on the whole, a "good thing"; and cynics and satirists of the calibre of Swift or LaRochefoucauld have sometimes been gingerly handled. Though obvious didacticism wakens a smile, moralism is commonly an unseen, powerful force in literary study. Thus, for a long time, every student of Restoration drama was supposed to come out with the verdict that, whatever its formal perfection, comedy was, as then written, immoral; and even today the graphic quality of a work like the Memoires of Casanova goes unmarked, whereas the edifying but empty platitudes of Dr. Johnson's essays are received as canonical successes. One may also be of the Catholic or the Protestant party, and an examination of histories of literature received in Catholic schools, at least in the United States, will reveal a set of emphases differing from those used by non-Catholics. Latterly, of course, there has been a general loosening of the taboos against literature portraying or analyzing sexual relationships, but this does not mean that the fiction of De Sade is commonly studied.

To understand how some of these pressures have come into being and to comprehend the present currents of literary study, it is necessary to examine certain historical facts. In the Western world (and, of course, in the English-speaking countries) literary study began by assuming that the masterpieces of classical Greece and Rome were alone worth the attention of gentlemen and scholars; only theories of literary beauty and of literary criticism based upon these masterpieces were received; and the "barbarous" productions of the Middle Ages, no less than the inferior productions of modern nations, were felt to sit so far below the academic salt as not to be worth studying at all, or, if studied, read only as a kind of extracurricular activity. In the English literary tradition proponents of the vernacular were never silenced, but they failed to conquer university prejudices rationalized into the theorem that a sound knowledge of Greek and Latin classics improved modern literature—a doctrine still with us. What broke the monopoly by Greek and Latin in the academic world was, among other things, the powerful force of romanticism, with its emphasis on the virtue of folk genius and the glories of nationalism as an expression and preservative of that genius.

In American academic life the struggle between classical scholarship and the rising radicalism of the modern languages was intense, but with the creation in 1883 of the Modern Language Association of America the Greeks and the Romans passed beneath the yoke. The MLA with its more than seven thousand members is today the most powerful organization of its kind in the United States and perhaps in the world. But the Modern Language Association came into being at a particular time. Though its original membership included persons of the catholic breadth of James Russell Lowell, "philology" in the European sense was the very breath of life in its nostrils, and "philology" as then conceived had important interconnections with certain favorite concepts of nineteenth-century science and philosophy.

One of these was philology in the narrower sense of a genetic approach to linguistic study. German romanticism had strongly supported the doctrine of a mysterious central focus which served, so to speak, as a distributing plant for the languages of mankind, and back to this mysterious central point (a scholarly mutation of the Tower of Babel) where dwelt the "Aryans," various languages, especially the great family of Germanic languages, could be traced. The duty of scholarship was to work up the stream of time; and as the archaeologist or the antiquarian constructed from fragments of papyri or scattered artifacts a complete, if artificial, work of art, so philologians delighted to trace significant variations in form, supplying them according to theoretical systems where they could not be found in extant sources until a whole genetic map could be plotted. Inevitably this interest placed a premium upon older documents, since these revealed older verbal forms; and in consequence the literature of the heroic ages—that is, the literary remains of Central and Northern Europe down to about 1000 A.D.—took on an academic value that had less relation to intellectual or aesthetic qualities than to survival as documentary evidence of linguistic change. Of course, heroism is heroism; and the *Niebelungenlied*, *Beowulf*, and the *Song of Roland* had, and still have, artistic value. It is difficult, however, to claim much artistic worth for Ulfilas's translation of part of the Bible into Gothic, for Anglo-Saxon riddles, or for Old Norse runes.

A second interesting commitment of the late nineteenth century was to racism. The languages and the literatures of the Germanic peoples were supposed to express the racial soul of democracy; and a line of descent was worked out from the *Germania* of Tacitus to, say, Theodore Roosevelt's *The Winning of the West*. Latin and Greek literature may have expressed the culture of a pre-Christian universe, but the world was to the strong Teutonic peoples; and scholars writing the literary history of the Germans, the English, the Scandinavians, and the Americans strove to discover in the national literature the expression of the national "soul"—that is, of national traits commonly interpreted as racial inheritances. Theoretically the same thing was possible for the Mediterranean world, and some scholars sought, indeed, to find in the continuity of French and Spanish literatures a continuing racial product. It was more usual, however, to interpret Romance literatures as expressing a cultural tradition descending from the ancients; and thus interpreters of French masterpieces found traits they identified as "reason," "clarity," or "universality," all thought to be modern versions of "classical" values.

The third commitment of the period was to science, and here the approach was genetic. Inheriting from classical scholarship the belief that the primary duty of the research worker is to establish the text of a literary document and then to discover how and why it came into being, scholars labored to create exact biographies and to give to the world the unfolding of a text. Every text had "sources," that is, documents or events that suggested particular passages or general ideas to the writer thereof, and to discover and establish parallels between some original "source" and the final work of art was a triumph of the new method. The method had its earlier successes in the medieval field, when plagiarism was a virtue and no author claimed to be original, since he would then lack authority; and if, with the incoming of modern notions of literary creativity, writers concealed their sources instead of boasting about them, this merely lent a new puzzle interest to the learned game.

The genetic approach was not confined to the single author, nor to the single work. Conveniently borrowing respectability from Aristotle, and more particularly from the little Aristotles of the Renaissance, scholars sought likewise to parallel biological science. Genera and species, two powerful words when the Modern Language Association was born, could, it was thought, be distinguished in literary history, since, clearly, there were such things as epics and comedies, odes and novels. To isolate and define the genre, to study the "laws" governing its development across time and space, to watch the coming in of new literary types, and to measure the success of a given work by its conformity to the typology thus created, seemed to do three things simultaneously: it paralleled the dynamic theory of Darwin about the evolution of species and so gave scientific assurance to scholarship; by uniting a "modern" notion of genres with the classical and pseudo-classical systems of the past, it gave depth in time to literary study; and by discovering the "laws" of literature it seemed to give point and focus to the activities of learned men. Today we have discarded this approach—perhaps ungratefully—because, since Croce, we are not so sure as we once were that literary works parallel biological phenomena. But the search for "genres" and for universal literary law had the effect of carrying literary study beyond nationalism into world literature; and to continue the analogy of comparative zoology, professors of comparative literature tried to do from a particular point of view what the advocates of the Great Books doctrine do today. But the complexities of interpreting the literatures of the Far East have not yet been solved.

In the American academic world of the 80's and the 90's the scholar was also the teacher, for there had not yet developed such organizations of pure research as the Institute for Advanced Study or the General Electric Laboratories. In literature academic respectability was greatest in the medieval field, and then diminished towards modern times. It was respectable to study Shakespeare, but less respectable to study Browning and not respectable at all to study most American writers. Rebellious youth found "philology" dry fodder, however scientific its intent; and younger scholars, nourished as graduate students upon a weird combination of Old Norse, Gothic, Old High Germanic, Old English, Middle High German, Middle English, and Old French, wondered what all this had to do with literary art. Moreover, if the aim was to discover universal laws of philology, the causes of philological change became by and by so complex that generalizations became rarer and rarer, nor did the search for universal principles in literary history turn up anything to which the scholarly world could agree. The "law" of gravitation was one thing, the "law" of rhotacism another, and whatever "law" appeared in literary development seemed to get nowhere, since, once you had established the truth that almost no author is a pure original but rather a being who reads books, listens to music, looks at pictures, and talks to people like anybody else, the presence or absence of literary originality was in no way a function of the number of sources a writer had employed. Who cares for the Ur-Hamlet when Shakespeare is available?

By the second decade of the twentieth century the modernity of nineteenth-century "philology" had become outmoded; and the departments of literature found a new way of being modern in that they came to include more and more works of art written in the lifetime of those living in the classroom. In this country the teaching of American literature rose from its seat as Cinderella among the ashes and rapidly turned into a leading figure at the literary court. Literary change ceased to be something sought on biological analogy and was more and more explicated as a problem in history and social psychology. By 1914 professors of literature could discuss the art of Thomas Hardy with professional zeal and not lose caste. Of course this movement of modernism, like all reform movements, suffered from enthusiasm: grave scholars in English discovered great genius in O. Henry; Jack London was by some thought to be a mighty man; Maeterlinck was elevated to the galaxy of the immortals; and Masefield's The Everlasting Mercy was admired as an expression of the natural man by savants who had never visited the slums. Vis-à-vis the clamor of the contemporary, the judgments of scholars did not appear to be better than the judgments of the book reviewers.

Beginning in the twenties, two movements of rescue were formed. One centered on the "New Criticism"; the other, on American studies. Inasmuch as the training of literary scholars in the American field had been handicapped by the fact that most of their training was in the British field, dissidents arose to take the education of experts in the cultural history of the nation out of English departments altogether by creating a separate program of "American studies." Repercussions in various English departments eventually gave the field of American literature a larger space in the sun, but meanwhile the effect of the American studies programs was in general to stress intellectual and cultural history rather than textual criticism; i.e., American literary works became documents in a larger context of social development. The effect was felt in other literatures as well.

The "New Criticism" proved to be more complicated. In general the assumption of the new critics, whose intellectual parentage was various, including the works of Ivor A. Richards, T. S. Eliot, and other aestheticians, philosophers, and moralists, was that historical scholarship (as they understood it) was all very well in its way, but that it led away from, rather than into, the text of a literary work. A poem should not mean, but be; a poem was not the expression of an extrapoetic idea culled from philosophy, religion, politics, or any other extraneous field; it was an immediate rendering of experience valid in its present terms, to be understood entirely in its own universe of discourse. Scrutiny of the text of a poem was, on the whole, sufficient, given the commonplaces of literary information; structure was something in the poem, not something imposed by tradition from without, just as the manipulation of figure and style, intensity or extensity—though these matters might be illumined from the practice of an age—lay uniquely within the universe of discourse of the work of art. This scrutiny of meaning was proved to be intensely necessary after Richard's disclosure of the wild variety of "meanings" even intelligent readers imputed to all sorts of poems, old and new.

The new criticism insisted that literary art is autonomous discourse, just as science is autonomous, but this truth placed them in an ambiguous relation to historical scholarship. It was all very well to say that the biography of a poet was not the same thing as the meaning of the poem, but clearly the meaning of the poem could be altered by what one knew of the biography of the poet. Moreover, the critics were, willy-nilly, compelled to employ the findings of historical scholarship even in the purest form of literary analysis, inasmuch as so obvious an element as the meaning of words depended upon the researches of the linguists. An uneasy truce prevailed: literary scholars demanded evidence for some of the dogmatic judgments of the new critics, and the critics continued to accuse scholarship of aesthetic coarseness; but both parties to the logomachy have managed to exist in the scholarly world.

The true difficulty, it presently appeared, arose not so much from tensions between old scholars and new critics as between the academic critics and scholars on the one hand, and the great reading public on the other. The minute examination of texts, however rewarding to a samurai class, did not prove attractive to the general reader; and during the last quarter of a century in the United States the split between high-brow and low-brow, as ancient as human nature, has widened rather than narrowed, despite the increased amount of time given to literary study in the grades, in high school, in college, and in university. The general public is, or can be, interested in "good books," but good books, a vague term, was not what the scholars meant by literature. Alongside the traditional scholarly canon of masterpieces, a second canon, satisfactory to the newer spirits, was created, particularly in poetry (which now mainly ceased to sell). Henry James went up and Thackeray went down; John Donne was proclaimed and Thomas Gray was slighted; Herman Melville became a mighty figure and Longfellow was ignored; special virtue was found in James Joyce and something less than virtue in George Moore. Nor was the transvaluation of values confined to the placement of authors only. It extended to reassessing familiar works and proclaiming the virtues, for modern times, of neglected masterpieces. Thus the "bitter" comedies or tragicomedies of Shakespeare—*Measure for Measure, Pericles, Troilus and Cressida* are examples—were found to have a special value and to contain a special, if enigmatic, message to modernity, and the values of *Julius Caesar, As You Like It,* and even of *Hamlet* tended to decline. But none of this interested the general reader.

The consequence was, on the whole, that literary study was pursued with passionate zeal by a consecrated few, but that, on the whole also, all indications are that the reading of books by American readers has declined in proportion to the population. Studies of the use of public libraraies, of book-buying habits, and of the actual reading of books indicate in the 1950's that among Western peoples the citizens of the United States read proportionately fewer books than do other nationals, just as they have fewer bookstores—something less than 1500. (If the United States supported bookstores as Denmark supports them, it would have 30,000.) The Americans have traditionally been readers of newspapers and magazines rather than of books, and apparently the cutting edge of literary scholarship has not altered their propensities significantly in this regard. Other forces also tended to check the reading habit, radio and television among them; and the drive in education towards a socially-adjusted childhood has not made reading—a solitary habit—attractive. All studies show a decided dropping off in the reading of books at the school-leaving age. Whatever the causes of this decline, the country does not today fulfill the expectations of its founders that enlightenment for its citizens was increasingly to come from books.

There has been a tendency to blame literary scholarship unduly for this failure. An association like the National Council of Teachers of English tends to be antagonistic towards literary scholarship, and an organization like the College English Association emphasizes "teaching" without inquiring too curiously into what is to be taught. Undoubtedly much that is published as scholarly research is of small value in the literary world—but of what area of discourse cannot the same thing be said?

Teachers, popular critics, and general readers are often the beneficiaries of scholarly investigation without being aware of it. Take the single case of Shakespeare. At the opening of the nineteenth century Coleridge wrote wonderful interpretations of Shakespeare, but this he did by imputing to Shakespeare Coleridge's own notion of poetic creation and by analyzing the characters of the plays with small reference to Elizabethan theories of psychology. Today it is possible to discriminate among Elizabethan motivation and psychology, romantic ascription of motivation and psychology to Shakespeare, and the motivation and psychology of Shakespearian characters seen from the point of view of contemporary theories of human nature. Inasmuch as a great work of art mirrors the intelligence of its reader, the difference is in one way of small importance, but one that a producer rehearsing *Macbeth* or *Othello* has to know in order to follow some consistent line. So likewise in the case of so familiar a work as Dickens's *Christmas Carol*, now largely "appreciated" as myth (like The Night Before Christmas). In the Victorian world it was an important document of social and economic protest, and the overnight reform of Scrooge, which seems to us part of the fairy tale, had meaning because the Christian psychology of 1843 made consistent sense. Contrariwise, in view of our knowledge of Tennyson's personality, we can now see in *In Memoriam* traces of spiritual agony not evident in 1850 to readers who took the poem as solemn discourse, for *In Memoriam* is in a special sense a great confessional document. Such interpretations slowly filter down from the graduate schools to the general reading public.

In the 1880's American literary scholarship looked with reverence to European savants for guidance; in the 1950's it does nothing of the sort. On the contrary, European savants come to the New World, and are delighted with the range and richness and variety they find here. Constant pressure is exerted by the editors of learned journals and the university presses toward a more agreeable literary style; and though the scholar seldom attracts the great, undifferentiated reading public, the cultural and commercial success of the university presses, in an era when general publishers have given up "prestige items," testifies that scholarly writing improves. The réclame of the New Critics has not ended the soberer investigations of orthodox research workers; and we know today vastly more about almost any literary period and about most literary figures than did the founders of the Modern Language Association. The greatest problem before literary interpretation is how to get the information now available to scholars and critics into the public domain and to put it to cultural use.

We began with a catalogue of the kinds of pressures or biases evident in literary learning; and one of the problems of popularization lies in the skillful avoidance of conventional responses to "literature" and "learning," or rather to a learned man. Learning is still something magical and mysterious; it sets its possessor apart and is supposed to demand from ordinary Americans a special social attitude towards the "professor." Literature is likewise remote. It is something distinguished from "reading"; it is something you are exposed to in the schools because it is supposed to do you good when you are young, but (with notable exceptions) it is not someting for the enrichment of daily life. In one sense, this is simply the old difference between high-brow and low-brow; in another sense here is one of the peccant humors of American culture. Neither Irving Babbitt nor George F. Babbitt can understand each other's interests or vocabulary.

Does this mean that the study of literature is an idle pastime? In part it does, if one believes that the primary purpose of literary study is to do immediate cultural good. But literary scholarship retains, or can be made to retain, all its original zest and flavor, and to the minority of the population that is steadily interested in it, whether as scholarship or as criticism or as both, it is more exciting now than it ever was before. Even if it gives up the assumption that investigation will eventually reveal "laws" in literature, there is still the pure intellectual pleasure in determining, so far as evidence exists, what an author was driving at, how he put his work together, why the work pleased or displeased its original audience, and what, if anything, it has to say to us now. Excessive claims are sometimes made for literary study. That literature or literary study is necessarily an instrument of international understanding in the world of the hydrogen bomb is at least a dubious assumption in view of the fact that, unlike music or painting, literature has as its medium language—perhaps the most emotionally charged channel of nationalism in existence. But that literary scholarship can still illumine human motives, enrich human enjoyment, develop sensitivity to beauty, and increase in some degree the wisdom of readers by revealing depth and variety in literary masterpieces—all this seems clear, even though these revelations are presently confined in the main to a minority of the population and to the academic world.

14

LINGUISTICS

Symbols Make Man

by John Lotz

LANGUAGE is like an iceberg. One part, the production of speech in the vocal tract, the accompanying gestures, the passage of the sound through the air and its impact on the ear, is open to immediate observation. But the vastly greater part, the formation of the utterance in the brain of the speaker, its reception by the hearer, and the association of the signal with experience—past and present, individually isolated and socially shared—is below the surface and can be fathomed only by soundings.

Human existence is welded to language. No normal person is without this faculty and no other species is known to possess it. Only the human infant is endowed with a babbling instinct; this prepares him for speech, but many years of learning and practice are required before the individual achieves the virtuosity of the adult in the use of his mother tongue. Once acquired, language becomes a constant companion to all human behavior. It is the possession of the individual, yet at the same time it is the bond which establishes society. Language depends upon, but is not determined by, the biological constitution of man, and differences among languages are not linked with physical differences among men. Any person can learn any language as his mother tongue.

The spoken word is the only all-inclusive medium of communication and it is the main focus of attention in linguistics. Speech is always available since it is produced by the human body without any tool; it can be varied from a soft whisper to a loud shout; it fills the entire space around the speaker, goes around obstacles, and thus does not require a direct line of connection with the hearer; nor does it depend on light, as do optical signals, and so can be used day or night; it leaves the body almost entirely free for other activities, and requires but little energy. Although overt speech may be foregone, as by Trappist monks because of religious vows or by widows in aboriginal Australia because of a taboo, even such persons have a need for communication and use substitute means of expression.

Spoken language is the necessary foundation for secondary symbolic systems. Among these, script, which lends permanency to the expression, is the most widespread, and increasing, literacy makes it a more and more important means of communication. For specific purposes script can be transposed into other media, such as the gesture language of the deaf, the Morse Code, or flag-signaling. The example of Helen Keller shows that the transposition of a full language into other perceivable media is possible. There are other language types, limited in scope and function, which are also founded on natural language: Pidgin English, the sign language of the Plains Indians, and scientific codes such as chemical symbols.

Language gives man, in addition to his biological heredity, another line of continuity which makes culture and the accumulation of knowledge possible. The use of simple tools and the occurrence of socially determined behavior—which used to be cited as marks of humanity—are phylogenetically prior to man, but the great complexity of human social organization and the extensive development of technology do presuppose language. Truly, language marks the birth of man, and in this sense one might interpret the opening words of the Gospel of St. John to mean: In the beginning was language.

Language not only characterizes all mankind, but also—the curse of Babel—divides it. After the stage of babbling, individuals become members of different language communities, and most often only of one. But contact between these communities is usually provided for by the presence of individuals who speak more than one language. The number of languages in existence is a more or less arbitrary figure; this is a reflection of the problems, linguistic and sociological, involved in defining language boundaries. In Scandinavia, for example, Danish, Norwegian, and Swedish, though mutually intelligible, are regarded as different languages because of their political status— whereas Lappish, which includes a number of nonmutually intelligible language communities, is usually counted as one language. Inventories of the languages of the world usually list from three to four thousand spoken languages; in some parts of the world many of the smaller language communities are rapidly disappearing. Some languages are used by many millions of speakers and may serve for international communication; others are spoken by only a small number and may be on the verge of extinction. In each language community, the language is differentiated into regional and social dialects, and may be employed in various styles. All languages seem to have unlimited potentialities of expression, but they show differences in the degree to which they actually cover the total range of human culture. Early world travelers reported languages so limited that speech had to be eked out with gestures, so their users could converse only by day or by the campfire; but trained observers have found no such language.

Language has always been one of the major factors determining human group affiliations. Those who did not speak the mother tongue were considered barbarians and, for example, in the Book of Judges we are told that a different pronunciation of the word *shibboleth* was the cue for the slaughter of the Ephraimites. But not until the development of effective media for mass communication and the shrinkage of distances by modern means of transportation did language differences become a critical force in international politics. In modern history, the definition of nationality is most often linked with language, though Switzerland can be cited as an example of a harmonious multilingual state. In Hungary at the beginning of the nineteenth century, there was a deliberate development of a vocabulary based on Hungarian patterns in order to render the language capable of replacing Latin and the proposed German as official state languages; and in a few decades ten thousand new words were introduced into Hungarian. Similar trends can be observed at present in Ireland and Israel. At Versailles, the Austro-Hungarian Empire was divided along linguistic lines, though the use of the word "ethnic" obscures this fact. The Munich agreement advanced further the realization of the slogan "one language, one state"; and after the Second World War, the wholesale expulsion and relocation of minority groups led even closer to this questionable goal.

Examples can be multiplied. Just as in English-speaking countries the acquisition of correct spelling is a time-consuming and expensive part of the education of the individual, so in Norway a large part of the national energy is spent on the tense and active disputes between the proponents of two very closely related language forms: riksmål and landsmål, which are roughly correlated with the political attitudes of the Conservatives and the Left. In recent European history, Danzig, Trieste, and the Saar have been explosive danger spots where language issues were greatly exploited. The Indic subcontinent, which was divided into India and Pakistan primarily on religious grounds, is beset by language problems; in India in particular there has been violence and bloodshed over attempts to redraw the administrative map along linguistic lines. This indicates that language has precedence here over geographic and economic factors.

Nowhere is the political significance of language more evident than in the Soviet Union, which is a federation of fifteen republics corresponding to the major language differences within the state. Below this level there are further administrative units, defined linguistically, in a descending hierarchy. Although in the smaller areas linguistic units may be subordinated to economic ones, the linguistic principle pervades the entire state organization and is also expressed at the highest level in the Soviet of Nationalities. Since its very inception the Soviet regime, recognizing language as a major instrument in the dissemination of the Communist ideology and in the integration of the state, has pursued a conscious policy of language and script reform. The special role of language was expressly recognized in the Soviet linguistic controversy, during which Stalin declared language to be independent of the Marxist concepts of the economic base of society and its various superstructures.

Very often the use of a language is associated with a religion. Sometimes a language no longer in everyday use is preserved in ritual, as Latin is in the Roman Catholic Church. Sometimes script serves as an expression of social realities. The close relationship between script and religion is well known. In Yugoslavia, for instance, the antagonism between the Catholic Croats and the Orthodox Serbs, so clearly demonstrated in the Second World War, is paralleled by their use of Latin and Cyrillic characters respectively. In Turkey, the introduction of Latin letters in place of the Arabic script was a big step in a deliberate program of severing old religious ties and emphasizing a new orientation to the West.

As a result of growing understanding of the significance of language in political affairs and international communication, a new field in the study of language is emerging: political and areal linguistics.

Man has no special organ for language. Speech is formed in the tract which is designed primarily for two of the oldest biological functions, eating and breathing. And like any other sound, speech is received by the ear, phylogenetically the most recently acquired sensory receptor. The air used for speech is manipulated mainly in two cavities, the pulmonary and oral-pharyngal; between them there is a flexible bundle of muscles, the vocal folds, which produces the voice employed in speech and singing. Two other cavities, which do not play an active role in speech, are connected with them: the nasal passage, which is not modifiable; and a fourth cavity, formed by the esophagus and stomach, which is generally kept closed. (The latter is never used in normal speech, though in some societies it is used in belching to express appreciation of food; esophagal air is employed in speech by some persons who have undergone laryngectomy.)

The body of air which is used for the production of speech is usually set in motion, for the purpose of articulation, on the outgoing breath; however, this is not exclusively so. In Swedish, for example, especially among women, the word *ja*, "yes," is very often spoken on the in-breath. Also used in speech are additional minor mechanisms which operate independently of breathing, such as the manipulation of oral air in the production of the click sounds which occur as normal speech elements in certain aboriginal languages of South Africa. During speech the passages of the larynx and the uvula are narrowed and the muscles kept tensed; this is necessary to build up the pressure required for the production of sound. The oral opening is used with much more diversity. Different languages make use of the mouth in various ways: Danish oral articulation is slack; English is vigorous but largely limited to vertical movements; and in French there is a striking alternation between rounding and spreading of the lips. And, due to the absence of labial articulation in Iroquois, it is said that a speaker can smoke his pipe while he talks without producing any distortion in his speech. The enormous variety of speech sounds is created in the mouth cavity by fast-changing configurations of the various organs, the most mobile of which is the tongue. It is noteworthy that in many languages the word for tongue also means language in general.

Only a very small part of the information conveyed by speech, less than one per cent, is used for linguistic purposes as such; the rest gives other kinds of information: about the specific characteristics of the vocal tract of the speaker, which enable us to recognize his voice; about his physical well-being, for instance whether or not he has a cold; about his emotional state; and his attitudes toward the entire context in which the speech event occurs. It can also carry other information about the speaker, with reference to the conventions of social class, occasion, and style—from the quiet voice considered good form in certain educated classes, to the overenergetic mannerisms of delivery of the radio announcer and the preacher. Such differences may also reflect the demands of very special circumstances or be closely tied to a particular tradition. Thus a trilled tongue-tip r was required in the stage diction of the Comedie Française, when all Paris was using the uvular r.

The musculature of the chest and the larynx controls the more inclusive phenomena of speech, such as intonation, stress, duration; it also is responsible for the syllabification, a rhythmical pulsation with well-defined peaks which underlies all speech processes, and provides for the basic phonetic categories of vowel and consonant. These phenomena also depend upon the conventions of the particular language. For example, the word corresponding to Christ in Japanese, a language characterized by an almost even alternation of vowels and consonants, is a four-syllable word, Kurushito.

Though the vocal tract functions as a whole, some languages make greater use of one or another part of it; Arabic uses the pharyngal muscles for its peculiar fricatives and "emphatic" sounds; French, the nasal passage, not only for consonants but for vowels as well; Russian, the raising of the blade of the tongue in its conspicuous palatalized sounds; and Abkhaz, a language of the Caucasus, uses both tongue-raising and lip-rounding in its impressive array of palatalized, labialized, and labio-palatalized consonants.

The vocal organs have been compared to the instruments of an orchestra, with each organ that can move and vary its shape contributing its share to the total sound. Phonetic transcriptions have been devised in the form of a musical score in which the bars represent the articulating organs, and the notes the manners of articulation. (Phonetic transcriptions, aimed at recording any speech sound by a graphic symbol, are enlarged alphabetical systems with many diacritic signs.)

The movements of the articulatory organs produce both a stream of air, which is useless for speech, and a vibration of the air which is perceived as sound. The sound produced in the vocal tract is radiated into the outside air mainly through the mouth, but some of the signal is emitted from other parts of the body. The oscillations travel away from the speaker at the speed of sound, so that when for instance the word so is uttered, the beginning of the s sound is already 120 feet away by the time the o sound begins.

The spoken utterance is an impact on the atmosphere, very short in duration and on a very small scale, in which the component sounds die away at different distances depending on their inherent energy. The oscillations produced by this impact are of small dimensions. (The human ear can perceive sound vibrations having an amplitude of less than one-hundredth of the diameter of a hydrogen atom, the smallest movement that can be detected by any of our sense organs.) But these vibrations are of the utmost complexity. Acoustic analysis resolves this tortuous oscillation in a three-dimensional framework of frequency, intensity, and time, in which each sound is characterized by a typical display of energy in various frequency regions along the unlimited time axis. The physical representation of speech resembles a fantastic landscape, with ever-curving, ever-changing mountain-like formations, plateaus, and isolated hills.

In the last few years new and powerful tools have been developed which provide us with a deeper insight into important aspects of the speech process. The sound spectrograph is a device which transforms auditory into visual patterns. It readily and rapidly gives us information about the physical composition of speech sounds, which previously either was not obtainable or could be arrived at only through time-consuming calculations. Another device, the pattern playback, allows us to convert visible patterns into sound and makes it possible to evaluate the contribution of various features in making speech recognizable and understandable. X-ray sound motion pictures of the human vocal tract permit us to investigate in great detail the formation of the sound and to subject this event to physiological, physical, and psychological study. In the field of speech analysis, the future looks distinctly promising.

Syllabic pulsation and the prosodic features form the basis of versification, the predominant form of poetic expression in many cultures. But the function of verse is by no means purely aesthetic; old Germanic law was couched in verse to prevent alteration, and modern advertising, for example, often uses rhythmical jingles. Verse is the numerical regulation of the syllabic peaks within certain syntactic constructions. In some metric traditions there is the added use of features of pitch, stress, and duration, which correspond on the whole to the physical dimensions of frequency, intensity, and time. The simplest type of verse is the syllabic, as in Serbian. In quantitative verse like the Classical Greek, not only the number of syllabic peaks but also the distances between them are relevant; in English the meter is based on varying sequences of heavily or lightly stressed syllabic peaks; and in the poetry of the T'ang dynasty in China, the numerous tones of the language were grouped for metrical purposes into two classes, even and changing, and verse was a contrapuntal construction of these tonal classes.

The origin and the perception of the speech signal are not observable directly. The hearer can report only his subjective impressions; and the little we know about the processes by which speech comes into being is derived from the interpretation of such marginal phenomena as slips of the tongue, and from the study of speech disorders. It has been established, however, that the speaker's reception of his own speech, both by bone conduction and through his hearing, provides the necessary controlling circuit without which speech deteriorates. Such a deterioration can be observed in persons who have lost their hearing; and a person born deaf can never acquire normal speech.

If we examine the neural basis of speech the cortex of the brain seems to be connected with symbolic function. Observations made on the cortex during brain surgery have shown that the areas corresponding to organs such as the tongue and the hands, which are used in articulate communication in addition to their primary functions, are disproportionately larger than those areas of the cortex that correspond to other parts of the body. Though biological and symbolic functions are intimately interwoven here—a fact which may account for some of man's peculiar psychological disturbances—these clinical observations may perhaps be used as evidence that there is a physiological foundation for the all-pervasive role symbolic behavior plays in human existence.

There are certain problems which are the proper concern of both medicine and linguistics. There is an increasing recognition among physicians of the importance of the language factor in problems of diagnosis. In psychiatry, language has always been given central importance. And linguists would greatly profit from careful medical investigations of speech disorders, especially the various types of aphasia, for a deeper understanding of the layers of internal organization cf language.

Knowledge about language did not advance beyond the mythical and magical stage until some centuries before Christ. At this time the Sanskrit grammarians, for religious reasons, designed a marvelous framework to preserve their sacred tongue unchanged; and the Greek grammarians, motivated more by philosophical and philological interests, constructed the system on which our school grammar is still to a large extent based. This study remained narrowly restricted to a few prestige languages, however, until the Age of Discovery, when explorers, conquerors, and missionaries assembled and made public a large mass of linguistic material from all over the world. Around the end of the eighteenth century a significant part of this material was evaluated by comparative linguistics. The major language families were established and the chronological perspective introduced. First, the genetic relationship among Hungarian, Finnish, and Lappish, which lay on the outskirts of Western Europe, was demonstrated and the Uralic language family recognized. This was followed by the recognition of other language families, primarily Indo-European which includes languages spoken over vast areas of the globe and of great cultural and political significance. Then later in the nineteenth century, in line with the era of historicism, the underlying regularity of language change was shown by the methods of historical linguistics, perhaps the only field in the social sciences in which such regularities have been so clearly demonstrated. (The recently developed technique of glotto-chronology, using about one hundred common words as a basis of comparison, aims to determine more exactly the time depth corresponding to differences among languages.)

In the nineteenth and twentieth centuries an enormous increase in information about various languages was brought forth by philology, dialect geography, phonetics, and anthropological field work. The treatment of the material was neither uniform nor consistent, however, and it was not until about a quarter of a century ago that structuralism, the most modern trend in linguistics in both Europe and America, introduced for the first time a universally applicable method for the description of all languages. The major results of structuralism have been in the analysis of the spoken utterance—but it has also brought results in semantics, as well as in historical and comparative linguistics.

The methodological principles underlying structuralism can be stated as follows. Language is to be analyzed according to specifically linguistic criteria, and is not to be regarded as a conglomerate of disparate physical, physiological, and psychological phenomena. This analysis arrives at a definite number of discrete units, which provide for the quantization of the stream of the utterance. These units are interdependent parts of a relational structure, and each language is characterized by an internal order of its own which is imposed upon the physical and behavioral phenomena and organizes these into linguistic categories.

The new insights are utilized for practical purposes, for example, in language teaching and in Bible translation. The concepts of structural linguistics have also been employed to some extent in other fields of inquiry: the study of literature, especially metrics, and ethnography, especially folklore. There is also considerable interest in interdisciplinary studies involving structural linguistics, as in psycholinguistics and ethno-linguistics.

What then is the blueprint of language design like?

All utterances of a language, from short greetings to long speeches, consist of one or more sentences of varying degrees of complexity.

The sentence is the largest unit within which there is an organization imposed by the conventions of the language. The parts of any given sentence do not figure in the syntactic constructions of any other; though some elements may refer forward or backward—for instance certain pronouns—each is an integral part of the sentence in which it occurs. The sentences may be marked by a special intonation or pause; however such features are optional in some languages. The internal organization of the sentence ranges from the careful formulation used in scientific discourse to the endlessly overlapping waves of Molly Bloom's monologue in Joyce's *Ulysses*.

Linguists today use two concepts, the *morpheme* and the *phoneme*, to account for the structure of the sentence. These units, together with the rules of their arrangement, technically known as *distribution*, enable the linguist to describe any utterance.

The morpheme is the smallest element with which meaning can be associated, and it is characterized by a specific distribution. In the following example the morpheme divisions are indicated by hyphens:

The-cat-s-are-purr-ing

A morpheme may appear in varying phonetic shapes—for instance, *knife* in the singular but *knives* in the plural. The concept of the morpheme enables the linguist to use a single ascending hierarchy of operations to account for higher syntactic constructions. (The word, which was a focal concept in traditional linguistics, is no longer considered basic by many linguists; it may perhaps be defined for all languages as a construct characterized by inner coherence and stability.) Compounds such as *lighthouse*, phrases such as *the big bad wolf*, clauses such as *that he is coming*, and finally, sentences, all are higher order constructions composed of morphemes. These constructions are frequently marked by certain phonetic features, such as stress or intonation, which indicate the distinction between different levels of the syntactic hierarchy, as the stress pattern differentiates between *blackbird* and *black bird*. As a rule, such groupings are constructed according to very simple principles: most often two units of one level are grouped together to form a unit at the next higher level, and so on up to the sentence. For example, the structure of the line in "The Tyger" of Blake is as follows:

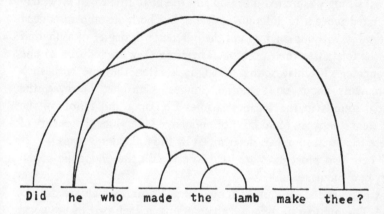

Did   he   who   made   the   lamb   make   thee ?

All morphemes are made up of phonemes, with the exception of marginal sound-gestures like the bilabial trill used when shivering: *Brrr!*. The concept of the phoneme, the cornerstone of structural linguistics, was operationally defined only a few decades ago, although it has been tacitly recognized ever since man began to reduce speech to writing, as consonantal and alphabetic scripts indicate. Each language organizes in a specific way the sounds it utilizes, and each language uses only a definite number of phonemes. Modern linguistics compares different fractions of utterances to discover the *significant contrasts* utilized by any given language. For instance, in English the final sounds in *cat* and *cap* distinguish two utterances which differ in meaning, and are therefore said to be phonemically distinctive; no such distinction can be attached to the difference between the final sounds in varying pronunciations of *cat*, one with a released, the other with a non-released *t*.

The procedure of establishing whether or not two sounds are phonemically different in identical positions is supplemented by a second which enables the linguist to subsume under one phonemic unit sounds occurring in different positions. In order to carry out this operation, it is required that these sounds share a unique phonetic feature, and that their differences can be accounted for in terms of their position relative to other sounds. For instance, the initial strongly aspirated p in pop and the final unreleased or weakly aspirated p occur in different positions; but both are stops produced at the lips without voicing, and the difference in degree of aspiration can be related to their position. Therefore they are reduced to one phoneme. This may sound trivial, as is often the case with such statements about one's mother tongue. Consider, however, the initial sounds in the Japanese names *Fujiyama* and *Hirohito;* the difference between f and h is not phonemic here, since the quality of these frictional sounds is determined by the following vowels.

These two procedures are used to establish the phonemic inventory of a language.

A phoneme is the sum of those sound features which are distinctive. The number of different articulations in each part of the vocal tract utilized for contrastive purposes in any given language is extremely limited; the choice is usually between two alternatives. For instance, there could be a continuous range of vibration of the vocal cords from full voicing to the lack of it, but there are no known cases where there is more than one contrast in voicing. The relation between these simple alternatives is called *opposition*, and a term in such an opposition is called a *distinctive feature*, which is the minimal unit in the structure of speech. The number of these oppositions is very small; it is less than a dozen in any known language. The inventory of the distinctive features and the way in which each participates in the total system is unique to a given language. Thus, in Cantonese tone contrasts distinguish morphemes, while in English tone differences serve only to mark clause types; on the other hand, voicing in English serves to distinguish morphemes, but in Cantonese all stops and fricatives are voiceless and all other sounds voiced, so that voicing is not distinctive.

Thus the structure of language symbols exhibits a pervasive economy. A few distinctive features are combined into a few dozen phonemes which have no intrinsic meaning. Certain combinations of these phonemes form a few thousand morphemes which refer to various segments of our experience, including language itself. Stable morphemic constructions, the lexical items which are listed in dictionaries, occur in all languages and greatly outnumber the morphemes. The morphemes and morpheme constructions are then combined into sentences, the number of which is nonlimited, and which can be correlated to a nonlimited repertory of experience. A free flow of sentences then comprises the complete utterance. This multistage, three-level construction involving phonemes, morphemes, and sentences characterizes natural language. The single-word, or better, single-morpheme sentences of the young child—who uses phonemes, but does not combine words into sentences—and the cries of animals, which, however numerous and varied, cannot be analyzed into phonemes nor combined into sentences, do not represent full language.

In some languages the morphemes show very little variation, as in Mandarin. In others morphemes behave like chameleons, taking many shapes according to the particular environment. Morphemes are combined into cohesive sequences in a variety of ways. Thus Turkish attaches a string of subordinate morphemes to an initial root; —e.g., from the root *sev-*, "to love," can be formed *sevistirilemedikle-rinden*. (This word is jokingly said to express the whole cause of the Crimean war: "because of their not having been able to be made mutually to love one another.") Still other languages intercalate morphemes into interlocking constructions: for instance, Egyptian Arabic combines *k-t-b*, "write," with the in-fixed elements *a-a*, to form *katab*, "he wrote," and with *u-u* to form *kutub*, "books." Syntactic constructions are sometimes marked by an agreement as onerous as the German gender or as monotonous as the Latin *illorum magnorum virorum*. In certain languages the whole sentence is constructed in a single syntactic key according to the class of things spoken of, as in Ilamba of Northern Rhodesia:

> mōnto wākoe mokōlu omoe wakakēla ekāna
> "His one big man is greater than the child."

kēnto kiakoe kekōlu kemoe kiamekēla enomba
"His one big thing is greater than the house."

The phonemic system also shows variety from language to language. Some languages have a very small inventory of phonemes—thus Hawaiian has only five vowels and six consonants; at the other extreme, Abkhaz, spoken in the Caucasus, has sixty-eight consonants and just two vowels. The number of phonemes in most languages is about two or three dozen. The arrangements of these phonemes again differs from language to language. Egyptian Arabic requires a consonant at the beginning of the utterance; Vogul of Western Siberia, the closest relative of Hungarian, does not tolerate initial consonant clusters; Finnish vowel harmony requires that the back vowels and the corresponding front vowels should not occur together in basic morphemic constructions. In Kabardian, also of the Caucasus, the order of articulation in consonant clusters—except for an initial sibilant—must be from the lips backward. Extremely long consonant clusters occur in Georgian, another language of the Caucasus: vbrdgvinav, "I roar." Some languages use initial clusters, like mb, which appear strange to us, but would not allow sp. In some languages whole sentences may occasionally be constructed of consonants alone, as in the Czech sentence: Strč prst skrz krk. "Stick a finger through the throat." (The r-sounds are the syllabic peaks in this sentence.)

The increasing amount of well analyzed material makes possible the construction of a refined framework for the typological characterization and classification of the languages of the world. In addition, observations of a general nature begin to emerge. Among these may be mentioned: the fact that languages are extravagantly restrictive in their employment of the potential combinations of phonemes and morphemes; that there is a well established order in the sequence in which the child acquires the sounds of his mother tongue; and that certain linguistic features are distributed over wide geographical areas, irrespective of genetic affiliations—such as, in the Balkans, the occurrence of the definite article in final position, and the absence of an *l–r* distinction in most languages of the Far East.

The numerical and statisical characteristics of the language signal are also receiving an increasing amount of attention. Mathematical linguistics, using the results of information theory, is discovering numerical regularities underlying language: the very high redundancy in English resulting from the restrictions on phoneme combinations, which provides a margin of safety for the comprehension of the message; the simple mathematical function which exists between the frequency at which a certain number of words occur in a long text and the number of words which occur at this frequency; and the statistical properties of the choice of words which characterizes the style of a given writer. This last method, for instance, has provided corroborative evidence that Thomas à Kempis was the author (or perhaps the editor) of the *Imitation of Christ*.

The structure of meaning, because of its greater complexity, relative inaccessibility, and integration with all experience, is not so well understood as is the structure of the signal. However, there has been definite progress in semantic theory. The arbitrary connection between meaning and the sign vehicle is generally recognized. We have not as yet achieved a grasp of the over-all semantics of language, which is presented under the two traditional headings of the grammar and the dictionary which to a certain degree overlap. Grammar treats the compulsory categories, the framework into which a large part of the language material is molded, and the lexical items single out aspects of our experience.

Morphemes and morpheme-constructions are connected to what they signify in an arbitrary and purely conventional way; if this were not so, all mankind would use only one language. Similar sounds may stand for different things in different languages, and, in the case of homonyms, they may mean different things in the same language. Even sound-imitative words vary: thus the English *splash* corresponds to Hungarian *loccsan*. These are constructed according to the same principles as the other words of the language, though occasionally some of them are unusual, like *pssst* or *cockadoodledoo*. Interjections also, though we think of them as spontaneous, are dictated by linguistic convention; a Frenchman is more likely to say *ai* when a German would say *au*, and an Englishman perhaps *ouch*. Beyond language proper, the gestures accompanying speech are also conventionalized, and the vividness and variety of gesticulation differ from one area to another. A nod of the head may mean yes or no, and a body posture which simply indicates proper respect in one cultural setting may be interpreted as hostility in another.

The arbitrary and conventional nature of language symbols shows clearly that any word can stand for any notion, a fact that is further corroborated by etymological research. The results of such research, though often uncertain, can reveal surprising origins. *Kangaroo* is a perfectly good name for the animal; it does not matter to the speaker whether it is true that "kangaroo" was the answer given by a native, when asked by Captain Cook for the name of the strange beast, and that it meant simply "I don't know." The English word *person* which expresses individuality as such to us, goes back to the Latin *persona*—from which we also get our word *parson*—and it referred to the mask worn by an actor in a play; here it was the mark not of the individual, but of a conventionalized type. Words can originate in many ways; for instance *snob* may have been originally an abbreviation for *sine nobilitate*, written after a name in the registry of fashionable English schools to indicate that the bearer of the name was a commoner. And "Pakistan" was made up of elements taken from the names of the five western provinces: the initials of *Panjab*, *Afghania*, *Kashmir*, and *Sindh*, and the final part of *Baluchistan*.

With reference to the semantic spectrum of lexical items, we know that some words have a concrete and definite reference while others have a less easily defined range of application. We also know that the use of metaphorical transfer is correlated with associative ties in our sensory perceptions and is reflected in the way lexical items are used. For instance, *soft*, primarily referring to substances or textures, and *sweet*, primarily a property of taste, are both used in describing sound qualities. Language is sometimes called a cemetery of dead metaphors. The outlines of the organization of the vocabulary into semantic fields begin to emerge as we take into account not the isolated meanings, but their mutual interrelations. In addition, we begin to understand the general orientation and organization of the vocabulary.

For polar opposites, for instance, some languages have a pair of terms—good-bad, beautiful-ugly—as does English; others have a single designation for the whole dimension, like Latin *altus*, "deep" or "high"; still others take one term of the opposition as basic and express the opposite by its negation. Thus in some Eskimo dialects the negative concept is taken as the point of departure—perhaps as protective magic—and the positive term is derived by its negation, "beautiful," for instance, being expressed as "not-ugly." Some languages treat the dual sensory organs as a unit; in Hungarian, for instance, the two eyes are expressed in the singular, and a single eye as "half-eye." In some languages there are differences in a large part of the vocabulary for various groups of users; in Thai, there is an intricate system of honorifics involving frequent reference to the social relationship between the speaker and the addressee; in Yana, an Indian language of California, men and women use an entirely different vocabulary. All languages show an abundance of terms relating to areas of experience which are of particular concern to the members of the culture: like the extensive terminology in Lappish for the reindeer, in Classical Arabic for the camel, and in Eskimo for snow—and in our culture, the vocabulary of the sailor and the automobile mechanic. Some stimulating work has been done showing that certain closed and well defined fields within the vocabulary, such as kinship terminology and terms for spatial relations, can be resolved into a few semantic features in analogy with the dissolution of the phoneme into distinctive features.

The grammatical relations are much better understood than the semantics of the lexicon; and it is in the field of grammatical analysis that modern structural methods have proven most fruitful. The grammatical categories pervade the entire language, and lend to each its distinctive character. These categories vary from language to language. The notion of number, for instance, may be presented in terms of a singular-plural dichotomy, or there may be other special categories of number such as dual or trial; or the category of number may not be expressed in the grammar at all, but in the lexicon. Hungarian, for instance, has two number categories: one for unspecified plurality, and the other for specified number including singularity and numerically explicit plurality; thus, when the speaker wishes to say "nine men" he uses the second category and says something like "nine man," *kilenc ember.* (By expressing number only once in the construction, Hungarian has less redundancy than, say, English.) Some languages distinguish between two kinds of *we,* one including the person or persons addressed and the other excluding them. The missionary who said that "we" will be punished for "our" sins, using the wrong kind of *we,* was rewarded with more sympathy than converts.

Language influences the total psychological makeup of man. The influence of language categories upon behavior was demonstrated, for instance, when color-recognition tests were given to both Zuni and English speakers. The members of each group did better at recognizing colors for which their language had a specific designation. But the influence of the native language may be more pervasive than the naming of experiences. It is reported, for instance, that in an experiment where three staccato beats of equal intensity were presented to a Czech, a Pole, and a Frenchman, these were interpreted by them in accordance with the stress-pattern of their respective mother tongues. The Czech, whose languages stresses the first syllable of the word, said the first beat was strongest; the Frenchman, whose language has terminal stress, heard the last beat as loudest; while the Pole, in whose language the last syllable but one is stressed, chose the middle beat as the strongest.

The exact role of language in thinking and logic is unknown. Though linguistic analysis and logical analysis have developed from a common ground, and nominalistic philosophies have constantly reappeared in the history of philosophy, the frequent assertion that "if Aristotle had been a Mexican, our logic would have been different" seems to rest on dubious grounds. Serious questions may also arise in connection with the currently popular speculation about the extent to which language determines our world view. It seems reasonable to believe that the habitual patterns of the mother tongue have a strong effect upon the behavior of the individual; but it is also clear that language is not a straitjacket, and that beyond the formation of expressions dictated by linguistic tradition, new creation is constantly taking place—in poetry, in science, and in everyday usage.

A glance at the communicative system of the bees serves to give us another perspective on human language. As von Frisch's marvelous observations and experiments have shown, bees are able to communicate information to each other about the distance and direction of places where nectar or pollen are abundant, and also the quality of these; and in addition, during swarming, the location of a suitable new home.

Nectar and pollen are directly transmitted in small samples to the other bees; distance and direction are indicated by an alternately rotating movement which is like a dance. The closer the food, the faster the dance; the farther away, the slower. A distance of 100 meters is represented by 38 turns per minute, a distance of 6 kilometers by 8 turns per minute. If the distance is more than 75 meters, the direction is also given, by a wiggling motion of the abdomen. The angle by which this wiggling deviates from the vertical indicates the direction in which the other bees must fly, using the sun as their point of orientation. If the honeycomb is not vertical, the dancing bee points directly towards the place where the food is to be found, provided the insect can see any part of the open sky; but the information conveyed by this method is less accurate. If neither gravity nor the sky afford guidance, the bee points helplessly at random. If there is an obstacle such as a mountain, extra flying time is added for the route around it; and if a wind is blowing, the additional time needed to reach the goal is indicated. In swarming, when many scouts are sent out, their verdict must be unanimous before the swarm will take possession of the new home.

The story of how the "language" of the bees was discovered is also very interesting, and may be instructive to those linguists who exclude the study of meaning from linguistics proper. In 1923 von Frisch was able to observe and describe in accurate detail the dance of the bees. After his first hypothesis was refuted, that of a two-word code, with the round dance standing for pollen and the wiggling dance for the nectar, the dance was interpreted as a symptom of general excitement, without further meaning. In 1946, however, von Frisch himself was able to prove that the dance represented a method of conveying very explicit information.

This communication system is ingenious in its simplicity. It uses sampling for nectar and pollen and a kind of transfer-mapping for distance and direction. It is straightforward; only the disturbance of normal conditions or deliberate interference by a human observer can cause confusion, and falsehood does not occur. It is functional; it serves the basic needs of the society for food, storage, and shelter.

At the same time it is a closed system; no new signal types can be added, no new types of information are conceivable. It is stereotyped, and in all probability involves no learning. No conversation is possible; only directives can be given. If confusion arises, no corrections can be made. Its effectiveness is restricted to the few bees that can be in direct contact with the body of the dancing bee. No time perspective can be indicated; the dance always refers to the immediate present. And, in spite of the fact that the system of communication in all the varieties of bees is fundamentally the same —with minor "dialectal" variations—the transfer of information from hive to hive takes place only rarely, when a messenger strays into an alien hive.

Such a system would not suffice for the vast and complex needs of human society. Though something like the technique of sampling is detectable in onomatopoetic words, it would be impossible, in a Swiftian scheme to dispense with symbols by displaying the things meant, to carry samples of everything to which the speaker might have occasion to refer. A mapping procedure is probably involved as the amorphous complex of thought and feeling unfolds in time and is projected upon the sequence of the linguistic elements—but the order of these is highly conventionalized. The essential means of human communication is the symbol.

There is no set limit to the number of symbolic elements in a language. Symbols can be added, mixed, borrowed, or newly created in any language; they can also shift their center of reference. The ability of English to absorb foreign elements is well known. This capacity of adding symbols without any set limit is a practical necessity, since the functions in which language is employed are similarly nonlimited.

Language serves as the vehicle of abstract thought, exalted mysticism, and poetic inspiration—but it is used as well in the ravings of a maniac and the mutterings of a drunkard. It is expressed overtly in speech and writing, it also occurs subvocally in thinking to oneself. It is stable enough to make understanding and continuity secure; it is flexible enough to permit adaptation to new circumstances.

Language serves many uses, and the clear-cut referential aspect is only one of them. Hence, it is an illusion to hold that a clarification of the semantic sphere would be a panacea, as the General Semanticists claim. The resolution of the differences in the use of the word "democracy"—an international fetish word—would not alleviate the tension between opposing political systems. Various attempts at an international language like Esperanto or Basic English either end up as incomplete replicas of natural languages or as primitive pidginizations. It would also be an illusion to believe that scientific languages could be developed independently of natural language. All scientific languages, such as mathematical symbolism, are necessarily "parasitic" superstructures on natural language, and the clarification achieved in the semantic sphere is paid for in limitation of scope and function. The possibility, suggested by an eminent mathematician, that children might be taught the language of Russell and Whitehead's *Principia Mathematica*, is certainly not workable.

Though communication between speakers of one and the same

language provides the opportunity for optimal understanding, the possibility of translation from one language to another permits communication within limits among all language communities. Due to the flexibility of language, and its potentialities for expansion, there is apparently no predefined limit to the kinds of experiences that may be communicated. However, as U.N. translators observe, different languages seem to imply different attitudes—the English pattern is said to be pragmatic and inductive, the French generalizing and deductive, the Russian intuitional and particular. These differences make the common approach to a problem difficult but do not in themselves preclude a solution. And Bible translators, who are faced with the problem of transposing texts embodying a Jewish-Christian ideology and reflecting a special ancient culture in its Mediterranean setting into languages associated with the most differing societies, usually find an expression which approximates the intent of the original by mobilizing the resources of the language collective. Thus Luther, whose Bible contributed enormously to the development of German, instructs the translator in his famous *Sendbrief:* "One must ask the mother in the house, the children in the street, the common man in the market-place, and watch their mouths as they talk, and translate thereafter; then people understand it, and know that one speaks to them in their [mother tongue]."

Symbols, however, demand their sacrifice. Because of their enormous number and complexity, symbolic systems are difficult to master; and, as Talleyrand remarked, they can serve the purposes of disguising thought as well as those of clarifications. Words may assume a magical importance, and symbols and names may carry on a substitute existence. In modern India, a large animal called the "blue cow" was renamed the "blue horse" so that its name would not remind people of the sacred cow, and it could be killed to protect the crops. The world is supposed to have been created by the Word, and the name of Jahveh could be spoken only once a year. Names may carry emotional significance, as do the assumed names in the higher echelons of the Soviet hierarchy. And a change in name may reflect an important change in the relationship of the individual to his social environment; witness the cataclysmic name changes given in the Bible—Saul to Paul, Jacob to Israel—and the frequent practice of taking a new name at the turning points of the life-cycle of the individual in primitive societies. A slogan, easily expressed in simple linguistic form, like the "four-minute mile" in track, can be instrumental in setting up a particular goal, fervently sought after by many athletes. In countries using the metric system, different goals are set for field and track events—goals which are within reach and which can find an easy expression.

Though there are no set limits to what language can speak about, there is one sphere of knowledge which, like the elusive white whale, will always remain unattainable because of the nature of symbols: the exploration of what can be proven by language. Gödel has shown in his famous theorem, in which the mathematical form is a particular kind of language symbolism, that however one shifts or broadens the array of symbols, there will always be black nebulae in the cosmos of language which can never be illuminated.

Thus linguistics, which deals with expression and communication, is a basic science along with those which deal with truth and knowledge, individual and social experience, and the nature of our physical and biological environment. It does not have a decisive voice in the council of the disciplines as the nominalists claim, but neither does it deal with a subordinate and negligible tool as the realists assert. It has a vital contribution to make in the analysis of the role that language by necessity plays in every science. Linguistics differs from all other disciplines in that its topic is language itself, while for the others language is a mere vehicle; but it has in common with all of them the fact that it too is presented through language.

15

MATHEMATICS

The *"Empty" Science*

by Anatol Rapoport

M ATHEMATICS exhibits one of the most curious aspects of the human mind. Most sciences are defined by their subject matter. Mathematics is defined by its method. Indeed, if by subject matter is meant a class of events, like "the living process" (the preoccupation of the biologist) or "the production and exchange of commodities" (the concern of the economist), then mathematics has no subject matter at all.

To be sure, old fashioned text books say that mathematics deals with numbers and magnitudes, but such a description misses the point. It is possible to deal with numbers without any idea of what mathematics is about. We now have machines that do the most complicated computations with unimaginable speed, but these machines are not mathematicians. On the other hand, it is commonplace for a great mathematician to have trouble in adding up a grocery check. Reckoning is not mathematics.

It has not always been this way, and the only means of understanding the new departures in mathematical thinking is to see clearly how we got where we are. There was a time when reckoning and measuring were all there was to mathematics. But there was also a time when the strongest and bravest were the best warriors. That time has passed. The whole concept of war has changed from a match of physical strength in battle to a vast coordination of production, transportation, diabolical invention, and diplomacy, and so the old concept of the warrior has disappeared. In mathematics it was a similar story. The whole concept of mathematics has changed. The modern mathematician has no resemblance to his prototype who was clever at numbers and at surveying.

If numbers and magnitude are not the chief themes of mathematics, what are? As we said, mathematics has no subject matter. Bertrand Russell was not joking when he remarked that in mathematics we never know what we are talking about nor whether what we are saying is true. He meant it literally. How, then, if one takes Russell's epigram seriously, is one to avoid the notion that mathematics is an empty pursuit? If mathematics is as ambiguous as Russell's statement seems to imply, how is one to understand the eulogies which hail mathematics as the proudest achievement of the human mind and the assertions of some philosophers that God must be a mathematician?

The key to this paradox is found in the nature of abstraction and of symbols. Once one understands the nature of abstraction, one fathoms the soul of mathematics, and when one understands what mathematics is truly about, one cannot help exclaiming "What hath man wrought!"

Think of a small child's conception of a game of chess. The child sees the game as two people facing a checkered board, on which they shift the positions of the pieces. The child imagines that he too "plays chess" as he moves the pieces around on the board. After a while (probably not before the eighth year on the average) the child can be made to understand that he is not really playing chess unless he follows certain rules. But only considerably later the idea sinks in that the pieces and the board are not necessary. The rules are the game. A chess game reported in the newspaper consists simply of letters and numbers indicating the moves, which need not have reference to any physical objects at all, but are only communcative symbols.

This progressive emancipation of concepts from particular situations depends on the maturation of a certain ability peculiar to human beings, the ability to abstract, that is, to perceive *relations* quite apart from the objects which are related. This ability appears also in the progressive mastery of language by the child. A young boy who has one brother, if asked "Have you a brother?" will say "Yes." But if asked "Has your brother a brother?" he may well say "No." He still does not think of *himself* as his brother's brother. He is he; the brother the brother. Only later he comes to understand that "brother" does not have to be any one in particular. "Brother" is not a name of a person; it is a name of a relation among persons. Abstraction, then, involves the ability to think and reason about relations apart from the things which are related. The maturation of mathematical ability follows a similar course.

First, there is counting, always with something to count. Two oranges and three oranges make five oranges. Two bicycles and three bicycles make five bicycles. It is an immense feat of abstraction to realize that two of *anything* and three of the same make five of the same. And since "anything" is nothing in particular, there is no point in mentioning it at all. Two and three make five. We still have words in our language inherited from a distant past when this leap into abstraction had not yet been made. We say a married *couple*, a *pair* of shoes, a *team* of horses, *twin* sisters, *double*-u, and, if we want to be fancy, a *brace* of pheasants. All these words mean "two." The many words for "two" indicate that the words were in use before the common meaning of "two" in all the different contexts was recognized. There is no such multiplicity of names for "thirty-six," probably because we learned to count only after we could abstract number from the objects counted. There are still people in remote places whose only counting words are "one," "two," and "many."

The concept of number as something apart from and independent of the objects with which it is associated is then the first step in mathematics. Once we have torn the numbers away from the objects and from such intermediate aids as fingers or pebbles, we attain much greater freedom in manipulating numbers. You can't divide seven cows evenly among thirteen men as long as you think of whole cows. But once seven ceases to be a number of objects and becomes a "magnitude," you can slice it as finely as you wish. Fractions are born. If you think of how much money you have, you cannot imagine having less than nothing. But if you abstract from "money" to "assets and liabilities," you can represent your "worth" by a magnitude which is less than nothing (if liabilities exceed your assets). Negative numbers are born.

The abstraction from objects is now complete, but now the numbers themselves appear as particular things with particular names. Any statements made about particular numbers will pertain to those only and not necessarily to others. Now the way forward in any science is toward a situation where more and more *general* statements can be made, that is, statements pertaining to more and more things simultaneously. The mental mechanism which makes this possible is abstraction. After arithmetic abstracted numbers from their context, algebra performed the next step of abstraction by divorcing symbols for numbers from particular numbers, so that a symbol could stand for any number. Let us see how this is done.

When I write $3+5=5+3$, I am saying that whether I add 5 to 3 or 3 to 5, I get the same result. But when I say $a+b=b+a$, I am saying that if I add two numbers (any two numbers), I get the same sum whether I add the second to the first or vice versa. To take a somewhat more complicated example, if I say $(5+3)(5-3)=5^2-3^2$, I am saying that the sum of 5 and 3 multiplied by their difference is the same as the difference of their squares. You can verify this and obtain 16 in both cases. But when I say $(a+b)(a-b)=a^2-b^2$, I am saying that the sum of any two numbers multiplied by their difference is the same as the difference of their squares.

If now you ask, "How do you know?" you invite an answer about the very nature of mathematics. So let us pursue this question. How do I know that $(a+b)(a-b)=a^2-b^2$? If I were worried about whether this was true, I could proceed to verify the statement by substituting "any" two numbers for a and b. We have seen that it is true for 5 and 3. Let us try 17 and 11. The product of the sum and difference is $28 \times 6 = 168$. The difference of the squares is $289 - 121 = 168$. It works. Let us try with two "ones." The product of the sum and difference is $2 \times 0 = 0$; the difference of the squares is $1 - 1 = 0$. It works again. If you are still in doubt, try two fractions, say $\frac{2}{3}$ and $\frac{1}{2}$. I assure you, you will get the same result.

Now does this settle the matter? If not, how many pairs of numbers shall we try before we can say with certainty that the formula $(a+b)\,(a-b) = a^2 - b^2$ is true in all cases? Let us see how we answer a similar question in other situations? How many times will you put your finger in the fire before you come to the conclusion that fire is hot? How many times must a chemist perform an experiment to be assured of the result? Your answers to such questions may be "once," "twice," or "many times." Experience may or may not justify your answers. But a mathematician gives an entirely different answer to such questions. Verification in special cases is never sufficient to establish the truth of a general mathematical statement, unless *all* cases have been verified.

Since we obviously cannot try all pairs of numbers to test our formula (there is an infinity of numbers), it follows that verification of the formula can never establish its truth for a mathematician. In this respect, the mathematician differs from all other scientists. The biologist, for example, having observed that in all observed instances rats give birth to rats and never to mice, and so on for other species, is able to assert his general proposition: Each organism reproduces after his own kind. When a chemist says that acids and bases react to produce water and salts; when the economist says that when a product which is in demand becomes rare, its price generally rises, they are stating generalizations from experience. True, if they are devoted to the spirit of science they will always have some reservations about any such general statements. They will be ready to modify them in the face of new evidence. However, in the face of repeated and consistent verification, a general statement in any science except mathematics will be at least provisionally accepted as "true." This method of establishing truth logicians call "induction," that is, arguing from many particular cases to the more general assertion. Because mathematics is not bound to the particular, this method is prohibited in mathematics. It violates the mathematician's rules of evidence. The only way a mathematical truth can be established (except where all cases can be verified, which is rarely) is by "deduction," that is, by arguing from the general to the particular.

To return to our example, the truth of the statement $(a+b)$ $(a-b) = a^2 - b^2$ cannot be established from any number of verifications with particular numbers. It can be established from the more general rules of addition and multiplication. These state that to multiply $(a+b)(a-b)$, you sum all the paired products, affixing to each its proper sign (*plus* if both members of the pair are of like sign, *minus* otherwise), thus: $a^2 - ab + ba - b^2$. Furthermore, $ab = ba$, so that $ab - ba = 0$. This leaves $a^2 - b^2$. The crucial feature of this proof is that the particular numbers for which *a* and *b* may stand *never entered the argument*. The reasoning holds no matter what numbers *a* and *b* stand for. Therefore it becomes unnecessary to verify the formula in any particular case to establish its truth.

The preceding example was from algebra. Indeed, much of algebra deals with establishing the results of operating on any numbers in a prescribed way. However, the earliest recognition of the nature of deductive proof and its role in mathematics appeared not in algebra but in geometry; so let us turn our attention to geometry.

The word "geometry" comes from the Greek words for "earth" and "measurement." It is said that geometry developed first as an art of determining land areas. We are told that it arose in ancient Egypt in response to the need of establishing field boundaries after they were erased by the annual overflows of the Nile. Now, just as reckoning was once simply a skill, involving only "know-how," not "know why," so was geometry. Many rules were known by which to compute lengths, areas, and volumes. The Egyptians knew that the area of a rectangular field equals the length times the width, that the circumference of the circle is about $3\frac{1}{7}$ times the diameter, that the volume of a pyramid is the area of the base times $\frac{1}{3}$ the height, etc.

We say this knowledge involved only "know-how," not "know-why," because the rules were not proved but only tested. This is not to say that "know-how" is in any way "inferior" knowledge. To a people engaged in the pyramid-building business for fifteen centuries, knowledge of how to compute the volume of a pyramid must have been important, proof or no proof. However, as a *mathematical* achievement much more impressive is the early knowledge of the Babylonians who, more than a thousand years before Pythagoras and Euclid, were acquainted with general theorems such as that the angle inscribed in a semicircle is a right angle, or the theorem for which Pythagoras later became famous. This general intellectual interest of those early Mesopotamian mathematicians, as opposed to the practical problems of weighing, finding volumes, or computing areas, is shown by their search for methods of determining numbers satisfying the Pythagorean relation, $A^2 + B^2 = C^2$.

In Greece, the whole approach to geometry was different. The Greeks "built" their geometry. The "bricks" were the propositions (or theorems, as they were called) and the mortar was logic. Greek geometry was as different from the Egyptian as a temple is different from a pile of bricks. The foundation of their "temple" consisted of a few simple propositions, which they thought were "self-evident." Thus it seemed impossible to deny that the shortest line between two points is a straight line; that if the same quantity is subtracted from two equal quantities, the remainders are equal, etc. Starting with these "postulates" (statements about primitive geometric notions) and "axioms" ("self-evident" statements about relations among quantities), Greek mathematicians proved more complicated statements about geometric figures, that is, they showed by means of logical argument that if one accepted the truth of the postulates and the axioms, one must accept the truth of the theorems. Then, using the propositions thus proved as "stepping stones" of reasoning, they proved still more complicated ones. Theirs was a process not unlike our building complicated machinery from manufactured parts. The parts are put together in subassemblies; these are united into assemblies, etc. Each step of the process starts where the last left off, making possible a division of labor and therefore an increase in complexity and efficiency. In the same way the introduction of the deductive method stimulated the rapid growth of mathematical knowledge. Such growth is not possible if knowledge depends on mere accumulation of facts and rules. The memory capacity of a single person is limited, and even if storage facilities (such as catalogues and libraries) are available, their usefulness diminishes as the bulk of accumulated information becomes unwieldy. If you want to get a feeling for the difference between logically connected and arbitrarily gathered information, try to memorize a hundred-word speech (the Declaration of Independence through "the pursuit of happiness" is 106 words) and then try to memorize one hundred randomly selected words and see the difference in the work involved.

Again it is time for an illustration. Let us prove the simplest of the propositions of geometry. If two straight lines intersect, the vertical angles are equal.

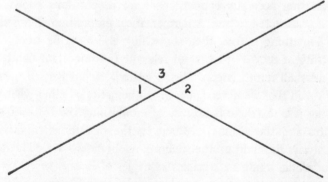

In the figure, one pair of vertical angles is labeled "1" and "2." Angles are measured by how much of a circle they span. Conventionally the circle is divided into 360 degrees, so that a "straight" angle, that is, one whose arms make a straight line and thus span half a circle, has 180 degrees. To prove the proposition, we need two axioms: 1) quantities equal to the same quantity are equal to each other; and 2) if the same quantity is subtracted from two equal quantities, the remainders are equal. We note that the sum of Angle 1 and Angle 3 is a straight angle, therefore we write: Angle 1 + Angle 3 = 180 degrees.

Similarly: Angle 2 + Angle 3 = 180 degrees.

Now we use axiom 1) and conclude that Angle 1 + Angle 3 = Angle 2 + Angle 3.

Now if we subtract Angle 3 from both of these quantities, we must conclude, because of axiom 2) that the remainders are equal, namely, Angle 1 = Angle 2 and our proof is complete. We are forced to say that the vertical angles are equal, not because we have measured them, but because their equality is a logical consequence of the axioms, which we have accepted. Note that the actual size of the angles does not enter the argument, any more than the values of a and b entered the proof of the formula $(a+b)(a-b) = a^2 - b^2$.

Simple as this simplest of geometric theorems is, it illustrates perfectly the nature of mathematics. Mathematical truths are arrived at by drawing necessary conclusions from propositions known or assumed or accepted as true. A mathematical proposition always says that if something is true, then something else must be true. The actual truth of the "if" part is not relevant (an important point, to which we shall return later.) This is what Bertrand Russell meant when he said that we never know in mathematics whether what we are saying is true (there is no way of establishing the truth of the postulates and the axioms). Moreover, the definitions in mathematics always depend on other definitions. Fractions are defined as ratios of whole numbers; triangles as triples of lines intersecting in three points, etc. If we try to break each definition down, we finally arrive at terms which cannot be defined, or else we would have to have an infinite number of definitions. Since mathematical propositions make sense only if all the terms are precisely defined, and since some terms must remain undefined, the ultimate meaning of mathematical propositions is about nothing in particular. If we take the point of view that what is real must be realizable, that is, must exist in some particular case, then it follows that mathematics does not talk about anything real. This is what Russell meant when he said that in mathematics we never know what we are talking about.

So far I have been stressing two seemingly opposite facets of mathematics. On the one hand, I have illustrated the power of mathematical reasoning, which enables us to make propositions without resort to verification about potentially infinite classes of things (for example, about all pairs of numbers and all pairs of vertical angles.) On the other hand, I have insisted that in the last analysis these propositions have no "real content," that is to say, while in early times mathematics (or what was then mathematics) was concerned with real sets of objects or real measurements, the growing abstraction of mathematics finally tore it away from its subject matter.

This "voidness" of mathematics is necessary for its development as a science in its own right. It is impossible to have a sophisticated arithmetic or algebra if one must always depend on fingers or pebbles for mathematical operations. Nor is it possible to have a sophisticated geometry if geometrical propositions must always be illustrated by diagrams. Yet mathematics is more than a game with fixed rules, a mere exercise in reasoning. Mathematics does provide a link between man's reason and the world in which man lives. In elementary geometry this is obvious. True, there is no such thing in the world as a mathematical "point" (since a point is assumed to have no size) nor are there perfect squares or circles or ellipses (about which mathematical propositions are made); yet there are objects which can be thought of as points, lines, circles, etc. A surveyor thinks of the boundary between two lots as a "straight line," even though it cannot be anything of the sort; every shift of a speck of dust distorts it. An engineer thinks of a wheel as a perfect circle. In computing the orbit of a planet, the astronomer thinks of the planet as a point. Physical objects are not mathematical objects, but they can be thought of as such. Then reasoning about mathematical objects can be applied, leading to certain conclusions. These conclusions say what would be true if the assumptions were true.

Whether the assumptions are actually true depends on how well the "mathematical picture" fits physical reality.

For example, if the earth were a perfect sphere, and if its diameter were exactly 4000 miles, then the area of the earth's surface would have to be 201,061,930 square miles to the nearest square mile, as a consequence of a proposition of geometry which relates the surface to the radius of a sphere. Now the earth is certainly not a perfect sphere, nor is its radius exactly 4000 miles. But the earth is sufficiently like a sphere, and the radius is sufficiently close to 4000 miles that we can be certain that the surface cannot differ much from 200,000,000 square miles. (Incidentally, mathematical reasoning enables us to estimate the magnitude of the error in the surface from the magnitude of the error in the radius.)

Thus the power of mathematics (think of the labor involved in measuring the surface of the earth directly!) lies in the fact that many relations in the real world can be translated into a mathematical picture, to which mathematical reasoning can be applied, whose results can be then retranslated into conclusions about the real world. When mathematics is used in this way, it is called "applied mathematics."

The science which relies most heavily on applied mathematics is physics, which deals literally with "what makes the world go around." Everything we know about motion, whether of planets or of atoms, of artillery shells or street cars, we know through physics. Everything we know about heat, electricity, light, sound, strength of materials, and nuclear energy we have learned through physics. Physics makes it possible for us men to harness the forces of nature to work for us and so for philosophers to think in leisure without having to depend on slave labor to provide the necessities of life. Yet great as this service has been, physics has rendered an even greater one. Before physics man saw the universe through the eyes of a child. Natural phenomena appeared to him as the work of gods, demons, and spirits. His cosmic horizon was limited to an idea of a flat earth with the sky for a ceiling and often a hell for a basement. It was physics which revealed the absurdity of this picture. As the vastness of the universe became apparent, man's conviction of his own importance and of the importance of the speck of cosmic dust on which he lived dwindled. But with increasing humility came also another kind of self-respect and a sense of power no longer based on self-deception. The universe was revealed as more awesome than anything previously imagined, but its laws proved themselves to be more and more reliable. The universe could be understood, and what can be understood can be to a certain extent controlled, if one is mature enough to accept what must be accepted, namely the laws according to which the universe is "run." This is what Francis Bacon meant when he said, "Knowledge is power."

The prodigious growth of physics, which ushered in the Age of Science, would have been impossible without a parallel development in mathematics. Modern physics may be said to have been born when men developed concepts for dealing in an exact fashion with change. In Antiquity velocity was measured by distance and time but no one conceived the need of studying the way in which velocities might change from one instant to the next. Although they knew that a falling body, starting from rest, that is, zero velocity, would hit the ground with some finite velocity, they were incapable of conceiving the stages whereby a falling body underwent a continuous change in velocity. By the time of Galileo, this radical concept of a velocity changing continuously from one instant to the next, while the rate of change was constant, had become part of physical thought. Galileo's great achievement was to show that a falling body, insofar as it was not affected by air friction, had a continually increasing velocity in which there was constant acceleration. Thus, although the velocity changes, the rate at which this velocity changes is constant. Starting from rest, such a body will attain a speed of 32 ft/sec. at the end of the first second, 64 ft/sec. at the end of the next second, etc. This condition is described mathematically by saying that the speed is proportional to the time.

Since it is impossible to measure the speed of a falling body at successive instants, Galileo resorted to the test of another relation which he derived by mathematics. He was able to show that if, as he expected, the speed of a falling body increases uniformly with the time, then the distance through which it falls must be proportional to the square of the time. The test he offered was not that of a body falling freely, because events occurred too quickly in such a case. Instead he "diluted" gravity by allowing a body to roll down an inclined plane and discovered that he could verify the prediction that the distance through which the body had rolled was in fact proportional to the square of the time elapsed. Since he trusted his mathematics, he assumed that he could with confidence assert that this experiment gave sufficient ground for believing that the velocity is proportional to the time.

These results of Galileo were used by Newton in establishing his principles of dynamics, or the science of forces producing motion. Newton, who was born within a year of Galileo's death, drew from Galileo's research a number of bold assertions. The first of these is that, contrary to most accepted ideas, a body (any body) if left alone would move in a straight line always with the same velocity, the one it started with (if it was at rest to begin with, it would remain at rest). Accordingly, if any body were seen to behave differently, if it moved in a curved line or speeded up or slowed down, some external force must be acting upon it. Earlier philosophers also talked about forces, but they conceived of forces as causing the motion itself, whereas Newton maintained that forces cause only *changes* in motion, either in speed or direction or both. The question, "Why does a body move?" then became profitless. To the question, "Why does the motion of a body change?" Newton answered, "Because of the forces acting on it." But even this question became unimportant. The all-important question became, "*How* do bodies change their motion when forces are acting on them?" Newton stated a general relation between the force acting and the rate at which the velocity was changing (acceleration). Acceleration turned out to be directly proportional to the force.

In addition to Galileo's discoveries, Newton had at his disposal the life work of Kepler, a great German astronomer, who, in turn, had summarized the careful life-long observations of the Danish astronomer, Tycho, in the following three mathematical laws of planetary motion:

1. Each planet moves in an ellipse, in which the sun is at one focus.

2. If a line is drawn from the sun to various positions occupied by a planet at moments separated by equal intervals of time, the areas of the sectors are equal.

3. The square of the period of revolution of each planet is proportional to the cube of the major axis of its orbit.

Newton's achievement, thought by some to be the greatest achievement of the human mind, was to prove (strictly by mathematical deduction) that the planets could move as they did if there was a force acting on each of them always directed toward the sun, always proportional to the mass of the planet and inversely proportional to the square of its distance from the sun. This was the famous law of gravity, later extended by Newton to apply to every pair of particles in the universe. Thus the problem of planetary motion which puzzled the keenest minds of mankind was solved, although the mystery remained as to what causes bodies to attract one another gravitationally.

To perform his calculations Newton forged a powerful tool. We say "powerful" by analogy with physical tools. We feel that a crowbar gives us "power" because with it we can exert a force much greater than with bare hands. Newton's tool gave us mental "power" to deal with problems which we could not attack with our "bare minds." This tool is called the calculus.* The calculus is a technique for solving problems in which the answer sought is not a quantity but a relation among quantities. To be sure, such problems were attacked also in Antiquity. For instance, the Greek mathematicians, who were interested primarily in geometry, asked "How can we calculate the volume of a sphere?" The question is not about a particular sphere but about any sphere. The answer, therefore, cannot be a particular quantity but must be a relation among quantities. The answer, $V = 4\pi r^3/3$, says that the volume V is related in a par-

---

* It is noteworthy that in his great published work, *Principia*, Newton did not use the calculus but relied on geometrical arguments.

ticular way to the radius r, namely it is the cube of the radius multiplied by 4/3 and by a number called π (which is approximately 3.14 and can be calculated to any desired degree of accuracy). Here V and r are called "variables," because either of them can assume any value. Only the relation indicated by the formula remains the same.

In the calculus such problems are extended to cover the cases where not only relations among variables are involved but also rates of change of one variable with respect to another. A typical problem in elementary calculus is the following: "If the speed of a body is proportional to the time elapsed, what is the relation between the distance traveled and the time elapsed?" If the speed were constant, the distance could be found by ordinary algebra, since in that case $s = vt$, where s is distance, v the speed, and t the time. But in our problem speed is variable; it changes proportionately to time. You can't multiply such a quantity by time to get distance, because, speaking crudely, it won't stand still as you multiply. The calculus enables us to deal with such situations by an operation called "integration," which performs multiplications and additions a tiny bit at the time, something like the way the motion picture camera captures a constantly moving scene "momentwise." The solution of the problem looks like this.

$$v = at$$
$$s = \int_0^t at \, dt = \tfrac{1}{2}at^2$$

This is the problem of falling bodies, with which Galileo was concerned. Galileo still did not have the calculus at his disposal but was able to solve the problem because the variation of velocity with time was of the simplest kind possible. The calculus, however, enables the mathematician to treat much more complicated problems of this sort.

Eighteeenth-century mathematicians and physicists were largely occupied with developing and sharpening the tools provided by Newton. Prodigiously complicated problems of motion (mostly involving heavenly bodies) were posed and solved. The existence of mathematical techniques made possible not only the solution of problems already posed but also the posing of new problems. It was so with the magnetic compass: the compass enabled people not only to go safely to places they had wanted to visit, but also made them want to discover new places to go to. The story of the discovery of the planet Neptune is a fine example of how far the mathematical techniques advanced in the century and a half after Newton. Neptune was actually "discovered" with the help of pencil and paper before it was discovered through the telescope. In order to account for the irregular behavior of the planet Uranus (irregular because it was not in accordance with what it should have been under the gravitational influence of the sun and the known planets), astronomers had to postulate the existence of another planet. The position and the mass of this hypothetical planet were calculated by Adams in England and by Leverrier in France, who then communicated the findings to the German astronomer Galle in Berlin. On the evening of the day when he received the communication (September 23, 1846) Galle pointed his telescope as Leverrier indicated, and on the next evening Neptune was discovered (a day had to pass to allow Neptune to shift his position and thus betray himself as a planet and not another fixed star).

The mathematical method of reasoning was not confined to astronomy. After the Industrial Revolution increasing attention was paid to physics as the basic science of technology. Our entire electrical industry is the result of researches in electricity and magnetism, which could not have been accomplished without the mental and symbolic tools of mathematics. The existence of radio waves was actually discovered in the equations of Maxwell, which dealt with the propagation of light. This is one example of how mathematics, being independent of the subject matter to which it is applied, makes possible by-products of discovery, which are often even more important than the original aims of the investigation. Mathematics not only provides answers about the way phenomena occur but also often changes our whole way of thinking about phenomena. For example, it was known for a long time that work could be changed into heat, as every boy scout knows who tries to build a fire by rubbing sticks. However, a mathematical investigation involving quantities of work and quantities of heat showed that heat could also be changed into work. Our heat engines (steam engines, turbines, internal combustion engines) owe their existence to this discovery. The release of nuclear energy is another dramatic example of a similar kind. In 1905 Einstein published a paper which dealt with the nature of time and space and the propagation of light. As a by-product of his analysis he deduced an equation which asserts the equivalence of mass and energy. It is now common knowledge that the possibility of release of nuclear energy was predicted by that equation.

All these examples of mathematics as a mental tool are taken from physics, because the achievements of the mathematical method in physics has been the most spectacular. It is difficult, however, to name a science concerned with establishing orderly relations among events where the mathematical way of thinking has not been applied in one way or another. Chemistry has been "mathematicized" almost to the same extent as physics. Large areas of biology have been "conquered" by mathematical methods, notably genetics and the associated theories of evolution. Physiology, to the extent that it deals with the physics and chemistry of the living process, relies heavily on these disciplines and therefore is amenable to mathematization. Of the social sciences, economics has become increasingly mathematical, largely because economics deals with clearly defined variables, such as price, rates of production, consumption, and circulation of goods, etc. Those branches of sociology which deal with demography (growth and distribution of populations) and other matters which can be studied quantitatively, such as voting behavior, the distribution of certain opinions or attitudes, progressive changes in economic or social status, etc., became increasingly ripe for the application of mathematical methods. The same is true of psychology to the extent that it deals with measurable aspects of human behavior (perception, performance, progressive acquisition of skills, memory capacity, etc.). Where the phenomena studied are not easily quantifiable, the very existence of mathematical methods sometimes encourages the students of those phenomena to redefine their questions in such a way that quantitative and mathematical methods can be applied.

The adventures of mathematics in all these fields of inquiry are no less interesting than the story of physics. But we must return to the principal theme of our discussion, the "nonexistent" subject matter of mathematics. We are now ready to attack the paradox underlying the nature of mathematics. On the one hand it appears that one can think mathematically about almost any class of events, and on the other hand it is asserted that mathematics has no subject matter. However, a little reflection reveals that this combination of universality and "emptiness" is not a paradox at all but a consequence of the mathematical method. The process of counting oranges is the same as that of counting bicycles. This means that counting has nothing to do with either oranges or bicycles but is applicable to both. Why? Because sets of bicycles and sets of oranges have something in common which is neither bicycle nor orange, namely number. Similarly, the process of calculating the relation between the pressure and the temperature of a given volume of gas and that of calculating the relation between the demand for and supply of eggs at a given price are similar procedures. But the procedures have nothing to do with either the property of gases or the price of eggs. They have to do only with the way certain relations among variables follow from certain other relations.

Two important points concerning the nature of mathematics flow from this circumstance. The first of these points we have already stressed. A mathematical statement never says that something is true, but only that if something is true then something else must be true. Therein lies both the limitation and the power of mathematics. Its limitation is that it can never tell us what the facts are. The facts must speak for themselves. The power of mathematics is that it enables us to guess something which we cannot observe. It does so by calling attention to what ought to be observed if our guess is correct. Thus mathematics does not tell us that the pressure of a gas is proportional to its temperature; it tells us that if gases have certain properties (which usually cannot be observed directly), then the pressure ought to be proportional to temperature. If, as usually happens, a gas has other properties, then mathematics tells us what other relation between pressure and temperature we ought to observe. Through mathematics and observation we are given corroborations or refutations of guesses which we make about the "causes" underlying observed events. The growth of any science is essentially a collection of such corroborations and refutations.

This characteristic "oughtness" of mathematical statements was not always realized. We mentioned the fact that the Greeks based their geometry on postulates which they took to be "self-evident," that is, actually and absolutely true. The absolute truth of these postulates was accepted without question until the nineteenth century and was even incorporated in Kant's philosophical system. Curiously the "self-evidence," if not the truth, of one of these postulates was repeatedly questioned, namely, that through a point external to a given line exactly one parallel line could be drawn. Through the ages there were many attempts to "prove" this postulate, that is, deduce it as a theorem from the other postulates. All these attempts failed and only in the nineteenth century was it shown why they failed. The Russian mathematician Lobachevsky and his contemporary Bolyai in Hungary did an unprecedented thing.* They constructed a "geometry" based on another postulate, namely that through a point external to a line two lines could be drawn such that none of the lines falling within the resulting angle could ever meet the given line! Preposterous? Why? This postulate contradicts experience, one might object. But what experience? No one has ever had any experience with straight lines (there just aren't any such objects) much less with parallel lines, which are not supposed to meet even if produced "forever" (no one has experienced anything "forever").

* Unprecedented in print. The great German mathematician Gauss anticipated them but did not venture to publish his results.

It was some time before the legitimacy of "non-Euclidean" geo-metries (whose postulates contradicted Euclid's postulate of parallels) was accepted in mathematics,* but when this came about the walls of mathematical orthodoxy came tumbling down. Mathe-matical systems began to be created instead of supposed to be given by nature. Thus it is not unusual in modern mathematics to work with spaces having an infinite number of dimensions or with systems where the product of two factors depends on the order of the factors (ab does not equal ba) or where there are only a finite number of numbers, or where there are several orders of "infinity," or where the whole is not greater than several of its parts, etc. The emancipation of mathematics today has gone much farther than a break with the concrete world; it also involved an emancipation from established mathematical ideas. This emancipation was made possible by the "noncommittal" character of mathematics. The mathematician is responsible only for drawing logical consequences from his assump-tion, not for the truth of the assumptions.

The second point is that the method of mathematics is not con-fined to the manipulation of "quantities." What is manipulated is symbols and what is important is not what the symbols stand for but the rules of manipulation. To be sure, the earliest symbols of mathematics stood for "natural numbers," i.e., 1, 2, 3, . . . But as mathematics grew, the meaning of the symbols was extended to fractions, to negative numbers, to irrational numbers like π, which cannot be expressed by any fraction, to "imaginary numbers" like $\sqrt{-1}$ which seem absurd according to the rules of elementary algebra, but which persistently demanded the assignment of meaning and thus made necessary the extension of the rules. Finally, the meaning of the symbols can be extended to things which do not even resemble numbers, such as relations or even propositions. There is a branch of mathematics (or of logic, as you may prefer to call it if you are a logician) called mathematical logic, in which the symbols

---

* Later still other geometries were constructed, for example, by Riemann, who assumed that there are no parallel lines to a given line. Riemannian Geometry became an important mathematical tool in the Theory of Relativity.

stand for propositions or combinations of propositions, such as "If a man wears green socks, he never beats his wife." The operations of this branch of mathematics look like the operations of algebra, but they serve not to calculate quantities but to disentangle the implications among the propositions. Here is a problem in mathematical logic. Suppose it is true that:

1. If a man wears green socks and beats his wife, then he wears a red tie, but he can't beat his wife and bet on horses.

2. If a man beats his wife or does not play the drums, then he either does not wear a red tie or he bets on horses.

3. A man either wears a red tie or green socks or else he does not bet on horses.

4. If he does not wear a red tie but beats his wife, he bets on horses.

5. If a man does not beat his wife, he does not play the drums.

When does a man beat his wife?

It is possible to get the answer by ordinary verbal reasoning, but it is not easy. There is a branch of mathematical logic called Boolean Algebra, a peculiar algebra in which the variables can assume only two values, "1" and "0." By means of this algebra it is possible to obtain the answer ("Never") in a few minutes and also to deduce other by-product propositions, such as that there are no drum players and if a man wears a red tie, he bets on horses.

The content of the problem is silly, but the method is serious. In fact the same method is today used both in disentangling legal clauses involving the payment of insurance benefits and in constructing electrical relay circuits for automatic machinery. What have green socks, drum players, wife beaters, etc. to do with insurance or with electrical circuits? Nothing. But relationwise, the situations are similar, since they are all described in sentences of the same type: "If so, then so, unless thus, in which case that, but not this, etc."

It is the structure, not the content of such propostions which has been mathematicized.

The algebra of mathematical logic has been extended to deal with "partially" true propositions, that is, ones characterized by a certain probability. An example is "An unmarried girl aged twenty has seven chances out of ten of being married during the next five years." The algebra of such propositions is called the theory of probability. It is the foundation of an important branch of applied mathematics called statistics. Statistics is used not only in insurance, where it has been established longest, but also in production quality control, in evaluating the significance of scientific experiments, in determining the effectiveness and the safety of a drug, and to a large extent in modern physical theories. Like other branches of mathematics, probability theory and statistics have given man a more sophisticated outlook on the nature of cause and effect. To the primitive mind, any event may appear the cause of any other event if the one precedes the other. Once such a "causal relation" is established in the mind, every pairing of the events "confirms" it, and the other cases are ignored. If a man is convinced that walking under ladders causes accidents, he will notice all the cases where accidents followed, even years afterwards, and forget all the times when nothing happened. Statistics provide a method of separating real causes from coincidences. It also provides a means for evaluating the importance of one among several causes. Thus no one can assert that "smoking cigarettes causes lung cancer." Millions of people smoke cigarettes without ever developing lung cancer. But statistical studies which compare the incidence of lung cancers among cigarette smokers to that among others do indicate that cigarette smoking may be a significant factor influencing the chances of developing this disease. Thus mathematical reasoning makes possible the translation of emotion-packed arguments about what causes what into careful reliable analysis.

Two other matters must be touched upon. One has to do with the nature of mathematical progress, the other with the inner limitations of mathematics or, for that matter, of any deductive system.

One of the most widespread misconceptions is a notion that

mathematics is "cut and dried," a subject so definitive and rigid that only those devoid of sentiment and imagination are seriously attracted to it. Even a superficial acquaintance with the history of mathematical thought should dispel this idea. Ever since people contemplated mathematics as mathematics, that is, as something of interest in itself, the development of this science has tapped the most profound sources of human creativity. And it still does. The creative character of mathematical research and invention is inherent in the very "mathematical attitude," which can be summarized thus: a solved problem is a dead problem. There has hardly been a time when mathematicians did not pose new problems faster than old ones were solved. This is all the more remarkable, because mathematicians do not usually solve problems one by one but attack a whole class of problems. Thus the discovery of the formula for the solution of a quadratic equation solved at once all quadratic equations. But then this class of problems (being solved) became just another problem in a larger class, namely to solve by formula an algebraic equation of any degree. As it turned out this more general problem was proved to have no solution, but in the course of proving this a whole vast new field of mathematical research was opened up: the theory of groups and of algebraic fields. One of the most fascinating things about mathematical research is that when something is proved "impossible," the event turns out to be a great mathematical achievement and often signals some new fruitful development. The great unsolved problems of Antiquity (squaring the circle, doubling the cube, trisecting the angle) have led to such "impossibility" proofs. On the other hand, some old problems have stayed unsolved and still challenge the keenest mathematical minds. Two of them are so easy to state that their prodigious difficulty is hard to believe. One such problem, called Fermat's Last Theorem (of which Fermat said that he had a proof which was never found) is to prove either that there is no set of whole numbers, x, y, z, n ($n > 2$) which satisfy $x^n + y^n = z^n$ or that there is such a set. Obviously there are such sets for $n = 2$, for example, $3^2 + 4^2 = 5^2$. But no set for *n* greater than 2 has ever been found, nor has any one ever proved that there are no such sets or that there must be some.

Another great unsolved problem is to prove that every even number is a sum of two primes (numbers divisible only by themselves) or else to find one which is not. For example, $16 = 11 + 5$, $68 = 37 + 31$, $100 = 41 + 59$, etc. But no one has ever proved that every even number can be so broken up, nor shown one that cannot.

Aside from these curiosities, however, progress in mathematics is a constant stream of new *kinds* of problems. As these problems are solved, the ideas underlying the solutions become techniques or routines. It does not take a mathematician today to solve problems involving only arithmetic computations or, for that matter, any operations that have become sufficiently routinized. This has become especially true with the advent of mathematical technology, the "mechanized brains" to which more and more computational work is relegated. And just as industrial technology has in the long run resulted in an enrichment of human work (even counting the loss of certain kinds of craftsmanship), so the computing machines are today enriching mathematics. For it is necessary to design them, to study their capabilities, limitations, and eccentricities, to design "languages" in which to feed them instructions and, of course, to pose problems to keep them busy.

The other matter is of more philosophical significance. We said the "emptiness" of mathematics gives it its power. Released from the responsibility of picturing the world as it is, the mathematician builds colossal edifices of deduction, the "systems"—large collections of conclusions resting on a foundation of a few postulates. The more topheavy the system, the more numerous and varied the theorems and the narrower the postulational foundation, the greater is the mathematical achievement. But then the greater the danger that the entire edifice may come tumbling down if only a single contradiction is discovered among the postulates. Accordingly the mathematician wants his systems to be both complete and consistent. A complete system is one in which every propostion involving the terms defined in the system can be shown to be either true or false. For example, the proposition that every even number is a sum of two primes has not yet been proved or disproved. But if the postulates of arithmetic are complete, then it should be possible *in principle* either to prove or disprove it. And certainly the system should be consistent, that is, it should not contain any contradictions. Now it is possible to prove certain systems consistent by means of propositions derived from postulates of *other* systems, but this only raises the question of whether these other systems are complete and consistent. The problem that has haunted mathematicians and logicians ever since Leibnitz has been to construct a system so comprehensive that it would be possible to prove it both complete and consistent.

In 1931 it was shown by Gödel that such a system is impossible to construct. Given any logical system, it is impossible to prove within the system itself that it is consistent: another proof of impossibility, a milestone in the development of mathematics. These impossibility proofs are perhaps the most characteristic achievements of mathematical thought. They endow the mathematician with that mixture of humility and hope which marks all great human endeavor.

Mathematics, then, is a creation of the human mind evolved in the experience of analytical thinking, that is, thinking which breaks up a complex experience into simple components and investigates the relations among the components. Mathematics is the heart and soul of specifically *human* thinking, liberated from the distorting influences of prejudices, fears, and passions, and therefore admirably suited to the pursuit of knowledge. To the extent that mathematical thinking has revealed to us many of the most profound truths about our world, some philosophers stand in awe of it and even declare mathematics to be akin to divine revelation. Others, no less humble before the magnificence of these truths, confine themselves to the point of view that the world is knowable, and that mathematics, like language, is a biological peculiarity of the human mind, which enables us collectively to accumulate knowledge about the world. Needless to say, this knowledge can be put to good or evil uses, depending on how the passions of men are directed.

16

PHILOSOPHY

The Growing Center

by Susanne K. Langer

KNOWLEDGE grows with exploration, adding new facts, correcting old beliefs. It grows like a tree, at every tip, so the crown seems to spread out an ever-growing fringe.

A human being is not a tree; our growth is more complicated. We have more than vegetative functions, and therefore more than a vegetative form of growth. But the analogy between physical growth and cultural growth, organic life and mental life, really goes much further than the picturesque figure of the "growing edge of knowledge." The constant multiplication of facts, often effected by breaking up big observations into more exact, measured data which lead in their turn to general but precise information, is the spectacular process in our scientific expansion. It takes place chiefly at the points of newest interest, and this growth of our store of knowledge is like the physical growth of new tissue by proliferation of the cells that compose it.

But in the higher organisms, such as a human being, the whole process of development—the whole *life*—is controlled by a complex organ whose parts pervade most of the body. This is known as the *central nervous system*. It comprises the brain, the spinal cord, and all the nerves; the special organs of sight and hearing, though not made entirely of nervous tissue, are extensions of the brain.

The central nervous system does not increase by multiplying its cells. From infancy to old age we have essentially the same nerve cells we started with at birth. (There are a few nerves, for instance in the face, that repair their tissue, but in general destroyed nerve-cells can never be replaced.) The nervous system has no "growing edge."

Yet obviously the nervous system of a man is bigger than that of a baby. It has grown somehow. The brain is bigger, though proportionately not much, and the spinal cord is longer. The nerves that reach the man's fingers have further to go than they used to. In the controlling central organ there is a different kind of increase—not by addition of new cells at the nerve ends or on the surface of the brain, but by growth of the original cells themselves. They stretch. They stretch to keep pace with the growing society of the cells that divide and multiply, and that extend the compass of the body as a growing population extends the compass of a city, suburb by suburb. The nervous system is a growing center, that holds all the advancing other parts in mutual alliance as one organism, living one life.

In the cultural life of our day—one of the very surprising days in man's history—the most breathtaking events arise from the sudden increase of scientific knowledge. One discovery leads to another. Every new fact suggests others to be established. When whole series of demonstrable facts fall into line, they exemplify natural laws, which are simply the most general facts we know about the universe. Then the "growing edge" ceases to be a fringe of more or less random facts and solidifies into a new part of the body of knowledge.

But in the growth of culture, as in the growth of a high organism, there is something that does not increase by addition of elements, but by modification and stretching: that is mentality itself, which comprises much more than knowledge. Pure factual knowledge, however wide, would not constitute a mental life.

Neither a single mind nor the collective mind of a society is solely or even primarily "a blank tablet on which experience writes" its record of ready-made facts. Knowledge of facts is a requisite for the activity of a living brain with all its involvements. The greater, older mental functions are feeling and imagination. Not that these several factors are really separate, or even separable; they are at best *distinguishable*, in a normal mind. If they fall apart, or if one interferes with the natural development of another, there is mental disturbance, which may range from a brief moment of disorientation to the gravest, lifelong imbalance.

Imagination is probably the greatest force acting on our feelings— greater and steadier than outside influences, like fear-inspiring noises and sights (lightning and thunder, an on-coming truck, a raging tiger) or direct sense pleasure, even including the intense pleasures of sexual excitement. Only a small part of reality, for a human being, is what actually is going on; the greater part is what he imagines in connection with the sights and sounds of the moment.

Imagination makes his world. This is not to say that his world is a fantasy, his life a dream, or any such poetic pseudo-philosophical thing. It means that his "world" is bigger than the stimuli which surround him, and the measure of it is the reach of his coherent and steady imagination. An animal's environment consists of the things that act on his senses. Absent things which he desires or fears probably have no proxies in his consciousness, like their images in ours, but appear, when finally they do, as satisfactions of his driving needs, or crises in his more or less constant watching and reacting. He does not live in a world of unbroken space and time, filled with events even when he is not present or when he is not interested; his "world" has a fragmentary, intermittent existence, arising and collapsing with his activities. A human being's world hangs together, its events fit into each other; no matter how devious their connections, there always are connections, in one big framework of Space and Time. (The modern concept of "space-time" is a refinement of thought that we shall consider later.) An animal's environment is not really a "world," let alone "the world"; his environment is a momentary reality, part of his own activity, influenced by previous experiences but not in ways that bring them back as a "past," and directed toward future experiences but not toward a "future." Past and future, events and states, perhaps even things in their relations to each other, have no part in his perception. *The world* is something human.

What makes the difference is the peculiar tendency of the human brain to use the sense impressions it receives not only as stimuli or obstacles to physical action, but as material for its specialized function, imagination. We not only see things, but at the same time we imagine them to have all sorts of properties that one cannot see. Animals respond to outside stimuli either overtly or not at all; but men respond largely in a cerebral, invisible way, producing images, notions, figments of all sorts that serve as *symbols for ideas*. The result is that we live in a web of ideas, a fabric of our own making wherein we catch the contributions of outside reality, sights, sounds, smells, etc. Actual perceptions come and go, and are beyond our control (except insofar as we may open or shut our eyes, touch things or not, and cause a few changes to happen), but symbols may be found or produced at will, and manipulated with great freedom; by means of them we supplement our fragmentary sensations and build up around each perceptual core a structure of ideas. That is the sense of saying we have ideas *about* what we actually see.

The symbolic rendering of experience is a vast topic that we cannot possibly enter on here. A good deal has been and is still being written about it, for the importance of symbolization is a recent discovery. Suffice it, then, to touch the high points of that all-important process. Its most spectacular product is the great systematic symbolism known as *language*, which engenders the whole mental development that sets men apart from their zoological brethren. The line between animals and men is, I think, precisely the language line. (Animals probably communicate only intentions and direct emotional excitements, not ideas *about* things.) Language serves far greater purposes than even the most elaborate system of signals whereby we might make our wishes known and control each other's behavior. Its first and most astounding function is to shape the human world.

Sense perceptions are only part of the world. They are indispensable elements, but by no means its whole substance. The world for human beings is made up of facts; and facts are as much a product of conception as of perception. Facts are "about" things, as our immediate knowledge is "about" our sensory experiences. Our world is not a random collection of things, but a great nexus of physical facts, historical facts, legal and political facts, and especially, for each person, the ever-approaching phalanx of practical facts that he has to meet from hour to hour. What we call "the world" is a conceptual structure of space and time in which events occur, and develop into situations from which new, more or less spectacular events arise; this development is the order of cause and effect as we conceive it, and what develops is Reality, the web of facts.

Reality contains all the deliverances of our senses, but its framework is not something visible, tangible, or in any sensuous way perceptible. Its framework is something intellectual, perceptible only through symbols. To say it is intellectual is not to say it is reserved for an intelligentsia, or even for civilized races; a common intellectuality belongs to all human beings that are not mentally defective, and impresses itself on their experience at the elementary level of understanding words.

It is sometimes said that words stand proxy for things and acts, and that consequently a dog to whom a word means an object, a person, or an act to be performed understands language. But that is a slipshod argument and false conclusion. The words that a dog "understands" are functioning as signals, like dinner bells and automobile horns. They tell him of the things they designate, but not about them. They may make him expect his dinner but they cannot inform him that it will be late, nor that yesterday's dinner was good. The human use of language, by contrast, is essentially to express ideas about the things mentioned—to call attention to their relations, parts, properties, aspects, and functions, and to the intricate relations of those constituents and functions to each other.

Relations are known to us primarily through words, our most

ready and powerful symbols. Though we implicitly take account of relations in action, explicitly they cannot be singled out and pointed to like physical things. Set up a large flowerpot and a small one, and try to *point out* the relation of "larger than": a person looking where you point—from one pot to the other—may see "different," "same shape," "side by side," "brick-colored," or even "two, a pair," as readily as "larger than." Relations are abstract, and abstract entities are embodied only in symbols. The profound difference between speech-gifted beings and speechless. ones is due to the power of words to set forth relations, which cannot be seen and touched, yet are the bonds among our sensations that create "facts." Our world of facts is shot through and through with concepts comprehended symbolically; "nature" is far more a language-made affair than people generally realize—made not only for sense, but for understanding, and prone to collapse into chaos if ideation fails.

At the center of human experience, then, there is always the activity of imagining Reality, conceiving the structure of it through words, images, or other symbols, and assimilating actual perceptions to it as they come—that is, *interpreting* them in the light of general, usually tacit ideas. This process of interpretation is so natural and constant that most of it goes on unconsciously. Instead of having sensations and judging them to "mean" the existence of things or the occurrence of events, we really perceive *things and happenings*, and become directly aware of "facts." The whole intellectual framework of space and time, things and properties, change, cause and effect, etc., is implicit in the very way we use our senses. The perception of relations, connections, and especially of *meaning* takes place through any and all avenues of sense; this kind of perception is the *logical intuition* contained in human experience as such, the factor that makes it human, different from animal response. It is reflected by the ways people use words (the "syntax" of their particular language), of which there are varieties, but all varieties of syntax serve to formulate *propositions*, and give rise to discourse and discursive reasoning. All our experience—practical, ethical, or intellectual—is built up on an intuitively constructed logical scaffold known as Common Sense.

As human awareness differs from that of animals, so, of course, does human feeling and emotion. Since our environment is a World, we have feelings toward the world—not transient excitements, but a permanent emotional attitude toward a permanent "universe." This attitude is the deepest level of feeling in us, by virtue of which we have a continuous emotional life; and, like all human feelings, it is closely related to imagination. It is fed, in each person, by his envisagement of the world, and of human life, and of himself in that frame; that is to say, by his orientation in Reality. His experiences may be many or few; so long as they are capable of interpretation in terms of Common Sense, his knowledge of Reality can grow just by adding facts, without changing his world image or disturbing his sense of orientation, which is always the keynote in a coherent life of feeling.

Common sense is the unconscious use of categories and concepts that fit common experience. It has grown up through ages, from the earliest forms of characteristically human perception and reaction—that is, the earliest ways of thinking—to what we recognize as sensible, logical thinking today. Its gradual development is reflected in the evolution of languages, a fascinating field of study that has only recently been opened and promises to be rich in new historical and psychological materials. Philosophers, too, have harvested their share of ideas from the linguists' new researches, which coincide with the great work of Frege, Peirce, and Russell on literal symbolism, and Cassirer on symbolic forms as such, to give present day philosophy its semantical turn.

The use of words is always an index to people's intellectual power: the vagueness or precision of the distinctions they draw between one thing and another may be seen in their choice of distinct words for those things, or their tendency to let one word serve many purposes and shift its meaning without taking account of relevant differences. The centers of attention are marked by the "key words" in their discourse—nouns in our Indo-European languages, held together by verbs that symbolize our awareness of relations, and elaborated with modifiers to express further distinctions. There are other languages in which actions are named by the "key words" and things are grammatically expressed as conditions of the actions, that is, by modifiers. Societies that differ radically in the logical structure of their languages have really a different inheritance of Common Sense, and their mutual understanding presents a deeper problem than they themselves realize when they establish a rough vocabulary to serve both parties in commerce with each other. The words of that vocabulary have a core of practical meaning for both, but the connotations that accrue to a word in the course of its career probably tend to grow apart as long as each group continues to live with its own language.

The power of language to keep step with the expansion of human experience through the long course of history lies in the tendency of words to mean more than they designate, or symbolize directly; for they tend to symbolize indirectly *anything for which their direct meaning itself may be a symbol*. The word "light" designates a physical phenomenon we perceive with our eyes, but light itself is a world-old symbol for knowledge, intelligence, reason, logical intuition (John Locke called such intuition "natural light"), and also for a large class of feelings—joy, relief, love, and religious exaltation. All things that light itself commonly symbolizes accrue to the word "light," as its *metaphorical meanings*, so naturally and originally that in studying the history of words it is impossible to judge whether the physical or the emotional or some other meaning is the oldest. Max Müller, a great philologist of the nineteenth century, called the physical meaning the "root metaphor," taking for granted that words originally meant physical objects and physical actions, as they most readily do for our common sense. The truth, however, is probably that in the pristine sense of a word all those conceptions, which we now call its several meanings, were not several, but that they have gradually become separated out of a matrix of vague, great significance, physical and emotional at once, felt rather than understood. Daylight was probably experienced as joy and night as trouble before any primitive thinker realized that light is one thing and joy another, darkness one thing and trouble another, and that light gave him joy and darkness caused him trouble.

The root metaphor is the image conveyed by the word, and this image may mean a feeling, an act, an object, even a personality or a place. All sorts of things may appear in this image, that is, they may be imagined in this form. The essence of human mentality is the use of images not as sheer memory traces, but as symbols which may be put together freely, elaborated, and treated as mental pictures of the most various experiences; i.e., the power of seeing one thing in another.

The processes of nature, especially, may be seen one in another; and those which are hard to observe are generally understood only through a model. Death is seen as an eternal sleep, youth and age as spring and autumn or winter, life as a flame consuming the candle that provides it. The very framework of experience is only thinkable by means of models: Time is most readily imagined as a flowing stream, and is, in fact, so hard to conceive without that metaphorical image that many people believe Time literally flows. Space is usually thought of as a huge vessel that contains all things but could also be empty; the fact that a vessel is necessarily something in space, dividing an inside from an outside, does not disturb the naïve imagination. Space is a receptacle, and all matter is in it.

Because we see one thing in another—Life in the candle flame, Death is sleep, Time in the flowing stream, Space in a bowl or in the sky that we see as an inverted bowl—the vast multiplicity of experiences compose one world for us. Our symbolic seeing is what gives that world its fundamental unity, much deeper than the unity of its causal connectedness: the gnomonic "likeness in difference" that unifies a nest of tables, rather than the simple concatenation of links that unifies a chain. Most of the things we encounter have no obvious causal connections: the roar of a passing plane, and the voice from the radio advertising toothpaste; the thermometer at freezing; the dog scratching himself under the table. It is an article of scientific faith (and a primary one) that all events are causally connected, however complex the web of their connections may be. We really see causal connections only in a few chains of events. Something bites the dog, so he scratches; the scratching bothers us, so presently we nudge him; because we nudge him, he stops for a moment and then uses the other leg. That is a causal chain; but so far as our direct observation is concerned, most things "just happen" at the moment when they do, and could have been otherwise. We believe them to have causes, but their causes have to be learned, or taken on faith.

What we do see, however, is that the most various things repeat a few fundamental forms, by virtue of which we can use familiar events as *models* to understand new ones and tangible objects as symbols of intangible realities. This helps a person in two ways to cope with his world: in the first place, by making great and remote parts or aspects of it conceivable, and secondly, by giving its homely, trivial contents a symbolic value. When ordinary acts like eating and sleeping, and common things like fire and trees and water, become symbols for the round of nature, human passion, and what not, they cease to be silly and separate items of experience, and take on significance as integral factors in the human scene.

This import of everyday things, the reflection of a cosmic order in the order of common life, is what builds up a person's world image, the frame in which his beliefs and doubts and judgments all make sense. The possession of such a frame is *mental orientation*. It is usually unrecognized, or only vaguely recognized, but it is the first requisite for a concerted "inner life"; for the sense of general orientation in the world is the basis of our emotional security. Like the pressure of the floor against our feet, it is not normally in consciousness, but let it fail, and we are scarcely conscious of anything else; there is complete disorientation and everything joins the confusion.

The unity of nature is not all that we owe to our power of symbolic thinking, which spontaneously makes conceptual metaphors and models out of sensory objects. Our ideas of moral qualities, good and evil, blessing and bane, seem all to have been attained with the help of concrete imagery, often of a very earthy sort. The expression of values is so consistently metaphorical that words like "high" and "low," "straight" and "crooked," have almost more readily a moral connotation than a geometrical one; it is hard, sometimes, to tell which is their primary sense and which the derivative. Without the concepts they convey we would have no moral world. The same thing holds for our conception of intellectual functions and qualities: "bright" and "dull," "keen," "obscure," "hard," even words like "wit," of which the root-metaphor is "white," are obviously physical terms; but without them we could not have developed the characteristically human sense of intellectual and moral existence.

Metaphorical images penetrate deeply into our commonsense ways of thinking. Nobody questions the good sense of saying that a tree spreads its branches in order to catch as much light as possible; the model of a person voluntarily lifting his arms in order to receive something beneficent coming from above is forgotten when we talk about the tree as though it spread the branches for its purpose. In fact, this guiding image is so forcible that most people who do not believe the tree has insight and intentions and voluntary motions still cannot surrender the metaphor of purposive action entirely; if the tree does not act from choice, some intelligent agent must be making it grow one way rather than another, in order that it may catch the scant forest light.

We often oppose what we call "poetic metaphors" to "hard common sense." But common sense is built on poetic metaphors.

Yet common sense is not poetry. The power of seeing one thing in another, which begets our metaphors and conceptual models (the oldest of which are myths of nature and human life), leads also to a characteristically human thought-process known as abstraction. By logical intuition we see not only what is "the same" in two widely different things, as for instance a burning candle consumed by its flame and a living body consumed by its life, but also what makes them different. As soon as the differences are clearly recognized, the common element stands out against them, and can be conceived alone as that which both of these different things exhibit. In this way the concept, e.g., "matter being consumed by its own activity," is abstracted; and a mind which can make such an abstraction realizes that life is not literally a burning candle but is reasonably symbolized by one.

Language registers this logical abstraction in the growth of its vocabulary. The concepts with which we operate in our daily lives—concepts of things and properties, mind and matter, necessity, money value, moral value, good and evil—all may be traced back, through the history of the words that express them, to their origins in vaguer but usually richer "root-metaphors." The abstract sense of our words today has been derived by a process of distinction and separation that results in the establishment of at least one literal meaning, and often a number of recognized metaphorical uses. So we may find, for instance: "Bright: giving or reflecting light; figuratively, of quick intelligence." But here the figurative use is so common that most dictionaries today (e.g., Webster's, or Funk & Wagnall's) list it as a second literal meaning.

In discourse and even more in writing we continue to give words new figurative meanings; and as there are many ways of "seeing" a new object or event, there is often a wide choice of older things to which it might be assimilated. Who decided that the covering of an automobile engine was to be called the "hood" in America, and in England, France, and Germany, the "bonnet"? Who called a cover for certain smaller units a "cowl," then made "cowl" a verb and derived the verbal noun "cowling" for the same object? Who called the cover for the hub of the wheel a "cap"? No one knows. All these words denote headgear, the most familiar loose covering for a special part, and the analogy is obvious enough so we accept the extended meaning without difficulty. A cover fitting closely all around something is usually designated as a "shoe"; again, we find the figure of speech natural, and soon forget it is a figure. By metaphorical extension, "shoe" becomes the literal name of the fitted casings on tires as well as the fitted casings on our feet.

In this way language grows with conception, and usually conception keeps pace with new experiences. The repository of all our concepts, old and new, quite abstract ones and inveterately poetic ones, is common sense, the generally accepted basis of reasonable discourse, knowledge, and good judgment.

But common sense is not a perfect conceptual system, self-consistent and coherent, by which all of reality could be understood. It is built by a spontaneous imagination that draws on many sources, and the images it employs are often incompatible, so it is really a rough-and-ready instrument that is prone to yield absurdities when its concepts are tested for all they imply. Their implications are often in flat contradiction to each other, or lead to a jumble of bizarre, unrelated beliefs. For instance, people who have studied just a little bit of psychology—say, an introductory course in college —can see by common sense that the concept of "the Will," as a distinct faculty or power, is untenable; but in moral and religious debates they continue to worry and argue about "freedom of the Will." They cannot drop the traditional commonsense assumption that an entity called "the Will" is the real agent behind their acts— not part of the body, but somehow inside it, moving it—although in another context they have seen clearly that this assumption makes no sense.

The fact is that any ambitious and sustained intellectual work soon overstrains the capacities of common sense. As soon as one thinks at all seriously and strenuously about nature, society, mind, truth, or any other big and complex subject, the traditional ways of conceiving it prove to be too muddled to allow any distinctions and definitions that might reveal hidden relations, or make obvious ones intelligible. The thinker, therefore, is confronted by the task of criticizing and correcting, perhaps even rejecting, the accepted images and tacit assumptions and building up a new, more abstract, more negotiable set of concepts.

Such a systematic critique of common sense is philosophy. As William James said, "The word means only the search for *clearness* where common people do not even suspect that there is any lack of it." Philosophy is the pursuit of meanings. It is not a process of finding new facts; the discovery and generalized statement of facts is science. Philosophizing is a process of making sense out of experience, rather than adding to experience itself as factual learning and experimental investigation do.

"The search for clearness"; that is, indeed, the constant quest, to which all the special techniques of philosophy are bent. Those techniques constitute a discipline, anciently known and taught as *logic*. Though the study of logic is old and venerable, its most spectacular advances belong to a fairly recent period, and are still in full swing. In the past, logic was almost entirely devoted to analyzing the formal concepts in general use—the abstractions implicit in grammar and syntax and ordinary concatenated discourse. With the growth of so-called "symbolic logic," however, logicians have gained a certain freedom from the influence of language, by using other than the traditional, linguistic forms of saying things—that is, other than the subject-and-predicate forms of positive and negative statements. This departure, which started from the invention of a powerful, quasi-mathematical symbolism, has opened up entirely new fields of logical work; it has turned the intellectual searchlights on the principles of abstraction, the necessity and limits of symbolization, and the possible combinations of abstract concepts in the frame of any symbolic system at all, not only what is commonly called a "language." Logical work today, therefore, is more than a matter of analyzing given forms; it consists largely of manipulating odd-looking abstract terms in new combinations, *constructing new formal concepts*.

Clearness, then, is not all that philosophical thinking yields, though that is its constant aim. Concepts may be clear but still inadequate. Suppose we could define to the point of perfect clarity the concept of "phlogiston"; if there is nothing in the world that exemplifies the concept, nothing that fits the definition, or if we cannot combine that concept with any others, its clarity is of no use; we still can do nothing with the term. Concepts must be not only clear but fit for some intellectual purpose. That is the core of truth in the doctrine known as "pragmatism," which asserts that beliefs are true if they "work." It is not the beliefs that are true, but the concepts involved in the beliefs that are valid, if—and only if —they work.

Some of the abstractions made by common sense might be made fairly precise and consistent; indeed, that is exactly what begot Euclid's geometry and Aristotle's logic, physics, and psychology. But as observation becomes wider and sharper, and facts pile up on facts, even a refined and codified version of our natural metaphors is not adequate to the growing task of understanding scientific connections. Concepts that begin in concrete images are too simple for the purpose.

At such times, the leaders of human thought do philosophical work. That is why great periods of philosophy follow upon periods of fast cultural growth or novel experience: the achievements of Democritus, Socrates, Plato, and Aristotle upon the rise of Greek civilization that culminated in the Age of Pericles, just before their day; medieval philosophy, from Eriugena to Aquinas, after the tremendous advent of Christianity; the so-called "modern philosophers"—Descartes, Bacon, and Hobbes, and all their intellectual progeny, slowly dwindling since the giant Kant—in the wake of the Renaissance, to master its welter of discoveries, adventures, and creative outbursts. A high philosophical period marks a stretching of the human mind, a more or less general reorientation in the world, and a new development in men's feeling for nature and for each other.

Such intellectual revolutions begin, of course, where higher abstractions and more negotiable concepts than those of current common sense are needed: among theologians, lawyers, mathematicians, astronomers, physicists, chemists, doctors, biologists, and other professional people dealing with intricate systems of facts or ideas. Experts as well as laymen, when they handle a purely conceptual subject like law or mathematics, invisible materials like those of theology, infinitesimal objects such as "atoms" and even parts of atoms, or inaccessible portions of the world, as one does in astronomy, necessarily resort to a model, i.e., a symbolic image taken from more familiar experience to represent an elusive concept. A scientist will demonstrate to himself and others the action of a heart by means of a simply constructed pump, with four valves and two loops of hose; or he will let a construction of metal rods and balls represent the tiny distances, and other relations, among whirling particles of electrically charged matter called "protons" and "electrons," assumed to compose the submicroscopic material elements which today bear the name of "atoms."

When the conceptual frame of our thinking is inadequate for understanding our world, the models that have served it in the past will not do any more. The first theory of atoms was propounded more than two thousand years ago, by the Greek philosopher Democritus;* his illustrations of the way atoms composed matter were taken from the sands of the sea, hard bits of stone settling by their weight into large masses, and from dust motes seen in sunbeams, exhibiting constant motion that he thought was "of their nature." His conception of atoms involved shape and motion, but not any inside structure or parts. In fact, the name he gave his material elements, "atoms," means "indivisible," i.e., without parts. Atomic structure, as we know it, could not be thought of without a new concept, or rather a whole set of new concepts—electromagnetic force, positive and negative charge, units of energy, and several other terms of analysis that were not current and, indeed, not possible in his day. Philosophical thinking had not reached the level of abstraction to which they belong.

Because we do operate with such notions, the old Greek models of physical substance are no good to us any more. Our philosophy of nature has outgrown them, and scientific observation shows us conditions they cannot represent. The chief reason, however, why physicists were never content with the ancient concept of the atom

---

* Or, probably, his teacher Leucippus; but the Latin poet Lucretius, from whom we have it, associates it for us with the name of Democritus.

was that this concept harbored a logical inconsistency. A simple substance, such as Democritus assumed, has really no properties except those of spatial extension. No matter how small such extension may be, it is never indivisible. One can imagine a particle of solid matter being indivisible in practice, that is, because we have no instrument that will further divide it; but in theory the end of its divisibility cannot be established at any magnitude.

This is a typical instance of the sort of conceptual problem that arises in science, religion, politics, or any other field of systematic interest, and presents a philosophical challenge. It is not enough to analyze the traditional concept, find it logically untenable, and reject the word "atom" as meaningless; "atom" does mean something that exists, but what answers to it in actuality cannot be a particle of absolutely hard matter, like an infinitesimal stone. At this point we have to construct a new meaning, one that will bear logical analysis and permit us still to use the word "atom" in describing the different forms of physical substance. This is the constructive work of philosophy. It is by far the greater part of that discipline; analysis shapes the problem and serves as a constant check, but logical construction is its real life. It requires imagination, skill in manipulating formal definitions, and above all a certain boldness and freedom of mind to depart from traditional ways of thinking and talking, dispense with the old misleading models, and even dismiss the promptings of common sense with lordly unconcern in the interest of abstract conceivability.

Ordinarily, in a normal and settled society, the limitations of common sense are of little concern to the average person. Even its paradoxes and absurdities do not disturb him, for he is not aware of them. The frame of his thinking, and therewith of his actions, passions, expectations, and all the business of his life, is rough but firm. It is chiefly a fabric of images taken from the most familiar aspects of existence: the space of his own living extended to larger and larger proportions is the space of his universe; years—measured by the turns of the earth about its axis—stretch into his own past and beyond it, and into his future and beyond it, to make Eternity. From his social experience he borrows the image of an imposed law regulating people's actions, and does not even know he is creating a metaphor when he calls the regularities of nature "natural law"; and as an authority imposes laws on people, he can hardly elude the assumption of a vastly greater authority imposing an absolute and perfect law on things, which consequently "obey" natural law in every point.

In times of rapid changes, however, when society is neither normal nor settled, the average person is driven to thinking about things beyond his own round of life—things that uphold this essential round, and suddenly seem insecure: Providence and its plan, the credentials of human authorities, the validity of morals and institutions, the value or vanity of work and of life itself.

Few men can think through such problems to a point of decision, any more than they could think out for themselves the reasons for expecting an eclipse on the fifth of next month at ten o'clock. But their mental security is not necessarily disturbed by this fact, so long as they believe implicitly that the major issues of life can be understood by those who really put their minds wholly to the task—that is, that there are answers, and human reason can shape them. That is the chief importance of the professional philosopher for the layman—the reason why Plato's doctrine of Ideas and Aristotle's teleology mattered to the merchants and soldiers of Greece, who had heard of them only vaguely if at all; why the Summa Theologica of St. Thomas was of vast importance to all Christendom, though probably only the higher clergy read it, and only in the Western church at that; and why, in the heyday of an expanding secular culture following the Renaissance, in a new world of science and modern commerce, Locke's Essay on Human Understanding was an intellectual bombshell, and Newton's Principia Mathematica, written in Latin and consisting largely of mathematical statements, intellectually affected people who were neither scientists nor mathematicians and had never studied a page of it.

Trained and specialized thinking is always in the vanguard of our conceptual development; what is abstruse and weird to one generation is usually quite acceptable to the next. It is the same in philosophy as in art and music: what we find comprehensible, the painting of El Greco or the music of Beethoven, was once received with reluctance or even violent protest as distorted modern stuff. John Locke had to plead against people's commonsense beliefs when he argued that the source of all our factual knowledge is sensation (that notion was old, but not popularly known); Kant, a hundred years later, had to fly in the face of common sense to call the same doctrine in question. Abstractly and logically developed concepts seep down into untutored thought only as concrete, familiar models are found to picture them. They seem reasonable to the average person just insofar as they are imaginable. And usually the advance of knowledge is slow enough to let such popular versions of new concepts take shape.

It is, after all, imagination that frames and supports and guides our thinking, not only about the practicalities of the day, but also about much greater things—good and evil, love, life and death, past and future, and human destiny. The average person probably does not contemplate such matters very often, but he has ideas about them, as we say, "at the back of his head"—gathered since childhood, from church, from impressive moments, and in sleepless nights. When he does have occasion to face fundamental issues of moral principle, hope or renunciation, self or society, the terms in which he thinks must make some clear sense to him; it is here that he needs a definite and adequately big world image.

We live, today, in an anxious world. Later generations will probably see our age as a time of transition from one social order to another, as we find the Middle Ages a "middle" between the Graeco-Roman civilization and the full-fledged European. But we cannot see the present that way, because what we are moving toward does not yet exist, and we can have no picture of it. Nor is the ascendency of Europe—the concert of nations consisting of white people, and their economic culture roughly coextensive with Christendom—as yet a finished act in history; but its form is broken. We feel ourselves swept along in a violent passage, from a world we cannot salvage to one we cannot see; and most people are afraid.

The deluge of novel experience that has overtaken us in the past two or three generations is, of course, widely recognized as the source of our general disorientation. Everybody knows how the social, economic, and physical aspects of life have changed—how artisan labor has given place to machinery, how new modes of travel and communication have revolutionized the social structure, bringing the most primitive cultures into direct contact with the most civilized, and how modern war and modern commerce, being worldwide, have mixed up all races and religions and tongues in a bedlam of fantastic adventure. These facts need no reiteration.

What few people realize is that the changed and still changing conditions of life are only one thing—the most tangible thing— that keeps us in a state of nervous tension verging on hysteria. There is a deeper source of anxiety, below the level of practical expectations and even of explicit thought: that is the growing inadequacy of words, and especially certain key words which have always functioned in our moral and political discourse, to express exactly what we mean in such discourse today. Perhaps the present popular excitement about "semantics" springs from a half-baked, but essentially sound, awareness of this profoundest trouble. It is a curious fact that really important philosophical issues usually evoke some echo from the public mind; indeed, the public at large has an uncanny way of feeling the importance of things about which it knows nothing explicitly. But cults and their campaigns—such as teaching huge audiences the first, superficial, often specious findings of semantic research—are quack medicine for grave philosophical ills. The inadequacy of words points to a more serious difficulty than the emotive use of language, and to get away from Aristotelian categories of thought requires more than a new formula which can be learned. The diagnosis may be essentially right, but the cure is an attack on symptoms.

What those symptoms reveal is a general frustration of our conceptual powers in the face of the new world, and that means, of

course, inability to reason clearly about it; consequently we lack
theoretical foundations to support any assertion about the things
that concern us most urgently—human rights, loyalty, freedom,
democracy, religion, nationality, culture. The cause of this bank-
ruptcy lies in two conditions: the speed with which practical changes
have overtaken the world, and the sudden expansion of thought.
Both actual life and theoretical thinking have outrun our powers of
imagination; so the average person—simple or sophisticated—is
unable to picture the universe, or even to conceive what the near
future is likely to be. The world image has collapsed.

Our chief disconcertment stems not from new experiences, but
from the fact that space and time, the implicit framework of all
experience, have changed; history actually unfolds faster than it has
ever done in the past. The development of political events is directly
influenced by the speed of communication and travel. Consider,
for instance, the difference between the Roman wars with the Goths
and with the Huns respectively: the Goths migrated with their
families, slowly pushing their westward frontier, always threatening
the established empire of Rome. When the Caesar moved against
them, the danger was obvious, but the crisis—the actual invasion of
Italy, the first march on the city—was still far in the offing. The
Goths moved at the leisurely pace of loaded wagons and of families
walking, and the political situation changed at the same rate.

The Huns came with the speed of riding men. The news of their
coming could scarcely precede them, for it could fly only at a
messenger's stretched gallop. Almost as soon as Rome knew it, the
Hun was at the gate. The political crisis was immediate.

Our history has sped up at the rate of our communication and
travel, which is so accelerated that we can no longer conceive it as
"twice as fast," "ten times as fast," as older ways. It is just out of
all proportion, so our old standards cannot even be modified to
take the new measurements. No matter how carefully we tell ourselves that things happen faster today than they used to, our ideas
of them still lag behind the change. This gives all current history an
air of extraordinary pressure, like a sudden emergency. The late

Franklin D. Roosevelt said, "You can't have an emergency for thirty years." True enough; but you can have a sense of emergency as long as that and longer.

Space, too, has undergone fundamental changes, not only in the realm of astronomy but in our earthly reckonings. Ever since the invention of steam power and the even more revolutionary gasoline motor, distances have been shrinking, as everyone knows. But recently something more radical than that has happened to the space of our living: the physical nature of places has changed. With the advent of air travel, our paths that used to be bound to the earth's topology now lie level in the upper air, and natural barriers —mountains, canyons, rivers, ice-caps and oceans—have lost their old meanings. Only the highest ranges present a "hump" in the space of our travel. The startling result is that *the earth has no secluded places any more*. Deep valleys and jungle-girded retreats lie open to peering eyes as they do to the sky. There are no more hiding places. Neither are there any real natural fastnesses; the old strongholds on cliffs and peaks are only the easier targets.

At the same time, scientific thinking, which in Newton's day was just gaining the status of "common sense" and displacing the more poetic, religious mode of thought of former centuries, has not stopped in its development. Kepler, Galileo, and Newton were only a beginning. Scientific conception has grown like Jack's beanstalk ever since, and soon left the vivid popular imagination behind. Modern mathematical operations are entirely alien to any metaphorical images we can muster. Yet we know something of this great mental adventure; for in civilized societies today almost everyone can read, and the radio spreads new ideas even to circles where reading is not commonly practiced, so everyone learns of what is going on, and the biggest thing going on is science. Our imagination is influenced by scientific notions that our reason cannot really fathom, especially as the most exciting ones have probably passed through the radio as through the meat-chopper.

The result is that the most advanced and thrilling thought of our day moves in a realm of its own. Its results come to us in the guise of "science wonders," "miracle drugs," and comic-book nightmares of interstellar wars or world-consuming explosions started by a mislaid grain of dust. The theoretical constructions behind the wonders transcend the very language we speak; they can be expressed only in mathematical symbols.

But the genuine scientific notions that have gradually become embodied in popular thought are straining it in another way: some of our most important ethical symbols have lost much if not all of their power. "High" and "low" have always symbolized good and evil; "up" and "down" therefore designated moral direction as well as spatial. The realization that "above" and "below" do not indicate fixed places, that the daytime sky and the night sky are different parts of space, and "up" and "down" mean, respectively, "away from the earth's center" and "toward the earth's center," has subtly, but profoundly influenced moral thought; for as the literal meanings of terms like "up" and "down" are seen to be relative, and what is more, relative to the earth, their symbolic sense, too, ceases to appear as something absolute, and implies a terrestial point of origin.

This is only one example, but others are not hard to find. Religion has always drawn on the model of patriarchal government, raised to the glorious degree of a monarch who owned his realm and all his subjects, a Pharaoh, a Solomon, a Caesar, a Louis. In an age that resents dynastic rule and extolls democracy, the divine ruler no longer appears in the image of something we admire, but in that of an obsolete personage or else a fairytale king. Except in a few countries that have not yielded yet to the prevailing trend, the once wise, omnipotent, and above all splendid king today is hedged about by restrictions of his power and checks on his wisdom, and walks in the garb of a somewhat formal and precise man of affairs. Earthly government is no longer a "natural symbol" of the cosmic rule once conceived in its image.

The old metaphors have lost their aptness, the old models are broken, and humanity—especially the most sensitive and thoughtful part of humanity everywhere—has lost its mental orientation and moral certitude.

Philosophy today shows violent symptoms of this intellectual collapse. Its most important exhibit is the tendency of serious present-day thinkers to base their whole philosophical undertaking not on human rationality, but on despair of reason. This makes philosophy itself not a process of constructing logical foundations for science, art, religion, and human relations, but a disciplining of the mind to accept unreason, a daily and hourly act of will to eschew reason and live either by faith or by some elected yet absolute "moral commitment." This attitude, rather than any doctrine, is the spirit of "existentialism" which pervades most of contemporary philosophy and literature in Continental Europe, and to some extent in the English-speaking countries too.

The tenets that unite the several philosophers who call themselves "existentialists"—notably Heidegger and Jaspers in Germany,* Sartre and Marcel in France—are programmatic rather than doctrinal. In doctrine these writers are often far apart. It is in aim, starting-point, and method that they belong to one spiritual movement.

Their starting-point is the recognition of existence as an ultimate inward experience; not only one's own existence,.but that of the world, which has the same character. Their problem is not to understand existence, because it is essentially irrational and therefore eludes understanding, but to accept and appreciate it. The deeper motivation of their quest is to put values into the world where they do not find them.

This is not an uncommon motive at any time, and in an age of cultural transition, full of tension, paradox, and uncertainty, it is a

---

* Both of these writers have lately repudiated the existentialist movement, as every active philosopher must reject a label that lumps his ideas with other people's. Though he was the founder of the school that bears it, Peirce rejected the label "pragmatist" after James published the "pragmatist theory of truth." Historically, Heidegger and Jaspers have been leaders of the existentialist movement, as Peirce was of the pragmatist.

powerful one; it turns thousands of people from their own vain efforts to cope with the world into the folds of religious faiths. But most people have little to sacrifice in this exchange; these men, quite otherwise, cannot easily rid themselves of their own reason that revolts against absurdity. Their writings are full of rational ideas and able arguments. Such thinkers find the acceptance of contradictions a heavy task. They have the temptation of rationality to contend with; and their philosophic method, therefore, demands a constant humiliation of reason. This humiliation is the free moral act, the constant choice, which the existentialist has to practice as the simple religious zealot practices constant prayer.

The promise of existentialism is individual selfhood, reorientation, the rescue of an emotional life that was disconcerted by fear of chaos, nothingness, and alienation. Its progress is a biographical one. The aim of this whole philosophical venture is to transcend personal limitations, meet personal needs, and solve personal·problems, no matter how many persons have the same anxiety to allay and the same "inwardness" to achieve. In this respect it resembles the ancient Hellenistic schools of Stoics, Cynics, Epicureans, and Cyrenaics; and like them, it does not contribute to theoretical thinking, because it is not a theory but an experience. It begins in "fear and trembling" and culminates in transcendence, or freedom, or affirmation of God, or self-realization in death, but not in any advance of thought; for thought is said only to build up paradoxes.

Existentialism is a movement of intellectual retreat. There may be wisdom in retreat; but at the present time there is, above all, grave danger in it. If the leaders of thought, the philosophers by vocation and training, despair of reason, who will maintain the nerve of all knowledge that it may stretch its reaches to keep the terrifying accretion of new facts in its command?

There are, fortunately, people philosophizing today who are not so consciously disoriented that the solution of personal problems dominates their systematic thought. They see philosophy as a critique of working concepts in all domains of life, especially those where old concepts are obsolete and new ones still incoherent and perhaps more than a little metaphorical. Paradox, which the existentialists regard as the end of all rational argument, is to these more extrovert thinkers its starting-point, not its stopping-place. Paradoxical ideas are imperfectly formulated ideas, and the philosopher's work is to analyze them, weigh what essential and unessential notions have gone into them (as in the classical idea of matter the concept of mass is essential, but that of unconsciousness or of ethical worthlessness is not), and define them without inconsistency. Their definition may sound strange to common sense, but at least it makes sense, and if it is adequate as well as self-consistent, then in another century or less it will even make common sense.

The most alluring, wide open fields for such new logical work at present are the natural sciences. Scientific concepts have sprung up like mushrooms in the realms of physics, chemistry, astronomy, biology. They have grown not only ahead of popular imagination, but ahead of all current academic philosophy. Great men of science have been their own philosophers. They are never afraid of ideas. Newton, Faraday, Einstein, Planck, and their peers—generation after generation—have invented the new concepts of physical science as they needed them. But of course they have limited their intellectual constructions to the requirements of their subject. Whether these bold abstractions can ever be squared with the economic, legal, moral, aesthetic and other forms of ideation that obtain in the rest of life is none of the physicist's concern; he is too busy in his own domain to play the metaphysician beyond it, and indeed, whenever he does so his imagination is as unguided by strict problems as anybody's, and is apt to lapse into traditional channels as soon as he ventures on foreign ground. Philosophy has its outposts in every special field, but its frontal advance is a task for its own scholars.

Establishing the rational foundations of scientific propositions is the work that engages the strongest philosophic minds today. It has taken them far into semantic problems: the effect of symbolic forms on meanings, the limits of logical systems, and the grounds for choice of systems. It has started a penetrating analysis of such concepts as space-time, measurement, simultaneity, location, equivalence, structure, dynamic pattern, element, form and function; but this analytic work is interwoven with the processes of new construction and logical imagination, which are naturally called for where sheer analysis can only reveal puzzles and paradoxes. Morton White, editing an anthology of recent philosophical writings, entitled the book *The Age of Analysis*. That designation of our age may be fair; analyzing concepts is our only formal technique; but few philosophers realize that their analyses are "loaded" with constructive intent, directed toward the formulation of new ideas in terms of which the scientific universe can be made conceivable again as a world, engendering and enclosing all things that are real to us.

While the sciences are striding along in seven-league boots, our social thinking seems to be stuck in a quagmire. Its very aims have become problematical. The development of practically limitless physical power has distorted and disrupted the traditional order of world power politics, which was founded on much smaller measures of violence and its effects. As Einstein once remarked, now that we know we can destroy anything we want to destroy, the threat of hostile destruction becomes something extravagant. Since the invention of atomic weapons, armed attack is no longer a reasonable diplomatic trump. A new political order, suited to a worldwide economic system and an essentially foot-loose, mingling world population, must be in the making; but so far we have no picture of it. If our old ideals and practices have become unreasonable, then unreasonable they are, but we still have them.

We are faced with an unintended, unguided, but irresistible revolution in all human relations, from the marriage bonds and family controls whereby personal life has traditionally been ordered, to the religious and patriotic loyalties that were wont to rule people's wider activities. Such a radical change in the human scene requires and effects a change in the concepts with which we operate practically and intellectually; but few people realize that their basic social conceptions have changed. While our profoundest metaphors have lost their moral import, something equally disconcerting has happened to almost all the strictly literal terms of social theory: they have become equivocal, for they no longer apply to the things we once applied them to, and the shift from old to new applications has shaken their exact sense. When we speak of "community," "society," "democracy," "freedom," we do not mean what our predecessors meant by those terms, but we still say the things they said. "A community" used to mean a more or less permanent group of individuals or families having special relations to each other that they did not have to families or persons outside the group. Can that notion be simply extended to humanity as a whole, the "world community"? "Freedom" used to mean freedom to act without restriction, as one saw fit, and take the consequences; do we mean anything like what the American pioneers called "freedom" when we propose to give people "freedom from want" or "freedom from fear"?

As space and time have changed their appearance and shaken our most elementary footholds in the physical world, language has changed its meanings without our knowing it, and thrown our literal, theoretical discourse into confusion. Our moral and political thinking lacks any sort of conceptual framework of its own. Even in special fields that we dignify with scientific sounding names—sociology, social psychology, social dynamics—there is no conceptual basis of powerful abstractions to implement deeper and deeper analysis, definitions that can be built up one upon another, like the definitions of mathematical terms or physical elements, and the building up of a highly articulated system of relationships. The terminology used at present in so-called "social science" is consciously artificial, but the concepts are still those of common sense, generalized but not abstract; that is to say, they are still prescientific.

As long as political affairs, morals apart from church doctrines, and social issues have no background of coherent, formal thought to which we can take recourse when problems become complicated, "social science" can be no guide to reasonable action. Where there is no theory there is no science, political or social or any other sort.

The usual explanation offered in excuse of this intellectual failure is that precise concepts are impossible and useless in political thought, because people are moved by self-interest or by emotion in politics, and do not act on grounds of reason. That is like saying that engineering can't build a power-dam, because dams are built by money and lobbies, not by mathematics. People are just as emotional in religion as in politics; this does not mean that theology must be unsystematic and confused. Engineering does not raise the money or pass the needed bills to get a power-dam built, but it does determine, precisely and clearly, what is involved in building the dam whenever we may decide to do so.

We need powerful concepts to cope with the welter of new conditions that beset us. At just this point, conception fails us; we have shifted too many old words to new applications, which their strict literal meanings don't quite fit, to know what we are talking about. So the bottom has gone out of our hard practical thinking. That causes the panic of distrust in reason, or, not uncommonly, a nostalgic desire to return to doctrines rationally and suitably built up in the smaller frame of a more stable world before reason became confused. Then one hears the watchwords: "Back to Kant!" "Back to St. Thomas!" "Back to Aristotle, Plato, Pythagoras!"

But we cannot go backward, except in dream. History moves forward, not backward.

Philosophy must go forward—boldly, over all obstacles—to make language adequate and literal thinking possible and effectual again. In those realms where theory is weakest, and where the terms of discourse are fuzziest, there is the greatest, most urgent work to be done. We must construct the morality of a new age, a new world; and that means a new morality. This cannot be done by adopting some simple new idea and making an "ism" of it—humanism, existentialism, Freudianism—and setting up a few general principles by which all familiar ethical rules are henceforth to be measured. It can only be done by analyzing and perhaps redefining not only obvious ethical aspects of life, but the nature of life itself, and individual life, and mentality, society, and many other subjects. Only in such long and free reflection may the abstract concepts emerge that will make social thinking as vital as physical science, and as mighty. Only by such unremitting work may we hope to engender "social sciences."

The problem of restoring the mental balance which humanity has obviously lost in this age is not psychiatric, nor religious, nor pedagogical, but philosophical. It is the inadequacy of our concepts that has finally caused all ethical and political thought to break down into rampant ideologies. The only antidote to ideology is active, purposive, confident ideation: that is the philosopher's work.

What we need today is not primarily a rebirth of good will, or a return to some ancient order of life; we need a generation of vigorous thinkers, fiercely devoted to philosophy, trained in logic, linguistics, mathematics, and prepared to learn whatever special skill or knowledge they may find needful on their way—trained as fully as any scientists, without evasion of dry subjects or stepwise procedures; people who can tackle terrible questions and fight through all the misconceptions and confusing traditions that mix up our thoughts and our lives. We must construct the scaffold for our new life, fast, ingeniously, and on big lines. We need big ideas—abstract, powerful, novel—in short, modern; that the human mind shall always encompass and control what human hands may reach.

The Symbol and the Substance

by George Hedley

It is hard to be objective about what is called the subjective, and it is impossible to be dispassionate about one's most passionate loyalties. Exact learning about religion therefore always has been difficult. Nevertheless in recent years the scholarly study of religion, as one of the fundamental ways of human acting, thinking, and feeling, and as our most rewarding way of reaching out beyond ourselves, has developed with a speed and scope unparalleled in the past.

The literature, history, and psychology of religion have become separate disciplines. The search for meaning has led to a new and intense interest in the philosophy of religion, and in the exploration of symbolic means of religious expression in liturgies, in the arts, and above all in theology. Because what we call "scientific method" has been most highly developed in the Occident, the scientific approach to religion hitherto has appeared most widely within the Hebrew-Christian tradition. This scientific enquiry indeed has issued recently in a sharp delimitation of its own capacities; but even the necessary strictures upon science have had to be, and have been, identified by scientific techniques.

The documents come first in the story. It is true that some of the Hebrew prophets violently repudiated parts of the Hebrew Law, and that the early Christian Fathers held conflicting views, and conducted completely free debates, about the authorship of many of the books of the New Testament. As time passed, however, the Bible came to be regarded as monolithic, infallible, and sacrosanct. In effect, the medieval Church left it in the background of a scene whose forestage was occupied by a mixture (scarcely a combination) of official dogmas and unofficial legends. Protestant rejection of the Church as final authority led to a new emphasis upon the Scriptures, but only slowly to new techniques in studying them.

The major leaders of Protestantism engaged in no slavish devotion to the *ipsissima verba*. Luther to all intents and purposes dropped the books of St. James, Esther, and the Revelation from his canon. Calvin saw no relationship between the Jewish Sabbath and the Christian Sunday. Wesley excised the imprecatory Psalms from his Psalter. Alexander Campbell, of the Bible-centered Disciples of Christ, in 1826 declared the King James translation to be "in many instances incorrect." It was easier, however, for the mass of Christians (including the majority of clerics) to rest upon a single authority than to investigate a plurality of problems. Thus for some three hundred years Protestantism in general assumed the Scriptures to be not only the Word of God, but also his words; and another century-plus has not disabused either the typical believer or the typical unbeliever of the misconception that this is the standard Christian position.

Fortunately most of the official schools of theology of the Protestant denominations have not remained captives of this type of anti-intellectualism. (The Roman Catholic path, for many years parallel and often pioneering, diverged sharply after 1907 when Pius X condemned "modernism" in his encyclical *Pascendi*.) From the early nineteenth century onward enquiring minds had seized upon the Biblical writings and grappled with the problems of their actual authorships, dates, and purposes. By a generation ago a number of findings of Biblical scholarship had moved from consensus into commonplace.

The "five books of Moses," plus many of the other narrative materials in the Old Testament, came to be seen as a weaving together of four major strands dating variously from 850 to perhaps 350 B.C., and representing not one but many different views both of the purposes of God and of the history of man. The book of Isaiah was separated into an eighth-century work of demolition and a sixth-century one of reconstruction, and interpolations and additions were recognized in almost all of the books of the prophets. In the New Testament the letters of St. Paul were arranged into chronological sequence, with only nine of the traditional fourteen now regarded as authentic writings of the apostle himself. The Gospel of St. Mark was recognized as a basic literary source for those of Sts. Matthew and Luke, while the Fourth Gospel was identified as being probably a Greek restatement of an originally Jewish faith.

One Old Testament example will show the kind of clarifying that ensued. As the record stands ostensibly, Abraham decides to offer his son Isaac as a sacrifice, but at the last minute learns better. Long afterward (five hundred years?) Moses forbids human sacrifice as the worst of Canaanite abominations. Yet two hundred years later still the judge Jephthah sacrifices his own daughter in fulfillment of a hasty vow, and is applauded for his fidelity if not for his good judgment. How sorely the sequence has confused and embarrassed many a sincere but uninformed Sunday School teacher!

Critical dating of the documents immediately makes sense out of this chaos. The Jephthah episode (Judges 11:29-40), latest in reputed occurrence, turns out to be earliest in its recording: about the middle of the ninth century B.C. A century later a sensitive pioneer in morality mildly suggests, in his tale of Abraham (Genesis 22:1-19), that human sacrifice scarcely is essential to please the God of the Hebrew family. Finally, after another two hundred years, the time is ripe for the jurists of the "second law" (Deuteronomy 12:31) to issue the flat prohibition which to their mind should have come from Moses. Criticism thus at once relieves conscience and straightens out the order of its growing.

Less easy for modern minds to digest, but not less important for religio-historical understanding, have been such contributions as the first notable one made by the many-sided Albert Schweitzer. Ostensibly a study of existing "lives of Christ," his *Quest of the Historical Jesus* (German 1906, English 1910) turned out to be the statement of a new and revolutionary thesis about the framework of Jesus' thinking. Schweitzer saw the whole gospel record in the light of Judaeo-Christian pessimism about the existing world order, and the correlative expectation of its immediate and cataclysmic ending. Jesus, contended the *enfant terrible* who has become the white-haired saint of Lambarene, took this popular Jewish position for granted and taught with it as his basic assumption.

This was fearfully upsetting to many scholars trained in the "liberal" Biblical tradition. They had made up their minds, long ago, that they were under no compulsion to agree with every view stated in the Bible. Many of them, however, had fallen into the habit of expecting that at least the important sections and persons of the Bible would agree with them. Few today would follow Schweitzer in making Jesus' belief in the imminent end of the world the touchstone for all his mission, but fewer now would deny that this element was present and important. The total effect, and a happy one for accurate evaluation and for religious insight as well, has been greatly to reduce the tendency to make of the man of Galilee a modern liberal Christian, and therefore to identify him the more clearly as a real citizen of Palestine in the first century. It is permissible to be amused that this current phase of historical scholarship about Jesus agrees precisely with the most orthodox theological view of his full humanity.

The first period of modern religious scholarship, within Protestantism, was heavily Bible-centered. The very study of the Bible, however, demonstrated that the Bible was at least as much a product as it was a producer. Attention then had to be turned to extra-Biblical factors: to materials other than the Bible in Biblical times, and to those later than the Bible in the history of religion.

As applied to religion, archaeology has clarified history and has amplified understanding. The prevalence of Canaanite artifacts at "Israelite" levels in Palestine demonstrates that there was cause for the recurring Scriptural protests against the adoption of Canaanite folkways and mores; and in particular the frequency of Astarte figurines illumines the passionate prophetic drive against Canaanite fertility rites. Another case is that of the seaboard settlement of the Philistines, who now have come alive as a powerful and able people, long the victims of enemy propaganda (Israelite, Egyptian, and Assyrian) coupled with their own literary silence.

One effect of Biblical archaeology, parallel to that in the classical field, has been to confirm a good deal of tradition which in early "critical" times had been regarded as completely unhistorical. The second excavation at Jericho, after World War I, revealed an almost total destruction of the city about the middle of the fifteenth century B.C. Fitted together with Canaanite complaints of marauding tribes referred to as "Habiri," this at once helped to support the Biblical account of the Israelite invasion of Palestine (though not necessarily of the wholesale character of the conquest), and to fix its date some four hundred years before David captured Jerusalem. The discovery at several Palestinian sites of small and identical weights labeled pim translated a previously obscure line in I Samuel 13:21, "and it was a pim for (sharpening) the mattocks," and confirmed the view that Philistia was in the Iron Age before Israel had attained to it.

Excavation in the Egyptian oases has revealed, through a mass of nonliterary papyri, that the Greek of the New Testament was precisely the colloquial speech of the Levant in the Hellenistic age. This not only served to establish the character of early Christianity as a religion appealing consciously and unpretentiously to the common man, but also provided new and vivid renderings for many New Testament words and phrases. Jesus crucified is, in Galatians, no longer merely "openly set forth" but publicly "placarded"; the Law as "schoolmaster" is a tutor-slave; St Paul does not "buffet" his body but "punishes" it as in a prize ring; and "Be not anxious" turns into "Don't skin yourself."

The most sensational find of recent years, and possibly the most important, has been that of the so-called "Dead Sea Scrolls." It will be a long time, thanks to the combination of political conflict, Arab peasant commercialism, and problems of physical handling and decipherment, before the full content of these materials can be known. It will take many times as long till the inevitable battles about their significance will have been fought out to the establishment of a scholarly consensus. Two points, however, now are reasonably clear.

One is that at last we have actual manuscripts of some of the Hebrew scriptures dating from almost a thousand years before those of the traditional ("Masoretic") Hebrew text, and so we are much nearer to the original readings, whether of disputed passages or of those that up to now have been taken for granted. The other is that, with the new light that seems to have been thrown upon the monastic community of the Essenes, the statements of Philo and Josephus about them have enhanced authority and take on additional meaning. The implication that Jesus was directly influenced by the Essenes, or that he may indeed have been a member of the sect, will require further and careful examination. The general effect to date is to reinforce the judgment which scholars long have held, to the effect that the recorded teachings of Jesus were unique in selection and implementation rather than in invention.

Another expansion of interest beyond the Bible has been into the history of the Christian Church in its first fifteen centuries. To most of the early Protestants this had seemed a period of decline and apostasy, well to be forgotten. The reaction of the Counter-Reformation long tended to make historical studies on the Roman Catholic side polemical rather than exploratory. Both antagonists now are doing better; the Protestants trying to identify the real nature of historic Catholic Christianity, the Romans applying to their own tradition the canons of literary and historical criticism. Partisan interests are not quite dead in either camp, but they are feebler far than they were a half century ago.

Christian scholars thus are newly aware, even if the Protestant laity isn't, that Christianity has not only a long history before Jesus, but also a long and critically important history after him. The teaching of the Church is rooted indeed in the New Testament, but its flowering and its fruits are not all to be found there. Many of them came long after, and new and sometimes surprising growth continues even yet to appear.

Patient and enquiring reading of the Fathers of the Church, and of the memoranda and decrees of the ecumenical Councils, has shown that the theological disputing of the fourth century was neither the warfare of absolute truth with absolute error, as many of the later orthodox had supposed, nor the senseless quarreling about trivia which recent liberalism had considered it. There were not only local quarrels, and cultural clashes between regions, and honest differences of opinion among churchmen. There were also basic and important differences in estimates of value. The notable case is that of the Trinitarian controversy, whose resolution in favor of "same essence" gave to the Christian fellowship an organic unity which it scarcely could have possessed if the Arian view of "similar essence" had prevailed.

The Byzantine tradition, long ignored by both Roman Catholics and Protestants as a fatty degeneration of the Christian heart and mind, turns out on reexamination to be rich not only in art works but also in important types of religious experience and expression. The folk faith of the Ethiopians, issuing in the elaboration of the cult of the Virgin; the liturgical riches of Constantinople and Alexandria and Malabar; the quiet quest of the Holy Ghost in the monasteries of Mount Athos; the development of the great Russian churches from a blending of Mediterranean domes and snow-covered gables; all these have captured the interest of scholarship, and all have much yet to yield in data and in comprehension.

To us the story of Western Christendom is more familiar, if not yet familiar enough. Others than G. K. Chesterton and Hilaire Belloc are realizing that the "Middle Ages" were not a void between

Classical Antiquity and modern times, but vital creators of the world we live in. The medieval scholastics and mystics and heretics are being restudied and ever and again reinterpreted. The "reformers before the Reformation," and the founders of Protestant movements large and small, are better known than they were and will be known better still. The broad churchmen of England, the social idealists of America, the sects of the underprivileged on both sides of the Atlantic, the modern monks of Einsiedeln or Solesmes, the theologians of Halle and Copenhagen and Göttingen and New York, are integral to the patterns of the religion in the West. None may be omitted if our knowledge and understanding are to be anywhere nearly complete.

Nor is the Judaeo-Christian tradition by any means all. "Comparative Religion," which began in medieval polemics against Islam, no longer is a tendentious comparison of the Christian ideal with the non-Christian actual to the necessary advantage of Christianity. Intelligence and conscience here again have combined to require a fairer and more accurate approach. The nineteenth century saw a vast amount of first translating of Indian, Persian, Chinese, and Arabic religious writings, and the twentieth is digging ever deeper into their meanings.

Embarrassing to "special creationists" in Christian circles, but greatly illumining to those who enquire to learn, is the discovery of many and great resemblances between the Christian and the "heathen" scriptures. Not only did ancient Babylonia have a flood myth comparable to the Israelite one of Noah, but the arid plateau of Persia turned out to have its own parallel in the "seven fatal winters." Both nationalism and universalism appeared in the Hindu Vedas much as they did in the Jewish Psalms, and monotheism was declared with the same rigor by Muhammad as it had been by the second Isaiah.

Something like the "Golden Rule" turned out to be nearly universal. Religious loyalty, at whatever cost to the individual, was as ringingly urged (if to our minds as puzzlingly expressed) in the *Bhagavad-Gita* as in the Revelation of St. John. Confucius evidently would have been quite at home sitting among the wise men who compiled the book of Proverbs, and Laotse would have said, of the *Logos* of the Fourth Gospel, "This is just what I mean by the *Tao*." Some there were who deprecated these similarities as mere matters of chance. To others they were new and encouraging evidence that God has not left himself without a witness among any people, that human values and aspirations are essentially alike wherever men think intently and live seriously.

Identity is not all, and comparison with Christianity is not the only, nor the necessary, technique in the approach to the religions of the Orient. A notable example of the study of an Oriental system in its own right is the work of Dr. D. T. Suziki, of the Otani Buddhist College in Tokyo, on that immediate-apprehension form of Buddhism which is known as Zen. The late Dr. J. B. Pratt of Williams College remarked that "there are two kinds of cultured people; those who have read Professor Suzuki's work on Zen Buddhism, and those who have not." Not a few Occidentals, including a striking number of psychiatrists, have found Buddhism, in one or another of its myriad types of expression, to be the religious answer they personally want. Whether or not there is such conversion, there needs to be quite as much scholarly work done on the proliferation of Buddhist movements as there has been on the multiple forms of Christianity; and the complexities of Hinduism and Islam, when they are duly recognized, turn out to be scarcely fewer or less intricate.

One persisting handicap in these fields of enquiry is that as yet there are relatively few adherents of the Eastern religions who have the thoroughgoing scholarship of a Suzuki, and who are willing to apply the canons of criticism sharply to their own traditions. The revised chronology of the sections of the Quran, established by Western scholars, is largely ignored by Muslims. The pluralism of Hindu religious origins is blanketed by most Hindu teachers in a clinging fog of philosophical monism. The Chinese in the past were prepared by the realism of their primary hero to be realistic about him, but there seems to be little objectivity toward the conservative Confucius today in the People's Republic. For the time being, then, it seems that the West will have to continue its leadership in the scholarly study of the religions of the East, though always under the necessary disadvantage of an approach made from outside.

Implications of historical analysis, as applied to the Bible, to Church history, and to the history of religion in general, could not but present themselves in the realm of personal religious faith and attitude. Probably the greatest single force in the recent development of humanistic studies has been the new science of psychology. Inevitably psychology has concerned itself with the phenomena of religion. The study of the psychology of religion has followed, as one would expect, the waves and currents of general psychological fashion. William James saw The Varieties of Religious Experience against the backdrop of his own somewhat romantic empiricism. The heyday of Watsonite behaviorism coincided with that of liberal modernism, whose mood combined a pedestrian factualism with a comfortable religious and ethical relativity. Freud changed all that; but then came Jung, and Künkel, and a host of others, to change the religious findings of Freud.

The psychologists of religion began to examine now not the works of official theologians, but those of the mostly unofficial persons called "mystics." The psychological processes at work in these were visible enough, and could readily be described in the jargon of Vienna and Zurich. They could be described, but it turned out that they were not thereby explained. How these men and women had searched for God was evident, and not only in Europe but also in India and Japan. What they had found nevertheless refused to melt away. The psychology of religion had helped to interpret some aspects of religion, but it had no more disposed of religion than the psychology of art has abolished aesthetic experience. Scientific honesty and humility then compelled the judgment that the indemonstrable was not necessarily the nonexistent, the unknowable not inevitably the unreal.

Another twentieth-century religious phenomenon to be examined, a parallel to mysticism, is a most rigorous form of Protestant theological doctrine. Karl Barth is unmentioned in a standard American *Dictionary of Religion and Ethics* published in 1921. (The same volume, incidentally, says nothing of the nineteenth-century Kierkegaard either. *O tempora, O mores!*) Indeed Barth's first book to be translated into English appeared only in 1928. Today his name and his work may be ignored by no one who would know anything of current religious life and thought. Out of the hammering of World War I there came, in 1919, Barth's *Römerbrief*; and out of that a new day in all informed Protestant thinking. This, at least; and the Roman Catholic theologians are indifferent neither to Barth nor to the movement he initiated.

The essence of Barthianism, described as "crisis theology" and more loosely as "neo-orthodoxy," is precisely the proposition that man's encounter with the divine is at once absolute and indefinable. God is the "wholly other," by no means to be captured within the formulae of men, yet always confronting man with the ultimate in moral obligation. Soon it was recognized that this was just what Calvin had insisted upon three hundred years before; and so neo-orthodoxy appears today as an authentic neo-Calvinism.

Because the mystic had seemed usually so assured of his direct contact with infinite reality, and so little dependent upon the guidance of either Church or Scripture, most of the contemporary neo-orthodox have been wary of the mystic way. It is possible, however, to suppose the kinship which they have thought to deny. Confident as are the mystics of their experience, they are emphatic that it cannot be verbalized with any degree of precision. Both for them and for the Barthians, God is at once totally real and almost totally indescribable. For both, the conviction of divine reality rests not upon scientific demonstration but on immediate inner contact. For both, then, the objective judgment about the subjective is that what is called the subjective is real, whatever scientific objectivity may have to say about it.

Can there be any nexus between Deity and humanity, intuition and research, spirit and body? Are we forever doomed to fall into the abysses that lie between such dualities? In the effort to aid the humanistic enterprise of understanding human nature, the problem of religious scholarship has turned out to be the very problem of religion itself. "Cur deus homo?" asked St. Anselm of Canterbury: "Why a God-man?" The seeker of today asks, "How does God come to man?"

Anselm's reply from the late eleventh century, which is one directed to both forms of the question, seems curiously to lead toward our most advanced twentieth-century thinking; but we shall have to trace it by a somewhat circuitous route. The way is that of symbolism. We do not know God, says Anselm, as we know physical objects, nor even as we know many of our abstract ideas. When we try to think of God, therefore, we think in terms of what we do know: of ideas and objects that are in the range of our comprehension and description.

This is the nature and function of symbolism. It may be as crass as the clay Astarte, as clumsy as the Aztec goddess of the corn; or it may be as subtle and articulate as the finest-spun passages in St. Thomas's Summa. It is symbolism in either case, the use of something else in the effort to reflect and represent something, of the object as the carrier of a value.

The danger of symbolism is obvious. It is ever that of idolatry. "These be thy gods, O Israel!" has been applicable not only to the golden calves of Aaron, but also to statues of St. Mary the Virgin, to the creeds of the Church, to days of fasting and festival, to the absolutist formulae of Midwestern fundamentalism. It always is idolatry to confuse the symbol with the reality.

The early Protestants saw this with reference to the images of the saints, though not all of them as to the phrasing of the Bible. The liberal modernists, more inclusive in their negativity, tried to sweep away all symbols because in themselves they were not finally real. But thereby the Protestants excluded from their ken not only the churchly statues but also the noble army of martyrs whom they represented, and the modernists soon found themselves left with no reality that mattered. Infantilism had assumed a one-for-one correlation between the immediate and the ultimate. It was surely a kind of adolescence that had reduced the correlation to zero. Slowly a renewed adulthood began to supervene.

One effect of the realization that man does not and can not get along without symbols has been a revival of interest in religious architecture and in the procedures of public worship. The fields of liturgics, of Christian iconography and music, or hymnology, have been cultivated with an increasing discernment and heightening enthusiasm. In one way these enquiries are factual and historical. In another they are psychological too, and ultimately philosophical in the fullest sense.

Even more important, the necessarily symbolic nature of every kind of religious utterance has become apparent. The historic creeds have come to mean not less, but more, as attention has turned from their apparent narration of events to their central assertion of meanings. Bowdlerizing of the Bible, a besetting habit in modernist circles, is yielding to a fresh appreciation of essential Biblical intentions. From the innocence of its childhood the Christian mind thus has moved, through the literalism of its schooldays, toward the sympathetic sophistication of the mentally and morally grown up.

This is where St. Anselm comes in. Why a God-man? The answer is myth, if you will; but it is the kind of myth that alone will lead us nearer to ultimate truth. The myth of incarnation, "that God became man by necessity," is the nearest that man yet has come to bridging the gap between himself and the creative and sustaining force which undergirds all being. "The Logos became flesh, and dwelt among us." This is considered philosophy. It is vaulting imagination. It is the core of the Christian faith.

Those of us who count ourselves Christian do not pretend that this central myth of ours includes all that is in the outer reality. The very limits of our knowledge, as marked out by scientific enquiry, prohibit any such claim; and religious intuition readily concurs. We are nevertheless persuaded that the actualities of human experience and the symbolic nature of human thought unite to drive us to this symbol of the God-man beyond all others, because it does more than any other to bring together the polarities of immediate and ultimate.

Historical, documentary, and psychological enquiry will go on to reap new harvests of learning, and philosophy and theology will continue to build new structures to contain them. None of these will avoid symbolism, both because they cannot and because our time is willing to rejoice in symbol once more. Nor within their inescapable symbolisms will they capture everything of the truth. What their history to date does argue is that the symbol of the eternal Christ revealed in the historic man Jesus is the one best designed to reflect the confrontation of finite man by the infinite God.

18

CONCLUSION

The Changing Canons
of Our Culture

by Lynn White, jr.

WHEN this book was planned, it was uncertain
that any "conclusion" or summary would be warranted. The sixteen
other contributors were selected not because they belong to one
scholarly clique or *avant-garde*, but because their researches and
their ability to write gave promise that they could tell the educated
public about the new questions, the new means of investigation, and
the new kinds of insight now developing in the many approaches to
the study of *Homo sapiens*. Moreover, save for casual correspondence
and conversation, each chapter was written independently. If common denominators emerge, they may therefore be the more meaningful for having been spontaneously generated, unpremeditated, often
implicit rather than explicit.

Little uniformity of thinking but an astonishing convergence of
intellectual tendencies is to be found in the preceding pages. There
is a pervasive conviction that our image of the person is changing.
One symptom of this change is the assumption that one can no
longer profitably discuss Man: one talks about people, about the
ways in which they act and interact, think and feel in terms of the
pattern of a given culture, and about how deviation from the norms
of that culture molds individuals and eventually may remold the

pattern of culture. Indeed, the most permeative idea in this book is the anthropologists' concept of culture: it has irrigated the whole field of humanistic study. Our new, image of the person may therefore best be described and understood in terms of basic changes in our own culture.

There is consensus today that although inevitably we are the offspring of the past, we are mutants as well. We are living in a time of general shift more fundamental than any since agriculture and herding displaced food-gathering and hunting as the habit of human existence. Not only the outer forms of living are being remodeled: our standards of values, thought and conduct, our criteria of judgment, all of our yardsticks are altering as well. The very canons of our culture are changing.

What are these changes of canon?

For one thing, ever since the days of the Greeks our thinking has been framed within the canon of the Occident. This is the unexamined assumption that civilization par excellence is that of the Western tradition; that history is essentially the stream of events which began with the siege of Troy and which gradually expanded from its first drama in the Levant to find ever wider stages in the Mediterranean of the Pax Romana, the Europe of medieval Latin Christendom, and the North Atlantic civilization of so-called Modern Times. All else—the epic spectacles of Peru and Mexico, of Islam, India and further India, of China, Korea, and Japan, even of that extraordinary Eastern Christendom of Byzantium and Russia— was either irrelevant or at best a cabinet of curiosities. To us, Man has really meant European-American Man: the rest were "natives." We may snicker at the California country pastor who habitually prayed "for the conversion of the heathen in the heart of Africa where the foot of man has never trod," but his naïvete illustrates what we are outgrowing. Our image of the person is ceasing to assume tacitly that the white man is made peculiarly in the likeness of God.

The canon of the Occident has been displaced by the canon of the globe. Today everything from communism to Coca Cola is becoming worldwide in its range. This has the ring of platitude only because we have accepted it so completely in the realm of international politics. Few of us realize the extent to which our most ordinary actions and thoughts are today being formed according to non-Occidental models. Admitting that we are change-prone, just why do we change as we do? There are superficial reasons indeed, but no really adequate explanations for such casual facts as that the use of vodka, for example, is growing so rapidly in America today, or that in any large liquor store one can buy saki, a beverage theoretically available but practically unknown among us a decade ago. Of making cookbooks there is no end; but why, suddenly, is there a market for innumerable ordinary kitchen-shelf cookbooks which, without cultural pretensions or hands-across-the-sea flourishes, simply assimilate the skewers of Armenia, the woks of China, and much else to everyday American cookery?

To be sure, no great culture of the Old World has ever been entirely isolated: borrowings have been constant. The eighteenth century loved chinoiserie and took to drinking tea out of porcelain cups—equipped, we may note, with unoriental saucers into which one might pour the tea if it were too hot. But this was consciously a fad; we today are different in the extent of our readiness to assimilate alien influences and our relative unconsciousness about the process. For several decades China and Korea have been the chief factors in furniture design from Los Angeles to Stockholm. A bride, recoiling from her mother's taste, today chooses the new without thinking of its Asian inspiration, which in any case is largely masked by the cliché of "functionalism." And Japan is the obvious source of most that is best in contemporary American and European domestic architecture. Not long ago a group of American ladies arranged to entertain some visiting Japanese students with a house-tour of the finest recently-built homes in their community. The students remained in a state of courteous boredom—after all, all this looked pretty much like grandmother's house on Kyushu—

until they burst into arm-waving enthusiasm over the sparkling gingerbread of an immaculately preserved Victorian villa which their hostesses had added to the tour to show how we had progressed. Clearly, while the Western tourist wails that the Orient is being "ruined" by Occidental influences, the Oriental may rightly feel that from his standpoint the West too is losing its distinctive and "picturesque" qualities by overmuch orientalization.

"But," objects the diminished ghost of Plato, "tacos and pilaff, crockery and bedposts, are not the essence of a civilization: it is ideas that are really important. Quite naturally our Asian friends have been taking over the superb philosophical concepts which are in the public domain of the West, but can it be shown that we are absorbing anything equivalent from them?"

For the moment, but only for the moment, let us refrain from looking at the structure of values which underlies the question: it can perhaps be answered in its own terms.

For more than a century, since the days of Schopenhauer and Emerson at least, the professional thinkers of the North Atlantic civilization have been consciously subject to Asian influences, but these have been regarded as an exotic rather than an integral element in our thought. In the last two or three decades, however, the psychoanalytic movement, the study of semantics, and the intricate skein of philosophies and theologies labeled Existentialism have combined to challenge the ancient Platonic-Cartesian dualism which polarized experience between mind and body, spirit and substance, time and eternity, man and nature, natural and supernatural. Because of all this we are at the moment peculiarly vulnerable to influences drawn from the stream of Buddhist thought which rose first in India and flowed in a broadening current through China to Japan, where it came to be known as Zen. With an almost unbelievable sophistication, but naturally in terms of their own tradition, the Zen thinkers faced and pondered many of the issues which are uppermost in the minds of Western linguists, psychologists, and philosophers today; and these latter, whether directly or by reflection, are finding light from the East. Prophecy is rash, but it may well be that the publication of D. T. Suzuki's first *Essays in Zen Buddhism* in 1927 will seem in future generations as great an intellectual event as William of Moerbeke's Latin translations of Aristotle in the thirteenth century or Marsiglio Ficino's of Plato in the fifteenth. But in Suzuki's case the shell of the Occident has been broken through. More than we dream, we are now governed by the new canon of the globe.

One reason for the subtly pervasive influence of Zen among us, even upon those who have never heard of it, is its challenge to a second major canon which we inherited from the Greeks: *the canon of logic and language*. For more than two thousand years in the West it has been axiomatic that logic and language are perfected instruments of intellectual analysis and expression. The training of our minds has consisted essentially of getting skills in logic, whether in its philosophical or its mathematical form, and in language, by which we have meant the European and, until recently, the classical tongues. Much of our present discussion of education is still based on the premise that the mind which has mastered logic and language is able to achieve clear and efficient results in any field.

But there is a new and more complex canon today, one which does not deny the validity of the canon of logic and language but which puts it into a wider context, just as the canon of the globe does not negate the canon of the Occident but changes its nature by amplifying it.

This second new canon is *the canon of symbols*. It insists that logic and language are neither perfected nor infallible, but rather that they are simply two most marvellous—and still evolving—human devices closely related to a cluster of similar inventions of symbolic intellectual instruments: the visual arts, literature, music, dance, theatre, liturgy, mythology, formulations of scientific law, philosophical patterns, and theological systems. A symbol may be a novel, a creed, a formula, a gesture, or a cadence, as well as an image, a word, or a crescent, cross, or swastika. We are beginning to see that the distinctive thing about the human species is that we are a symbol-making animal, *Homo signifex*, and that without this function we could never have become *sapiens*.

For we have not only a capacity for making symbols: we are under necessity to create them in order to cope humanly with our experience. An orangutang or a tiny child may manage in terms of things immediately sensed or remembered as sensed. But thought or communication involving relationships or generalizations, much less any complex imagination of what might be as compared with what is, seems to demand symbols. For practical purposes we do not and cannot deal with things in themselves: we must deal with signs pointing toward things.

The fact that these signs are arbitrary to the point of whimsicality is not a defect but a virtue: each arbitrary creation may open new vistas to the mind's eye. If this book were in Hopi it would still convey much the same ideas, but some probably a bit more lucidly and some a bit more obscurely; for each convention of symbols has its peculiar capacities and weaknesses. Our race needs both Hopi and English.

The mathematicians above all others have discovered the utility of developing different symbolic grammars which may be mutually contradictory but which are functional so long as they are internally coherent. In 1733, as intellectual sport the Jesuit Girolamo Saccheri challenged Euclid's axiom of parallels and, substituting the "nonsensical" axiom that through a given point two lines may be drawn parallel to a given line, he constructed a self-consistent non-Euclidean geometry. Unfortunately he laughed it off as a *jeu d'esprit*. Not until four generations later did mathematicians realize that he had made a great discovery. Then a whole constellation of contrasting geometries burst forth, and it was with the light of Riemannian geometry that Einstein found the mathematical key for the release of atomic energy. The most astonishing part of the new canon of symbols is the discovery that we human beings can deal with facts only in terms of fantasies. We have only begun to understand the instrumental validity of arbitrary symbols.

Indeed, even the way our senses report experience to us may be structured by the conventions of language, art, or the like. Recently an American psychologist studied changes in perception and methods of solving problems which took place among members of the Baganda tribe in Uganda as they learned English and came under European influence. He gave them pieces of cardboard of different shapes, sizes, and colors and asked them to separate them into piles. Those who had been in English-language schools almost always divided them according to color, as Westerners do. Those who had had few European contacts built piles on the basis of size or shape, but almost never according to color: the language of the Bagandas is almost entirely lacking in words for colors, and evidently the tribesmen are simply not equipped to detect such variations. If Homeric Greek makes no distinction between blue and green, can we be sure that those less blind than Homer were able to see the difference? And when, toward the middle of the thirteenth century, Villard de Honnecourt appends to his sketch of a lion the proud scribble, "Note well that this lion was drawn from life," should we be astonished that his lion is exactly one of those tame little poodle-lions, with a mane of symmetrical ringlets, universally found in late Romanesque and early Gothic sculpture? In every society there is a convention of vision, and perhaps of each of the senses.

A most important aspect of the canon of symbols, therefore, is our realization that while symbols are created by us, these creatures in a peculiar way come alive, turn upon us, and coerce us and our experience to conform to their anatomy.

For example, any man who makes it his business to observe American women closely will quickly discover that in our land women are emotionally dependent on men in a way quite different from that in which men are dependent on women. Despite all the proud talk of sex equality, women themselves refer to "hen parties" with contempt and to "stag parties" with a twinge of envy. The reasons for this widespread and unwarranted feminine sense of being secondary are many, but at least one of them is linguistic. The grammar of English dictates that when a referent is either of indeterminate sex or of both sexes, it shall be considered masculine.

The penetration of this habit of language into the minds of little girls as they grow up to be women is more profound than most people, including most women, have recognized; for it implies that personality is really a male attribute, and that women are a human subspecies. It is dramatized in the story of the suffragette fight in Britain, when a young recruit to the feminist forces burst into tears after a little clash with police over picketing. "My daughter, don't despair," said a seasoned campaigner. "Pray to God and She will give you strength!" It would be a miracle if a girl-baby, learning to use the symbols of our tongue, could escape some unverbalized wound to her self-respect; whereas a boy-baby's ego is bolstered by the pattern of our language.

Intuitions of this sort, related to the new canon of symbols, lead us on to the recognition of a third major change in the canons of our culture. From the Greeks, again, we inherit the canon of rationality which assumes that reason is the supreme human attribute and that anything other than rationality is "less" than rationality and to be deplored as subhuman. It assumes that disagreements are not fundamental, and that, with adequate reasonable discussion and examination of the evidence, a single truth will emerge acceptable to all men.

But now we dwell in a world dominated by the canon of the unconscious. Closer scrutiny of our mental processes has shown that a vast lot is happening in the shadowy irridescence, the black opal of the abyss which lies within each of us. Our scientists, in particular, have become fascinated by the problem of the genesis of original ideas, and have resuscitated the word "serendipity" to label one of the most curious aspects of intellectual creation: the seemingly instantaneous discovery of something entirely unexpected in the course of hard work toward a different goal. The word was invented in 1754 by Horace Walpole from the legend of the Princess of Serendip: she had three suitors to each of whom she assigned an impossible task; all three failed, but in the course of his heroic struggles each accomplished something even more marvelous.

Every scholar and artist has in some measure experienced serendipity: the sudden welling up into consciousness of insights, intellectual structures, visions which clearly would never have come had the conscious mind not been in travail, but of whose gestation we had no forewarning. Reason is not all of the mind.

For many centuries such thinkers as St. Thomas Aquinas, so rationalist that they perceived some limitations of reason, groped towards a picture of the human mind as a shiny sheet of metal, part of which is bent back upon itself so that it is mirrored in itself. Reason is the part of the mind which is capable of reflection, that is, of contemplating its own processes. The rest of the mind perhaps does not differ from reason in its essential qualities, particularly in creativity. But unfortunately we cannot yet easily watch it in action.

Aldous Huxley in his essay on mescalin has pointed out that, as the chemistry and physiology of our nervous system become clearer, experimental means of peering into these mysteries may be developed. To date, the psychoanalytic assault on the problem of the unconscious has been the most sustained and probably the most rewarding. Yet its very success has opened up new complexities: the unconscious seems to be as deeply conditioned by cultural forms as is the conscious mind. Surely the relative scarcity in America of the Oedipus complex, at least in its "classic" Freudian form, is related to the contrast between the paternal monarchy of the nineteenth-century Viennese family and the chaotic town-meeting government of the typical American family of recent decades.

The social psychologists, anthropologists, and historians are proving helpful in this exploration of the unconscious. For example, it is becoming clear that episodes such as the slaughter of the Jews by the Nazis, the four centuries of the witch-mania during the European Renaissance, or the recent resurgence of witchcraft and witch hunting among the Navahos, are intelligible not in terms of the functioning of the rational faculty but as group responses to spiritual crises, as means of coping with and "explaining" deep psychic disturbances produced by catastrophic shifts in the cultural foundations. The linguists analyzing non-European tongues have reached similar insights: language structures, social relationships, and cosmologies often have a related pattern among a given people, and the emotions and unconscious attitudes as well as the verbalized ideas of participants in a culture seem to be shaped by these as definitely as a Flathead Indian's brain is shaped by the headboard of his papoose cradle.

The human mind is not completely conditioned. It can achieve an extraordinary degree of freedom and "objectivity." But we have come to see that logical reasoning and rational confrontation of relevant evidence is only part of the task if true freedom is to be won. The idea that there are unconscious areas of the mind is not new, but in no previous era, of Western thought at least, has it loomed so large or challenged us so insistently. The realization of the scope, the dangers, and the potentialities of the unconscious is essential to our new image of the person.

It is significant that, more and more, we are using the word *unconscious* rather than *subconscious*. The latter is involved in metaphorical association of up-and-down spatial relationships with value judgments, and it thus might trick us into assuming that the unconscious is in some way *sub* and therefore inferior or unworthy. This aspect of the new canon of the unconscious illustrates the fourth, and final, major change of canon which is observable in our culture.

Although some of the earlier Ionian philosophers seem to have had a different bent of mind, ever since the great days of Athens we have generally thought, felt and acted in terms of the canon of the hierarchy of values. We have assumed and consciously taught that some types of human activity are more worthy of study and reverence than others because the contemplation of them seemed to bring greater spiritual rewards. This hierarchy of values, expressed most clearly in the ancient concept of the liberal arts, was codified in the Middle Ages, expanded in the Renaissance and post-Renaissance, and has continued to be manifest in emphasis on the importance of mathematics, logic, philosophy, literature, and the unapplied sciences. Within its self-imposed limitations, this tradition of personal cultivation and of education had an unsurpassed richness and intellectual magnificence.

But large parts of human experience and creativity were omitted from the upper rungs of this ladder of values which provided the pattern and rationale of our inherited culture. Anything, above all, which required the use of the hands was excluded, not only rigorously but with some indignation, from the area of prestige which was reflected in the older liberal arts curricula. It was shut out because the top brackets of culture and education were the perquisite of an aristocracy which used not its hands but its brains.

The Greeks and Romans, living in a slave economy, considered use of the hands banausic and contemptible. Primitive Christianity, largely a proletarian movement, had contrary instincts which were perpetuated by the medieval monks and by their Protestant ascetic offshoot, the Puritans. But the notion that "to labor is to pray," that work with the hands is integral to the good life, was slow to make an impression on our cultural tradition, presumably because society remained largely aristocratic or hierarchical in organization. Today we have forgotten, or can scarcely believe, the degree to which manual operations were once avoided by those who were, or aspired to be, of the upper crust. For example, old pictures of the dissection of cadavers in medical schools show not only that the professor of anatomy almost invariably stood lecturing from a medical text while a barber-surgeon assistant actually wielded the scalpel but that, at a slightly later period when this assistant had come to achieve a certain social status, he too, although present to supervise, delegated the actual dissection to a second assistant.

The secret of the almost explosive originality of our times is the wiping out (save in certain cultural backwaters) of the ancient barrier between the aristocrat and the worker. Americans, whose ancestors first created a large-scale equalitarian community, should take particular pride in this reunion of the human hand and brain into their proper organic whole: the ideal image of the person is no longer the armless Venus of Milo. Yet even in America our language and our presuppositions are still so permeated by the inherited aristocratic tradition that it is hard to put into words just what is involved in the fact that the combined democratic and technological revolutions have made both workers of us all and aristocrats of us all; that' the two sets of values, historically so sharply divided, are now confused and must be schematized according to a new plan.

This plan is emerging: the old canon of the hierarchy or ladder of values has turned at right angles to become a new canon of the spectrum of values. Whereas the old canon insisted that some human activities are by their nature more intellectually and spiritually profitable than others, the new canon holds that every human activity, whether changing diapers or reading Spinoza, whether plowing for barley or measuring galaxies, enshrines the possibility—perhaps not the actuality but the potentiality—of greatness: its proper contemplation and practice promise the reward of insight. "What is the Buddha?" asked the Zen novice. "Three pounds of rice," replied the abbot.

"All the road to heaven is heaven," said St. Teresa of Avila. The notion of a spectrum of values, as distinct from a hierarchy of values, challenges all the dualisms which, among us Occidentals, for over two thousand years have divided the seamless coat of actual human experience. The path and the goal, means and ends, becoming and being, process and purpose—all these fuse into nowness. We are no longer under compulsion to violate immediacy: each perception, whatever its nature, may be the beatific vision, each moment orchestrated for Gabriel's trumpet. Just as the economic and political revolutions of our time have produced an egalitarian society, so our intellectual revolution has insisted on—what would have seemed a logical and semantic absurdity to former ages—an equality of values. Indeed, we suddenly realize the weakness of our verbal symbols: clearly "value" is a monetary metaphor, inherently scaled up-and-down rather than sideways. Yet we have no other serviceable word, so we must use the term "value," understanding in what sense it is obsolete.

Just as aristocratic forebodings that a democratic social order would necessarily mean the end of personal cultivation and individualism have not been realized, so democratic insistence on the equal potential worth of what have been called "values" does not inevitably lead to mental or emotional drabness. On the contrary, it can open our eyes to the spiritual possibilities inherent in types of experience and creativity which, because of a divided society and class-centered education, could not be envisaged as a whole by any previous generation.

It compels us, for example, to redefine our notion of "genius" to embrace kinds of originality hitherto overlooked. Sometime about 1420 an unknown carpenter or shipwright, presumably a Fleming, invented the bit-and-brace, thus making possible continuous rotary motion in boring. By that act he invented the compound crank and precipitated the greatest single revolution in the design of machinery: by 1430 we find machines involving double compound cranks and two connecting rods. No unconscious "evolution" led to the brace: it was created by a leap of the mind which imagined and implemented a new kinetic pattern which has been fundamental to the development of modern society. Until we have learned to look at the carpenter's brace with a certain awe, we have not begun to absorb the cultural implications of the democratic revolution.

All four of the old canons which have suffered a sea change in the storms of our time were formulated by the first consciously Occidental society, that of Athens. In the realm of thought and emotion, twenty-four centuries of Hellenic dominance now are ended. The marvel is not that our vision is confused but rather that we are learning so quickly how to view mankind from vantage-points other than the Acropolis.

Whenever there is major change there is likewise risk of great loss. If we have made a correct analysis of the four mutations of canon which are going on around us, what are the cultural treasures which may be endangered by this flux?

Does the change from the canon of the Occident to the canon

of the globe in any way diminish the wonder, the amazing variety and spontaneity of the Western tradition in which we Americans stand? No; but it imposes upon us the difficult problem of how to become citizens of the world without uprooting ourselves from our native soil. A superficial cosmopolitanism is no adequate substitute for a cultural parochialism which makes up in spiritual depth what it lacks in breadth. How are we to become cultivated in global terms when most of us don't manage it in Occidental terms?

The canon of logic and language has become the canon of symbols. Are logic and language less important than formerly? No; now we can envisage and use them as parts of a vastly expanded set of tools of analysis and communication. But whereas once a person could confidently regard himself as educated if he were competent with these two instruments (including, of course, mathematics), how is each of us today to learn to handle the rest with facility, or even to know what is happening when other people are employing them? In a brief life which can accommodate only a short period of formal education, how can we learn the vocabulary, grammar, and semantics of drama, dance, music, and the like? How can we explore the mutually contradictory but often coherent thought structures of the major philosophers, and learn to use them, as a mathematician uses the different incompatible geometries, each to achieve a variant quality of vision? How can we find time or imagination enough to encompass the language of myth, which tells not what once happened but what is always happening? How can we come to understand, from the inside, why Newton considered himself almost more a theologian than a mathematician? The peril is that, like small children suddenly taken to a new land with a strange speech, we may become tongue-tied. Indeed, the state of much current literature, music, and art makes one fear that this is in fact happening.

Now that the canon of rationality has become the canon of the unconscious, does this mean that we should simply assume that we and all other people are essentially irrational and need no longer bother with the disciplines of reason? No; it means that we have come to realize more clearly than ever before the psychological, biological, and cultural context of the rational function. We have recognized the chances that self-interest or self-deception will mask itself quite honestly as rationality. That we name such cover-up thinking with the popular word "rationalizing" shows how deeply this conception has penetrated the general mind. We have put our idea of the conscious mind into the frame which in fact it has always had, and by this sharper delimitation of its bounds we can become more aware of the nature, the uses, and the glory of rationality. Yet, when all this is said, to many temperaments the canon of the unconscious is an invitation to let the reason become lazy.

Finally, since revolution has swept aristocracy into the cracks and corners, does the shift from the canon of the hierarchy of values to the canon of the spectrum of values mean that the values cultivated by the aristocracies of the past are obsolete? No; on the contrary, if we neglect them we are betraying the democratic revolution which was an effort to upgrade the masses and not to downgrade them. Yet in the long perspective of human history our revolution is so new that we do not really know what a high democratic culture would look like, much less what its formal education—that is, its organized plan for cultural transmission—would be. The task of understanding ourselves and the world we live in is vastly complicated by the democratic necessity of supplementing the well formulated aristocratic values with others, more nebulous at present because never adequately verbalized, which for millennia have been held by the common people to be equally necessary and worthy of respect. In general these latter values have centered not, like those of the aristocrats, in government, religion, and art but in the home, the daily relations of people in community, and the skills of production and craftsmanship. The task is not simply to add these to the traditionally cherished values of the upper classes, but rather to smelt all human values down and to recast them as a unit. Until this is done we shall continue in a state of cultural confusion; but the blast furnace is only now beginning to glow hot.

Each of these four basic changes of canon is a green apple in the bad case of intellectual, social, artistic, and moral dyspepsia from which we are all suffering at present: there is more to be digested than our bellies can handle. There are some, of course, who think that they can vomit the substance of the modern world and nourish themselves on savors wafted from the past. But most of us will say with Adelard of Bath, eight centuries ago, "I'm not the sort of fellow who can be fed with the picture of a beefsteak!"

Only one aid to digestion appears. Practically every book we read, every speech we hear, every TV show or moving picture we see, every conversation around us is formulated and phrased, at least on the surface, in terms of the four old canons of the Occident, of logic and language, of rationality and of the hierarchy of values. This outer form, however, is a violation of the inner substance. In theological terms, our culture has experienced transubstantiation and it is our spiritual task to recognize the actualities and not be deceived by the accidents. It would be useful as an intellectual discipline to apply to our analysis of what goes on about us the four new canons of the globe, of symbols, of the unconscious, and of the spectrum of values. Since each of them is no more than a cultural reflection of a changed concept of what a human being is, these canons may help us to understand not only our age but ourselves.

Starting at one end of the Christian system of theological symbols, the Westminster Catechism of 1647 poses as its first question, "What is the chief end of man?" and answers, with the rolling thunder of Calvinism, "To glorify God and enjoy Him forever." In diametrical contrast, the Anglican Catechism of 1549 had begun with a most deceptive appearance of simplicity: "What is your name?" The latter question is really no easier than the other, but, given the temper of our times, most minds of the mid-twentieth century must start their pilgrimage from this earthier point of wondering who we are. Perhaps this book may serve some as a *vade mecum*.

Index

Abraham, 289

Abstraction, 262, 267, 271; analysis by symbolic logic, 270; in economics, 141; in mathematics, 233-237; in social science, 284

Adams, Henry, 180

Adams, John, 164

Adams, John C., 247

Adelard of Bath, 316

Aesthetic nicety, Japanese, 37-38; Thai, 225

Aesthetics, 179

Agriculture, 70-71, 73; economic policy in, 140; prehistoric, 57-64; productivity, 125-126. See also Land use

Alberta, 121

Alexander the Great, 188

Amateurism, musical, 170-171

American Federation of Labor, 101

American Geographical Society, 123

American Legion, 101

American Medical Assn., 101, 102

American Political Science Assn., 108

American studies, 201-202

Ankor Vat, 68

Anselm of Canterbury, St., 298, 299

Anthropology, see Cultural anthropology

Anti-intellectualism, 288

Anxiety, 275-282; assumption of existentialism, 281; loss of symbolic meaning, 276; relieved by mores, 35

Apollonios, 156

Aquinas, Thomas, 152, 271, 274, 285, 298, 309

Arabia, 68

Arabic language, semantic elements in, 225; speech elements in, 213, 221, 222

Archaeology, 48-67; aerial survey, 54-55; applied to art history, 178-179, 187-193; analytic and synthetic methods in, 58-59; bias, 64-65; burials, 56-57; Carbon 14, 36, 54, 62, 69, 92; climatic reconstruction, 54; contemporary research, 52-55; limitations and strengths of, 50-51, 65-67; relations to history, science and anthropology, 49, 52, 54; subject matter of, 52-53

Archaeology of: Arabia, 68; Babylon, 64; Britain, 58, 61, 125-126, 188; Crete, 68, 187; Danube, 59-60; Denmark, 60-61; Egypt, 68, 291; Latin America, 65-66, 69; Palestine, 68, 291-292; Scythia, 52; Southeast Asia, 68; Soviet Union, 52; U.S., 53

Archimedes, 154

Architecture, 190-192, 299

Areal differentiation, 117-121; applications to planning, 120-122; medical implications of, 124

Aristocracy, 72, 279, 311-312

Aristotle, 94, 97, 114, 152, 153, 155, 160, 161, 199, 227, 271, 274, 276, 285, 305

Art Bulletin, 179, 181

Art history, 178-193; American, 179-182; archaeological data, 57, 178-179, 187-193; church architecture, 190; effects of, 187-190; empirical, 184;

317